LEFEBVRE, LOVE AND STRUGGLE

Henri Lefebvre was one of the most significant European thinkers of the twentieth century. At the centre of intellectual life in Paris for almost eighty years, he was involved with André Breton's Surrealism as a student, with the young Sartre and the formalisation of Existentialism, and in later years tutored Guy Debord's 'Situationists' and the activists of the 1960s and 1970s in Paris. Lefebvre carried ideas from generation to generation of the political avant garde and yet he remains largely an enigma.

Lefebvre, Love and Struggle provides the only comprehensive guide to Lefebvre's work. Rob Shields draws on the full range of Lefebvre's writings including many previously untranslated and unpublished works and correspondence. Topics covered include Lefebvre's early relationship with Marxism, his critique of the rise of Fascism, as well as his *Critique of Everyday Life* and the significant works on urban space for which he is best known today.

Rob Shields is Associate Professor and Director of the Institute for Interdisciplinary Studies at Carleton University, Ottawa. Previous publications include *Cultures of Internet, Lifestyle Shopping* and *Places on the Margin: Alternative Geographies of Modernity*.

INTERNATIONAL LIBRARY OF SOCIOLOGY
Founded by Karl Mannheim
Editor: John Urry
Lancaster University

LEFEBVRE, LOVE AND STRUGGLE

Spatial dialectics

Rob Shields

London and New York

First published 1999
by Routledge
11 New Fetter Lane, London EC4P 4EE

Simultaneously published in the USA and Canada
by Routledge
29 West 35th Street, New York, NY 10001

Typeset in Galliard by Routledge
Printed and bound in Great Britain by Creative Print and Design (Wales), Ebbw Vale

British Library Cataloguing in Publication Data
A catalogue record for this book is available from the British Library

Library of Congress Cataloging in Publication Data
Shields, Rob, 1961–
Lefebvre, love and struggle : spatial dialectics / R. Shields.
1. Lefebvre, Henri, 1905–1991. I. Title.
B2430.L3874S   98-20945
194–dc21   CIP

ISBN 0–415–09369–4 (hbk)
ISBN 0–415–09370–8 (pbk)

CONTENTS

CONTENTS

CONTENTS

PREFACE AND
ACKNOWLEDGEMENTS

> My wish to make sense of the outline I began with became a wish to
> make sense of the confusion the outline immediately produced: to make
> sense of such cryptic pronouncements, mysteries blithely claiming all the
> weight of history, as that made by Marxist sociologist Henri Lefebvre in
> 1975 – 'to the degree that modernity has a meaning, it is this, it carries
> within itself, from the beginning, a radical negation – Dada.'
>
> Greil Marcus *Lipstick Traces* (1989: 24)

Henri Lefebvre's humanistic Marxism highlights the importance of the felt
experience of dullness, boredom and estrangement as a source of utopian inspiration and revolutionary resolve. His purpose was to transform society, and he
contributed to several generations of intellectual and political movements in
France. He functioned like a conducting wire, passing a thread of consistent
ideas from group to group: from the rag-tag remnants of France's post-First
World War youth; from the Surrealist and Dadaist avant-garde poets of revolution to the grassroots of the Parti Communiste Français; from the activists of
the Internationale Situationniste to the students of May 1968. Then on to
inspire first Marxist geographers with his spatial analysis and finally more 'postmodern' thinkers fired by his grasp of the global forces of transnational capital
and the lived, local, experience of everyday life. Nevertheless, Lefebvre has been
dismissed by his detractors and too narrowly understood by those who championed his ideas. This book is a contribution to the development of a more radical
understanding of Lefebvre's ideas than orthodox Marxism ever allowed. It also
argues that there is much to be learned by social activists and theorists from this
radicalised Marxism.

This book has been written over a long period of time: fourteen years of
research and involvement with Lefebvre's ideas and legacy. The long gestation
period has allowed me to develop my thinking about his work, but I have
always found more to add every time I opened his books. This is not an 'autho-
rised biography' but the result of these readings. The translations are mine
unless otherwise noted or cited from English translations. This highlights the
way in which I have relied on the work of others, including those who have

been critical and from whom I have learned much. This is perhaps my greatest debt and I have done my best to present their positions and contributions faithfully. This book thus seeks to both summarise and to act as a point of departure for further readings of the most insightful and trenchant texts. Over many years, Lefebvre's *La Production de l'espace* has been a resident of my desktop, and it has more recently been joined by Donald Nicholson-Smith's translation and a stack of texts by Derek Gregory, David Harvey, and Sadie Plant. Works by Michael Curry, Alastair Bonnett, Joost Van Loon, Ian Roderick, Virginia Blum, and Heidi Nast have been essential eye-openers to new ways of seeing texts that had become too familiar or whose pages had lost decade-old tags.

Fredric Jameson first sparked my interest in a lecture course on postmodernism in the summer of 1984. A lengthy Masters thesis followed this and it is to the credit of Carleton University that they willingly allowed me to pursue the topic wherever it might lead. I got into a fist fight over Lefebvre with the external examiner at my Masters thesis defence. This book makes that worth it. Applying this resulted in *Places on the Margin* (1990), a first set of case studies of spatialisation based on Lefebvre's work. Over the years, I have benefited from conversations with Charles Gordon, Bruce MacFarlane, Adam Pōdgōrecki, Derek Smith, Jacques Chevalier, Derek Cosgrove, Edward Soja, Will Straw, Tony King, Peter Jackson, Kevin Hetherington, and at Sussex University, Peter Saunders, Peter Dickens, Joerge Dyrkton, Myung-Rae Cho, the late Allon White, the late Gillian Rose and far too many others to mention. I owe an incalculable debt to Marie Brisson, who introduced me to semiotics, postmodernism, Paris and much more. At Lancaster, I benefited from chats with John Urry, Scott Lash, Celia Lury, Mick Dillon, Sarah Franklin, Elizabeth Shove and others involved with the Institute for Cultural Research. A loyal group of Ph.D. students, including Anne Cronin, Derek McGhee, Paul Haynes, Monica Degen, Vince Miller, Turro-Kimmo Lehtonen, Jon Cox, Frederick Nilssen and Cressida Myles provided a chorus of feedback and interest. Erin Manning and Zoetanya Sujon have done remarkable jobs on the Index and Bibliography. In London, Dennis Hodgson's editing, Mark Ralph's organisation, Mari Shullaw's patience and Chris Rojek's foresight have been crucial. My colleagues in Culture and Communications, Dede Boden and Greg Myers, rounded this out with good counsel. Remi Hess and Michel Maffesoli and the Centre d'Études sur latuel et le Quotidien at La Sorbonne accorded me generous hospitality and assistance in Paris. My current colleagues in the Politics and Everyday Life Concentration, in the Department of Sociology and Anthropology and more widely at Carleton – in Comparative Literary Studies, in Geography, Architecture and in the School for Studies in Art and Culture – together with my co-editors at *Space and Culture*, know how much I have depended on their support.

I gratefully acknowledge the support of a Commonwealth Scholarship, the Social Sciences and Humanities Council of Canada Postdoctoral Research Fellowship, and the assistance of the Dean of Social Sciences, Carleton

University. Earlier versions of some chapters have appeared in numerous conference papers, and I deeply appreciated the engagement and feedback of those who attended. Finally, Bohdana Dutka has queried my sanity and seen me through the final push, all the while forcing me to acknowledge the luxury of this writing project in contrast to the basic needs of the poorest of this planet.

1

LEFEBVRE'S SIGNIFICANCE

I frankly confess, this communism so contrary to my interests and my inclinations, exercises a charm on my soul which I cannot resist. . . .

After Heine's *Lutece*

(1976: IX, 224 cited in Lefebvre 1995: 34 [1962i: 40])

This is a book about the ideas and intellectual practice of Henri Lefebvre. It is not a biography, but introducing both the man and the historical context of his life is important. Lefebvre would probably insist on the centrality of everyday life. His interest in the politics of the banal, and his opposition to the idea that politics should be an elitist activity, carried forward by a party vanguard, means that his own daily life, his politics, and his writing and teaching are all bound up with each other. Events, as Lefebvre once suggested, overturn theories and cause us to rethink our ideas.

Henri Lefebvre is significant as an involved participant at the centre of nearly a century of social, economic and intellectual change in Western Europe. The greatest problem in understanding his work is that his theories on particular subjects have often been studied without reference to his other works. Notably in English, there are many, many 'Lefebvres'; each is a partial understanding. If he is a Marxist – and there is no doubt about that – he began as a Surrealist, even a Dadaist.[1] His experience with artistic avant-gardes seeking a revolution through art, not politics, influenced him for the rest of his life. They gave his Marxism some unexpected twists, such as its intense focus on alienation and opposition to economism. He is never 'just' a Marxist or just an Existentialist or

---

1   While a student, Lefebvre associated with members of both avant-garde movements, writing commentaries on their work and attempting to draw philosophical inspiration from their rejection of conventionality, artistic norms and assumptions about the role of the artist before later criticising their elitism and disinterest in the fate of the working classes from a sterner, Marxist position. Much impressed by the notoriety of the Surrealist poets Breton and Aragon, who produced unedited 'automatic writing' and anti-rational works, he welcomed to Paris the Dadaist poet Tristan Tzara (a pseudonym of Sami Rosenstock), who, along with artists such as Marcel Duchamp, proclaimed nihilistic disbelief in all promises of progress or human redemption as the only possible response to the carnage of the First World War.

a Nietzschean. He is always more, and this surplus or excess has contributed to the difficulty of coming to terms with his work.

We can easily divide Lefebvre's work into periods and map out zones in his wide-ranging intellectual geography. There is an abiding interest in emancipation and the condition of the human. If early on his interest is focused on the self-liberation of the individual, this later shifts to his commitment to Communism and socialist forms of autonomous management. He develops an interest first in his mother's birthplace in the Pyrenees. From this 'motherland' he moves to a focus on the rural and peasant life, later to become best-known for his work on urban space. This led to him being cast as a geographer, but his fascination with linguistic systems and the ideological elements of cultural semiotics belies such a simple categorisation. Over a long life, he wrote prolifically on French figures, ranging from Descartes to the Romantics. And for a long time he occupied a position, stage centre, as 'the Father of Dialectical Materialism', his concise books on logic being translated into enough languages to make him the most translated French writer of his time.

These sprawling interests present an intellectual terrain in which different areas are actually interlinked, fed from the same springs of inspiration and tied together into life-projects that, once unearthed, are as indivisible watersheds. This geography also has its sweet plains and rough crags. In a long life, Lefebvre's interests and activities embraced the street marches of the late 1960s and the near revolution of May 1968 as well as the philosophical life of a scholar and the politics of French intellectuals. My intention is to take a holistic approach, surveying both the overall extent and the regional differences of this landscape, made up of Lefebvre's sixty-plus books and more than three hundred articles.

What unites all of his work – from his first to most mature works – is his deeply humanistic interest in alienation. Humanism transcends even his commitment to a long-lost love: the Communist Party, from which he was expelled. This, he argues, is the key motivation for Marx and for social change anywhere. It is not technological progress, the absence of war, or ease of life, or even length of life, but the chance for a *fully lived life* that is the measure of a civilisation. The quality of any society lies in the opportunity for the unalienated and authentic life experience that it gives all its members. Grounded in anything else, democracy falls short of what it could be. In cultural terms, this quality supersedes historically imposed measures of beauty or elegance. In political and economic terms, it is an index of liberty.

A second unifying theme is his methodological understanding of the work of Marx and Engels. They applied dialectical materialism to economics, he argues, and would have gone on to other areas of life, as Engels did in his study of the family after Marx's death. There are no 'red lights' in Marx that prevent us going on to apply dialectical materialism as a rigorous method for revealing the mechanisms of everyday life, our understanding of the environment, passions such as nationalism and even love. Marx's work is merely exemplary. Lefebvre applied dialectical theory to Marxism, arguing that dialectical *method* is the standard of orthodoxy. It is because of dialectical materialism that 'Marxism develops itself' (1934b: 29–30). If frozen into a dogma, however, Marxism quickly becomes an empty set of pieties.

This chapter asks 'Why should we be interested in Lefebvre's ideas?' What is his place in the larger politico-intellectual landscape of the twentieth century? I refuse to place Lefebvre's badly flawed character on a pedestal, but later we will outline his biography and sketch his involvement in some of the most important European avant-garde movements this century: Surrealism, Marxist theory, the Communist Party, Existentialism, the student revolts of the 1960s, and the development of research on the city, on social space and on globalisation, which laid the ground for postmodern theory. These passions will be examined in separate chapters.

Lefebvre's status

The range of Lefebvre's activities and contributions makes him a difficult figure to evaluate. He has been, and is, read in often contradictory ways. How then can we evaluate his intellectual contributions and his current status? His works are still often quoted. There is a curiosity about his complex position, and a thirst for both more clarity about what is known and about the vast bulk of Lefebvre's work, which is largely unread, unremarked upon and untranslated. Many have discovered that his position on the edge of orthodox Marxism has both a coherence and an enduring message. Its unorthodoxy lies in the absence of economic reductionism and dogmatism. For Lefebvre, the work of Marx and other radical thinkers continued to open up possibilities and provoke. This is in sharp contrast to the tendency of these works to be taught and imposed as stultifying rule-books. If we find a lively and ongoing engagement with Marx, Hegel – and equally with German philosophers of the early and late nineteenth century such as Schelling and Nietzsche, respectively, as well as an international cast of twentieth-century cultural theorists, including Bakhtin and Lacan – this pleasant surprise is followed by the enduring coherence of his focus on the saddest aspects of modernity: its alienated, dehumanising traits, which are then translated, as the young Marx showed, into economic exploitation and oppression. After the dogma, the collapse of Party programmes into the infighting of Party nomenclatura, Lefebvre's brand of Marxism continues to speak to and offer something for the dispossessed. In this sense, he has more in common with the Latin American Left than with Eurocommunists. In assessing Lefebvre's current importance, it is therefore a set of contrasts with the established Party doctrines of the Left and his long-standing criticism of Structuralism and economism that distinguishes him. This will be the source of both his strengths and weaknesses *vis-à-vis* better known Marxisms and post-Structuralisms of the latter-day Left.

A second element of importance is the length of Lefebvre's intellectual and activist career in and around Paris – stretching from the mid-1920s to the end of the 1980s. This spans a sequence of key artistic and philosophical currents centred in Paris, beginning with the artistic avant-garde of Surrealists and Dadaists to the philosophical interventions in everyday life made by Existentialists; it includes the politics of French Marxism, and the activism of the Situationists, the student movements of the 1960s and the independent Left such as Action Directe in the 1970s. Was he an inconsequential spectator or an important contributor? A 'Zelig' or a Leonardo?[2] I will argue that Lefebvre was an important 'conducting wire' of motivating ideas and sentiments from group to group and generation to generation. His limits are revealed by the lack of a clear position on feminism and immigration into France. However, he is cited by feminists, ranging from Donna Haraway (1991) to bell hooks (1990), not to mention Latin American and African Marxists. Lefebvre is important as a common reference shared across Romantic movements for self-transcendence through art and poetry, armed struggles for liberation and new social movements for justice. No greater claim can be made for any progressive intellectual.

From his central location in Paris, Lefebvre was in contact with three, even four, generations of European scholars and political activists. Even at the end of his life, despite a general crisis in Marxism,

> At least one exception, of signal honour, stands out against the general shift of positions in these years. The oldest living survivor of the Western Marxist tradition . . . Henri Lefebvre, neither bent nor turned in his eighth decade, continuing to produce imperturbable and original work on subjects typically ignored by much of the Left.
>
> (Anderson 1983:30)

More than an eye-witness of events, Lefebvre was involved at the grassroots level of political debate and social change. He was a key figure in the Communist Party's intellectual circles. For a time a taxi driver, he was active in the Resistance. He is perhaps most notoriously associated with his students – including Daniel Cohn-Bendit, who led the 'Festival' of May 1968. Outside, and sometimes excluded from, a position in the more comfortable university faculties in Paris, Lefebvre was in direct contact with many regional social

---

2 'Zelig' is the character, spliced into famous images of historical scenes, in the Woody Allen film *Zelig*. He appears as an 'unidentified figure' in the background of successive famous photographs propelled beyond his control or comprehension from event to event. Like Walter Benjamin's 'Angelus Novus', blown backward into the future with the debris of history stretching back like a wake at his feet, the character is condemned to be a powerless bystander at key historical moments, at which he is always caught off-guard and to which he has no adequate response and too slow a reaction time to intervene in. By contrast, Leonardo da Vinci worked across many different fields as an artist, inventor and engineer, proposing projects of direct historical and military significance to his patrons.

movements and various so-called extremists. He conducted years of research in industrial settings, on many factory floors, and in union halls and meeting rooms. He was a key adviser to East European leaders and even, some have claimed, a one-time tutor of Prince Charles. If he tried to explain the student protests of 1968 to the prince, Henri Lefebvre also inspired the 1980s politics of Class War punk activists in the UK, and the Green Party in Germany.

Not only was he long-lived, but he was broadly involved across several disciplines, and as mentioned above, not only in university life but also in activism, party politics and writing for the general public. In academic terms alone, he was closely involved in the development of dialectical logic and methods, in rural sociology, in the study of globalisation (*le planétaire*) and in the cultural sociology of everyday life, while dabbling in the sociology of literature and intellectual history. He was a key figure in the institutionalisation of urban studies and of applied sociology, directing the first Institute of Sociology, and the influential Institut de Sociologie Urbaine in Paris. He brought Marxism into the university curriculum, as the first to lecture on the topic at the Sorbonne and later as the first Professor of Sociology at the University of Nanterre, in the suburbs of Paris. Such 'firsts' and his institutional appointments suggest achievements.

The chapters that follow will examine these achievements for their contemporary importance, but we can briefly signal some elements immediately. In bringing French sociology into a closer relationship with ongoing struggles at the middle-range and micro-levels, Lefebvre helped to encourage not only an 'applied' sociology but also an engaged social science. Rather than simply passing comment, or serving as the national conscience, as French intellectuals do, Lefebvre took seriously the political nature of everyday life and developed social science contributions to the uncovering of inequalities, the monitoring of abuse and the resolution of conflicts – notably in cooperation with the union movement. He is, however, much better known for his theorisation of the importance of the spatial character of social life, setting his social concerns into the embodied, three-dimensional world rather than simply in words and pages of debate. Lefebvre's study of *The Production of Space* (1991d) illustrates his ability to synthesise different disciplines and approaches. Drawing on his philosophical position, he applied dialectical materialism to the amorphous case of body space and geographic territoriality. But at the same time he took seriously his social and political commitments. Rather than simply discussing the philosophical status of space – 'how many dimensions exist', or 'is space a "thing" or "void between things"?' – Lefebvre investigates social attitudes towards space, all the while not neglecting to emphasise the integral importance of physical dimensions and spatial categories such as boundaries and regions in everyday life. The project took several tries – books on the city, on the relation between urban and rural areas and finally on 'social space' as a whole. The end result is a lengthy book that presents a history of different philosophical understandings of space and ties each one to a set of practices. Each philosophy is embodied and concretised in everyday routines and modifications to the built environment and landscape. More importantly, this socially constructed 'second nature' is chock full of morally coded sites and political regulations concretised in the environment. Philosophical understandings of space have political implications. These syntheses are totalising theories: even while the history of social productions of space rolls on, Lefebvre takes a stab at all aspects of the phenomenon in an attempt to explain all and to make his theory impregnable to criticism (see Chapter 8). Even artists, such as the Surrealists, who shock and surprise are shown to draw their power from upsetting everyday spatial codes and expectations.

The response by critics and disciples alike has been to try to cut Lefebvre down to size. By attempting to fit his work back into the narrower ontological terrains of their disciplines and the reigning epistemologies and methodologies of the day, Lefebvre has been drawn upon on a piecemeal basis. In English, this has been exacerbated by the unavailability of translations of Lefebvre's most important theoretical works. In the chapters that follow, it will be shown that his applied work appears nonsensical if these theoretical works are not read. To continue the example of social space, while the concluding text *The Production of Space* was translated, and his small textbook on *Dialectical Materialism* is available in second-hand stores, few of his political economic works and none of his contributions to Nietzsche scholarship have been translated – including the first anti-Fascist appreciation of *Nietzsche* (1939a) and his synthesis, *Hegel Marx Nietzsche ou le Royaume des Ombres* (1975a). His very last book on space–time, *Rythmanalyse* (1992a; see also 1985a), is also unavailable (but see the translation of an anticipatory essay by Régulier and Lefebvre (1986a) in Kofman and Lebas' edited collection of his *Writings on Cities* (Lefebvre *et al.* 1996). English-language translators and scholars make glaring errors in their reception of Lefebvre. Misunderstandings of Lefebvre are rife in Anglophone geography (for example, Curry 1996: 179; see Chapter 8), while Lefebvre has been ignored in political economy (for example, Jessop 1991; Clement 1986) and features as only an intriguing source in cultural studies however brilliantly quoted (for example, Ross 1995; hooks 1990). By contrast, my approach will be to attempt to present the breadth of Lefebvre's work across disciplines and approaches. Rather than emphasising this lack of fit, however, I wish to highlight the integral character of his approach. It is not an eclecticism.

Dialectical materialism is at the core of Lefebvre's project. All of his writing since the late 1920s are dialectical and cannot be understood otherwise. Even his style is based on the Socratic question-and-answer method of dialectics. This also reflects the manner in which he produced his texts, which were mostly dictated. His writing practice is anchored in the duality of his voice and the activity of his typists. Dictating all of his most important books and articles 'live' while his female companions typed, a conversation is implicit in the rambling quality of his works. If they are hard to read or analyse, this is because they are cut up by rhetorical questions and because they consist of dictated material, and discussions that were the unacknowledged contributions of those typists, which filled in a lengthy outline of key points that Lefebvre wrote up ahead of time (sometimes this is evident, for example in explicitly numbered sections and paragraphs).

Lefebvre's life history reveals him to be a hybrid, and ironically his focus on the dialectic was quite appropriate to the synthetic nature of his character. The following section outlines his life from post-First World War student through Surrealism to joining the Communist Party in 1928 and his battles against the party hierarchy to become the leading left-wing intellectual in France until he quitted the party in 1957 in disgust at its bureaucratic restrictions – a move that propelled him into the centre of the new 1960s student countercultures and allowed him to play a radical role in arguing for new understandings of the city, the state and globalisation in the 1970s and 1980s.

Following chapters examine in detail specific themes. Chapter 3 focuses on his early work and develops his proto-Existentialist ideas. Chapter 4 outlines his interest in alienation, spontaneity and what he called unalienated 'moments of presence'. Chapter 5 examines critically his idea of 'everyday life'. Chapter 6 explores his importance as 'father of the dialectic' and his criticisms of Structuralism. Chapter 7 examines his links with Sartre and their joint development of key Existentialist concepts and methods. Chapter 8 explores his revolutionary theory of social space. In addition, his position on key debates and the judgements that other important writers have made about Lefebvre's own arguments will be surveyed. In this manner, his more than sixty books and 300-plus articles will be drawn together. Great attention has been paid to cross-referencing and the reader is encouraged to examine the index and comprehensive bibliography of Lefebvre's works and the translations of his writings. More important than the mass of detail, however, is that Lefebvre personifies the twentieth-century search for freedom, the demand for grassroots democracy, identity, self-fulfilment and happiness. His untraditional life reflects the disorder of the century, with its wars, decolonisation, rise of multinational capital, oil embargoes, the Cold War, and the rise of mass media. He is perhaps the only Communist – certainly the only political economist – to have dared assert that all he had ever written about was love (Hess 1988: 26–30).

2

ADVENTURE, ART AND WARS
1905-45

Le soleil crucifié: The crucified sun

Henri Lefebvre was born in Hagetmau in Landes, a département in south-western France, to a well-off professional family. He did not like to be reminded of his birth date, 16 June in 1901, 'adjusting' it to 1905 by taking advantage of a felicitous and complementary error by librarians cataloguing his English trans-lations. He died on 29 June 1991 at the official age of 90 in Pau, the capital of Haut-Pyrenées, where he had lived in his mother's ancestral home in the nearby historic walled town of Navarrenx. His mother was part Basque and a fervent Catholic whom Lefebvre paradoxically described as 'almost Jansenist . . . puritan' (1989a: 247). The narrowness of his mother's religious belief was an early element against which the young Lefebvre rebelled. By contrast, his father was a pragmatic rationalist whom Lefebvre described as sceptical and anti-clerical, 'Voltairean' (1989a: 242).

Lefebvre's resistance to moral restriction was supplemented by an adolescent revolt against his father's bourgeois values and his parent's aspirations for a career in law for their son. 'It was necessary to reject what came from one side as well as from the other, the sceptics [*sic*] humour and mysticism, to retain what I could keep, irony and passion' (1989: 243). To the young Lefebvre, the ancient Gallic hilltop Christian crosses, which featured a circle centred on the cross, Celtic-style, were a disturbing image of himself and of this rational, puritan atmosphere. A circle on the cross – seen as the sun on the cross – represented the crucifixion of the sun to Lefebvre and to him, this symbolised vitality, youth and life crucified by morality and social duty: 'like my ancestors I continued to crucify the sun in me, and to carry in me the sun spiked to the cross' (1989a: 252-3). For much of his life, he continued this self-crucifixion, sacrificing his own voice to the Communist party line. Yet this revelatory 'moment' crystallised his rejection of traditional values and proved formative in Lefebvre's later life course, when he promoted a new generation of breakaway intellectuals.[1] He also searched out

1 These included Guy Debord, founder of the Situationists; Daniel Cohn-Bendt, leader of the student revolt in Paris during May 1968; and Jean Baudrillard, *enfant terrible* of postmodern theory. All figure prominently in the politics of 1960s and 1970s Paris.

ancestral heretics and independent thinkers, turning to rural sociology and to the sixteenth-century Cathar heresies of the Pyrenees.

The family moved north and, influenced by growing up in Brittany near the sea, Lefebvre persuaded his parents to place him in the academically oriented school École Saint-Charles at Saint-Brieuc with the aim of gaining him access to a professional education as a naval architect. But with the outbreak of the First World War, the 15-year-old was moved from the north-west coast to the well-known Lycée Louis-le-Grand in occupied Paris for safety. Paris gave him independence and exposed him to the new influences of metropolitan life, modern literature and classical philosophy – Nietzsche and Spinoza. These had a lasting impact on a very serious student. From these two, Lefebvre took his central dualism of 'lived experience' (*le vécu*, the lived) and the 'conceptual thought' (*le conçu*, the conceived), respectively. He was also influenced by Schopenhauer's idea of the importance of will.[2] Rémi Hess, Lefebvre's biographer, argues that the influence of *The World as Will and Representation* (Schopenhauer 1958, originally published in 1818) can be seen in Lefebvre's interest in creating a political project at the scale of 'the global' from the 1970s on. The influence of another great text, *Parerga and Parlipomena* (Schopenhauer 1970, originally published in 1851), can be seen in the question-and-answer structure of Lefebvre's writings and his early belief in adventure as the spontaneous expression of individual creativity (Hess 1988: 22).

Paris during the First World War was a depressed city besieged by shortages; it was damp, cold and undernourished. From the front, depressing news of the genocide of a generation filtered back into lists of the dead and missing. The hopelessness of trench warfare represented the dead-end of established lifestyles and systems of thought. Then, as a result of a series of respiratory illnesses, Lefebvre was forced to abandon his technical and engineering-oriented education in Paris and was sent south-east to Provence to recover in a more temperate climate. He was unable to complete the necessary exams. By 1918, Lefebvre had entered the University of Aix-en-Provence for the degree of *Licence* in Philosophy with new dreams. Under Maurice Blondel, a noted Catholic philosopher, Lefebvre's philosophical training was focused on Catholic theology. Blondel was theologically heretical, but he attempted to remain close to the spirit of Catholic faith. Blondel's 'internal dissidence' from within the ranks of the faithful was later re-enacted by Lefebvre in the Parti Communiste Français (PCF). Indeed, hierarchical Catholic obedience was mirrored by Lefebvre's later subservience to party discipline.

---

2 Schopenhauer's philosophy placed an emphasis on will instead of intellect. Will is essentially pointless, irreducible and without end. The irrationality of will could be argued to be the 'deep truth' revealed by the coherence of the mind's organised categories. Freedom was found in the escape, in part through art, from the compulsiveness of the will. Schopenhauer's work provided a basis on which the young Lefebvre could contest the sense of necessity and inevitability to the pursuit of socially prescribed goals and to work.

Figure 2.1 Key sites in France (shown in bold) associated with Lefebvre

From his studies of St Augustine, Lefebvre drew an antipathy for Aristotelian categories and the *logos* that was central to Aristotle's philosophy – that is, its emphasis on abstract concepts that emphasised formal logic and the unique, monadic identities of concepts and objects. The static quality of Aristotle's categories were the opposite of the dynamism, the change and development, that Spinoza emphasised. Nonetheless, an enthusiastic tone pervades his recollections of this period, contrasting the chill of wartime Paris with the warmth of Aix, first loves and the escape from a troubled era into philosophy and metaphysics.

In his recollections of this period, Lefebvre dwelt equally on Catholic mysticism, his growing interest in the Cathar heresies of his native Pyrenees and the confusion of unconsummated romances. The significance of the Cathar heritage, whose ruined castles dot the Pyrenees where Lefebvre spent his early summers and to which he retired, was their insistence on independent thought, free of the control of the Roman Catholic Church. About this period, Edith Kurzweil comments drily:

> What we know about his youth comes from that work, from self-conscious flashbacks that occasionally provide the background to his intellectual history. He earned his *licence* at the university in Aix-en-Provence but asserted that he did not choose philosophy, that it chose him through the person of the liberal Catholic Maurice Blondel, whom he saw 'through the eyes of the beautiful female students around him'. After about two years he left them all; the women he says he then loved but with none of whom he made love, and Blondel, with whom he had studied Augustine and Pascal, to go to the Sorbonne.
>
> (Kurzweil 1980: 60)

After the *Licence*, Lefebvre obtained his DES (*Diplôme des Études Supérieures*)[3] in philosophy from the Sorbonne in 1919. There, he worked under Léon Brunschwicq on Pascal and his Jansenist heritage. In these courses, he met other students with whom he formed the 'Young Philosophers' group – Pierre Morhange, Georges Politzer and later Norbert Guterman, and Georges Friedmann formed a core.[4] From the École Normale Supérieure, Paul Nizan and his much younger friend Jean-Paul Sartre added a further circle. All these young philosophers, or *les Philosophes* as they called themselves, reacted critically to the reigning approaches at the Sorbonne. The classical and intellectual tone set by Brunschwicq did not respond to the disordered lives of the post-First World War generation (see Mannheim 1956). Old concepts did not seem to apply. Struggles over definitions contrasted drily with the important struggles over the conditions of everyday life, continuing wars of liberation and the impact of the Russian Revolution. The only alternative to classical categorical logic offered by academic philosophy was the pure idealism of Bergson, which Politzer characterised as philosophy 'By postulate. By decree' (1959i: 41).

---

3 In France, the *Diplôme des Études Supérieures* (DES) is now equivalent to the coursework component of a doctorate (i.e. a Ph.D. a.b.d. – all but dissertation) or to an M.Phil. In the context of the 1920s, the DES represented the highest level of studies topped only by a major, published thesis or *habilitation* of many years duration, presented in mid-career. Lefebvre presented his thesis in 1954.

4 Morhange went on to produce spiritualistic and messianic poetry; Politzer, whose work Lefebvre later rejected, died in the Second World War; Guterman, a Jewish émigré from Russia who spoke several languages, contributed crucial translation skills and, after emigrating to the United States before the Second World War and joining the Hassidim, went on to join the editorial board of *Monthly Review*. Others included Mandelbrot, the Polish mathematician who shared a flat with Lefebvre and Politzer; Georges Friedmann; and Paul Nizan.

Lefebvre criticised it as an over-intellectualised formalism that ignored any experiential basis of 'lived time' in favour of concepts of duration, which remained abstract, disconnected from – and therefore irrelevant to – everyday life (Lefebvre undated a: 8).

What was wrong with Bergson? The closed philosophical system of Bergson appeared to lack exactly the element of 'lived experience' and spontaneous sense of vitality that Lefebvre found in Nietzsche. Even though Bergson attempted to include experience in his theory, he was embalming and entombing it as far as Lefebvre was concerned. By contrast, outside of the Sorbonne courses, key influences on the literature and science of the century waited. It seemed to Lefebvre that

> the young avant-garde simultaneously discovered Cantor, Einstein, Freud, Hegel, Marx, Lenin. And Novalis, Hoffmann. And Valéry and Proust. Pellmell. With these at hand, one could begin again from scratch. The Russian Revolution had made one past history a tabula rasa and was reconstructing a society; we were to follow its lead.
>
> (1959i: 31)

Throughout both the period in Aix and at the Sorbonne, it is difficult to separate Lefebvre's intellectual life from his pursuit of intelligent and beautiful women. It almost seems as if he chose his studies depending on the libidinous potential. Similarly, the *Philosophes* engaged in an endless series of irritations, pranks on and disturbances of Brunschwicq and particularly Bergson. They were undoubtedly noticed, but were not taken seriously. However, the willingness to turn a philosophical argument into a punch-up or an ongoing feud was good training for the years to follow. It anticipated the Surrealists' tactics of protest and demonstration, modelled on the mass actions of workers' movements and on the refined organisational model of the Suffragette movement for women's right to vote, which popularised methods of civil disobedience such as the occupation of important sites and the invasion of news conferences and public events.

What are we to make of 'philosophy in the bedroom'? Gallic flair, youthful exuberance or mere womanising? Late-century commentators have attempted to avoid both the sexual aspects of Lefebvre's life and the importance of *eros* – his taste for life, love and adventure. A radical response to the economic fragility of post-First World War France, and the abstraction of academic philosophy, can still be found in a union of mystical longing and sexual yearning. Lefebvre anticipated the sexual freedom of the 1960s, and in yoking lust with philosophy expressed the spirit of the most radical theorists of liberation, who hardly dared to explore the implications of their claims. Hess argues that Lefebvre viewed women as mediators between the world and ideas. Yet this personification of mythical figures such as Ariadne, or Beatrice, onto mundane relationships led to disappointment and conflict in his relationships. This ideology also redoubles the force of Lefebvre's specific appropriation of the feminine as 'the muse' within a framework that privileged masculine 'adventure' and active embodiment. This patriarchal ideology undermines his proposals for empowerment and dis-alienation and leaves the inheritors of those goals an essential task: the recasting of his theoretical frameworks in ways that open up his legacy and these important projects to non-European, non-male, non-white actors and agents.

If Lefebvre was radicalised by desire, as much as by education, its results can be seen in the issues of the journal *Philosophies*, which was published by the *Philosophes* between 1924 and 1926. The young philosophers believed that they represented their time, appealing to youth to abandon the dead past of philosophy and European classicism (Politzer 1924: 18). The inadequacy of philosophy was to be a lifelong position championed by Lefebvre. They believed in a new postwar world in which poetry and a new form of lived philosophy would come to the fore. Brawling, making love and dancing had more of the appeal of life lived in its fullness compared with dusty academic philosophers. The central theme of this self-published journal was the idea that it is possible to create lucidly one's life as a work of art. Lefebvre explored the implications of attempting to 'live' a philosophy (see 1925a), putting theory into practice – in a word, what Marx called *praxis*.

'Living out' their critique of Bergson and Brunschwicq may have meant only student pranks. These were dignified by their discovery of Dadaist manifestos and the work of the Surrealists. As only the beginning of a set of gross demonstrations of the importance of materialism, a tortoise that they named 'Creative Evolution' was paraded by Politzer and Lefebvre to classes, lampooning one of Bergson's key theories. Hess underlines the confusion evident in the journal and the pranks. Self-contradiction was a result of the mix of people involved. Pierre Morhange's spiritualism and belief in an absolute God lent a tone of messianism to a journal that nonetheless proclaimed itself to be iconoclastic (Hess 1988: 36–7). Yet Georges-Philippe Friedmann, who was to become one of the leading French intellectuals of the 1930s, singled out the *Philosophes* as the group most likely to resolve the questions behind the general malaise of the post-First World War period. This *inquiétude* of the time was diagnosed as a 'crisis of spirit' borne of the desire to replace the turn-of-the-century values that had given rise to the First World War. However, what was required was a movement beyond 'apolitical' critique and messianic hope to engage with the problems of daily life (Friedmann 1925: 125).

> Following the [First] World War, intellectuals found themselves unable to grasp the rapidly transformed world about them and sought individual solutions in pure spirituality, in narcissism and in the 'discovery' of intuition and psychology. This abdication . . . was the 'Crise de l'Esprit' heralded by Paul Valéry, which led . . . at best to 'onanistic mysticism' and self-satisfaction of the intellect: self-destructive, paranoid, impotent. This pursuit of 'pure passion,' 'Art for art's sake' and

'intimate being' was the very *cul-de-sac* that Lefebvre, Guterman and the 'Philosophes' admitted to having explored . . . and escaped . . . between 1925 and 1928. After the bordellos, the brawls, the ceaseless debates and disappointed hopes, they turned to Marxism as the theory that best explained the causes of the inquietude. In one stroke Guterman and Lefebvre succinctly accounted for their previous positions, performed a terse autocritique and relegated those who failed to make the same transition to the political and intellectual wasteland!

(Burkhard 1986: 244; see Lefebvre 1959i: 15–19, 99–100, 109)

After the First World War, the re-establishment of day-to-day routine in French civil life was on more monotonous, industrial terms than before the war. Marxist thought developed in France in response. Taylorism organised the workplace; production organised daily life. However, in a reciprocal movement, the everyday – the trivial aspects of life – affected productivity and thus production. One can see in the Charlie Chaplin films of this period a portrait of the reign of machine-like repetition, which threatened to crush independent human spirits. The central question for all radical thinkers was thus how to 'leave' the 'everyday world' in which people's creativity, spirit and social life was suffocated by the trivial routines of the new production lines.

In the only French biography of Lefebvre, Hess argues that the emergence of Surrealism was therefore not a gratuitous cultural event but a response to this alienation. As capitalism organised itself and began to organise all of social life, it posed similar problems for many European thinkers. Thus, at about the same time Heidegger began to elaborate his concept of *Täglichkeit* (the 'everyday', again with the overriding sense of the 'trivial') – a concept he had found in Lukács' work. In *Being and Time* (1928), he elaborated the notion of the 'repetitive' in which things and living itself became taken for granted (Hess 1988: 53). This notion of banality was also taken up by the Surrealists.

For the Surrealists, it was poetry that would 'delocalise' and change the everyday. By making the familiar strange, they attempted to retrieve a role for art in changing the consciousness of individuals and in breaking through the stultifying dullness of daily life. But this was not just any art. Instead, particular forms and modernist aesthetics were privileged over what the peasantry had known all along, producing folk art, dance and forms of self-organised festival. These satisfied them even if they did not live up to the compositional and political standards of the avant-gardes, which were not directed to the level of local communities but to the abstract politics of the state and emerging international art movements and, in effect, markets. For the *Philosophes*, the way out of the monotony of the everyday was through political revolution – again directed to the level of the state but mixing in, confusedly, the everyday and local. Looking to, and misunderstanding, the Russian Revolution, the *Philosophes* looked forward to the end of industrial labour and liberation from work. Work as it was organised under capitalism was argued to be so dreary as to amount to slavery.

Wage labour must be abolished. Lefebvre commented, in a late interview with Hess, that

> we thought of the revolution as a never-ending popular festival. From 1925, we wrote many things about the end of work. At this time, we saw that transformation of work as the revolutionary goal.
> (interview with Lefebvre, February 1988; cited in Hess 1988: 52–3)

Three routes existed from the monotony of the repetitive and the everyday: Heidegger chose the metaphysico-philosophical route, focusing his theory on the old question of the origin of Being and on the importance of history to developing a level of appreciation that would transcend the banality of everyday life. The second route was the 'living poetry' of the Surrealists: the poetic life in all its variations – love, travel, orality, poetry and performance. The third was a romantic revolution that would transform daily life. That was the initial route of the *Philosophes* (Hess 1988: 53).

May 1925 saw the last issue of *Philosophies*. After this, practically the same group launched a new review to proclaim the uniqueness of life against the monotonous time of everyday life under the title of *L'Esprit*.[5] This lasted only two issues, but in it Lefebvre and the other *Philosophes* continued their polemic against traditional philosophical practices, which privileged representation over action. This marked a transitional phase of reassessment. The *Philosophes'* notion of 'adventure' or a mysticism based on action had clearly failed to provide an ethical guide to action.

Life as 'adventure' provided a solution to the postwar malaise but only at the level of emotions and outlook – and only for men, as noted above. 'Adventurism' was the result of alienation from a militaristic status quo and the encounter with artistic avant-gardes which turned warlike tactics into revolutionary strategies. 'Adventurism' could be termed 'War as Art' just as much as it cultivated an aesthetic 'Art of War'. The ground tone of day-to-day living was recast. Banality was reconceived as the plane of immanence of Enlightenment, an important position for Lefebvre throughout his writings. The frustrations of post-First World War life were either rejected in favour of nonconformist 'bohemian' living or rationalised. But, not only did adventurism fail to provide an ethical formulation for social – that is collective – emancipation, it was powerless to effect changes in the grim material conditions of everyday life. Instead, it appeared as a privilege of those able to disengage: a long-term option only for a few, and quickly fatal for countless, homeless others.

Was the 'revolution' that the members of the groups around *Philosophies* and its successor, *L'Esprit* a Marxist 'revolution'? The clearest model at the time was the Russian Revolution of Lenin and Trotsky. But the *Philosophes* appear to have

---

5 Not to be confused with the journal *Esprit*, launched by Mounier slightly later.

still prioritised a revolution of the spirit over a socialist revolution, which would have required more than simply the abolition of work (a demand that sounds both more utopian and anarchistic than the Communists of the late 1920s, who felt themselves to be on the verge of an inevitable conquest of the state). Politzer, for example, argued that it sufficed to know the truth to accomplish the *Philosophes'* revolution. Here 'revolution' was a poetic and philosophical *fait accompli* divorced from economic or political change (Politzer 1926: 111).

The ambiguity of Lefebvre's early use of the term 'revolution' lent later credence to the 1950s accusations that Lefebvre had never been a 'true' Marxist. His involvement with the student uprising of May 1968 suggests that Lefebvre maintained a sense of revolutionary social change not led by a party vanguard or 'organic intellectuals' of the working class (cf. Gramsci) but that was rather something spontaneous, romantic. As Lefebvre explained it in *The Explosion: From Nanterre to the Climax* (1969d [1968h]) the 'romantic revolution' of May 1968 was not sparked by economic strikes but by the alienation of relatively privileged, middle-class students, artists and creative intellectuals. Their alienation at the 'new university' of Nanterre and the depressing surroundings spurred them to act. Set in the poorest area of western Paris, the campus still consists of

> functional buildings that are utterly devoid of character . . . were designed for the functions of education: vast amphitheatres, small 'functional' rooms, drab halls, an administrative wing . . . [Here] manifest poverty sharply contrasts with the utopian and mythical richness of officially proposed culture and officially dispensed knowledge.
>
> (Lefebvre 1969d: 106)

At the same time as a romantic revolution of adventure was promoted, Lefebvre and Guterman[6] published the first French translations – their first publication in any language – of many works of the young Marx on alienation in the pages of *Philosophies* and *L'Esprit*. Even if Lefebvre was later to emphasise Marx's method of dialectical materialism, the Marx he shared with Guterman was the young humanist Marx to whom alienation was the paramount problem. Guterman's Judaic ethical and spiritual influence – not to mention his editorial mark – is powerfully stamped on much of Lefebvre's work.[7] As a result of this hybrid interest in Marx, on at least two occasions the group attracted the puzzled interest of Communist writers and was criticised by writers speaking for

---

6 Norbert Guterman gave Lefebvre access to Russian and corrected his German. The Guterman papers in New York's Columbia University Library contain much of Lefebvre's correspondence to Guterman spanning almost sixty years as well as unpublished manuscripts (see Trebitsch 1992). Guterman and Lefebvre worked most closely together from 1930 to 1950, despite their geographical separation by the late 1930s – Lefebvre, a teacher outside Paris; Guterman, a refugee translator in New York. While Lefebvre tends to portray it as a gradual divergence of interests, Guterman's work always showed the influence of his Jewish background and spiritual interests, which culminated in his devotion to Hassidic Judaism.

the PCF. Pierre Naville (1926) criticised the 'confusion' of the *Philosophes*'
'Jewish philosophical jargon' with historical materialism.

Rémi Hess, in his definitive biography *Henri Lefebvre et l'aventure du siècle*,
argues that the texts written before the formal adhesion to the PCF allow us to
see what Lefebvre and his circle brought to Marxism that they would continue
to work towards after adherence to Marxist principles and what they would
sacrifice in the name of Marxism (Hess 1988: 64). Lefebvre has been called a
'romantic', but it is more appropriate to say that he was inspired, fascinated, by
the Romantic movement in nineteenth-century literature and the arts. In
Lefebvre's case, the sacrifice of these passions was in the name of the PCF. For
the PCF, Lefebvre functioned as an intellectual 'hired gun'. His willingness to
allow his critiques of fellow-intellectuals such as Sartre to stand as party
condemnation of independent thinkers remains Lefebvre's greatest character
flaw. Why? Lefebvre himself would later suffer the same fate: condemnation and
expulsion from the PCF for Marxist unorthodoxy. He continually fought against
dogmatism, yet he allowed his own work to be used as dogma by the party.
Lefebvre can easily be criticised for intellectual opportunism and engaging in a
war of 'every person for themselves', bereft of any ethical legitimacy whatsoever.

Nonetheless, Lefebvre's intellectual legacy remains. He contributed to separating Marx's insights from the party political doctrine of Stalinism. The result
was a new 'take' on Marxism – neo-Marxism, which inspired the counterculture
of the 1960s. His theoretical contribution to the understanding and development of dialectical materialism is of signal importance. Lefebvre made alienation
the central problem for progressive thought. His critique of everyday life and
the human condition under capitalism provides the foundation for a non-statist
Marxism that concretely addresses problems of human existence rather than
focusing on abstract macro-economics. With other members of the French Left,
including and even ahead of groups such as *Socialisme ou Barbarie* and the
Situationists, Lefebvre redefined the notion of the 'proletariat' as 'lack of
control' from its pure, Marxist, definition in terms of labour and the ownership
of capital. This opened and continues to offer the possibility of a Marxist renaissance – a *critical socialism*.

The *Philosophes* had become increasingly involved with other groups. Their
relationship with the Surrealists fluctuated over time, but they joined in some of
the Surrealists' spectacular 'scandals' and conspicuous petty vandalism. In this
call for revolution, materialist and spiritualist themes were mixed. Relations with
the Surrealists in particular, but also with *Clarté*, were good enough that a
merger was contemplated. In their collective manifesto, 'Révolution d'abord et
toujours' ('Revolution today and for ever'), published in *Clarté*, Marx,

---

7 Lefebvre and Guterman worked jointly on projects, and their correspondence in the 1930s
includes numerous editorial comments on each other's work. Michel Trebitsch argues that
Guterman's influence can be seen strongly in both Lefebvre's *Nietzsche* (1939a) and
Matérialisme dialectique (1939b) (Trebitsch 1992: 73).

Nietzsche and Rimbaud were among the guides favoured in a call to 'liberty calculated according to our most profound spiritual needs' (*Philosophies* 1925: 23; cited in Burkhard 1986: 48). This mixture of political with deeply personal change left its traces in Lefebvre's later Marxism – it is not surprising to find him involved with the students of the 1960s counterculture, who focused on the same themes.

With the outbreak of rebellion in French Morocco in the mid-1920s and the collaboration of the French and Spanish governments against the rebelling Rif tribesmen, the bickering groups of Parisian intellectuals found a common outside enemy (*Le Figaro* 7 July 1925; Sirinelli 1990: 96–101). Lefebvre had known Breton from the early 1920s, meeting 'in a bistro near Montmartre and at a small avant-garde theatre' to 'argue . . . elaborate' and decry the lack of alternative proposals to the postwar status quo (1991c: 36). The attraction was the independence of the Surrealists, their taste for adventure and their grasp of the new. They lived their poetry and philosophy. Iconoclastic not only in thought but in action. Lefebvre gravitated to what he called their profession of 'freedom in love. And this produced incessant amorous comings and goings in the group' – what they professed, they were trying to live (1991c: 38). But the *Philosophes* sought to maintain their independence and distinct identity, leading them to leave the united 'Front Populaire' and the Surrealists to split later with the '*Clartéistes*' (see Short 1966: 164). On the one hand, there were personality conflicts between the Surrealists and the *Philosophes*. Thus, Breton and Morhange competed to portray themselves as messianic figures – 'a factor which precluded a relationship of either equality or discipleship' (Short 1966; cited in Burkhard 1986: 310). Later, they all joined a united front formed as the AEAR, the 'Association des artistes et écrivains révolutionnaires', but this too was the scene of incessant bickering as Tzara and Aragon jockeyed for control. Organisational conflicts arose – Lefebvre accused the Surrealists of attempting to dominate and confuse the *Philosophes*. Rather incredibly, he argues that they even planned to take over the Communist Third Internationale (1959: 325–6), which was quashed by Russian, Stalinist interests anyway. Theoretical conflicts arose as the groups staked out divergent claims on the poetic end of philosophy (Surrealists), which diverged from the *Philosophes*' interest in social change. Stalling tactics on both sides further complicated the matter as each group attempted to take advantage of the other's resources and to capture the energies of each other's few adherents. Burkhard comments:

> The development and trajectory of the 'Philosophies' is strikingly similar to that of the Surrealists. However, it should be recognised [that] the 'Philosophies' [*sic*] coalesced later than the Surrealists and yet emerged as adherents of the PCF almost simultaneously, which suggests the politicisation of the 'Philosophies' core was more rapid and intense.
>
> (1986: 310)

Humanistic Marxist

Lefebvre joined the PCF in 1928, along with most of the other core members of the Philosophes group. Under the banner of forming a 'broad cultural front' in opposition to the growing nationalism and Fascism of the right, the Philosophes group joined with the Marxists of the Communist journal *Clarté*, and with both Belgian and French Surrealists, to demand radical social change. Lefebvre was drawn closer and closer to the mainstream of the PCF. Once a materialist framework had been accepted, there were few other groups or movements with whom any of the *Philosophes* could associate with in order to follow their programme of making a philosophy engaged with the realities of political life. This approach would lead Lefebvre to engage in social and cultural research, leading him beyond philosophy into sociology and urban studies.

Although he had come from a middle-class and professional background, Lefebvre worked as a taxi driver to support his family. Always a loner, Lefebvre and his biographers are oddly silent on his family life and coy about the identities of his wives and other partners (Hess 1988: 31). This remains true when women interviewed Lefebvre on his life and work (Latour and Combes 1991). This silence is only broken in his correspondence with his close friend and co-author Guterman, and in surreal interjections into his dialectical autobiography *Le Somme et le reste*. Speaking of his experience in military service, he suddenly interrupts his narrative: 'I still dreamt. During this time, a son was born to me. Something which would certainly change things. At this time, several days leave permitted me to get back into touch with the *Philosophes* (Lefebvre 1989a: 429).

During that time, his son Francis was born to Henriette Valet, with whom Lefebvre lived in the suburb of Fontenay when he was in Paris. Lefebvre also had various mistresses, such as Sofia Jancu (alias Etienne Constant), some of whom at times linked him in turn to senior figures in the PCF (see Trebitsch 1992: 75). It may have also partly been through the influence of some of these women that he maintained his lifelong links with populist grassroots activism instead of his contacts being limited to those within the intellectual circles of the PCF. His first son, Jean, was born in 1925. His sons Joël and Roland were born in 1926 and 1928, respectively, and his daughter Janine in 1930. More children would be born from later companions, including Danielle, with whom he spent much of the Second World War and who had Olivier and Frida in the 1950s. From the 1960s until 1975 he lived with Nicole Beaurain, half his age, who prepared all of his correspondence and with whom he had Armelle (1964). She remarried in 1977, by which time he was living with Catherine Régulier, who although even younger was much more his collaborator than a typist, and whom he later married in turn.[8]

Henriette Valet was a telephone operator turned novelist – and his typist for

---

8 Source: Letters to Guterman, Guterman Papers, Butler Library, Columbia University, New York.

his books on both Lenin (1938a) and Hegel (1938b). The 1937 novel *Mauvais temps*, published under her name (but likely to have been written by or at least co-authored with Lefebvre (1937i)), dealt with his favourite themes of alienation and everyday life. He wrote of the two years it took to write while teaching in a *lycée* at Montargis, and of his concern that he would be accused of doing too many different things and not be taken seriously as a philosopher if he published fiction under his own name.[9] At this time, Lefebvre's economic status was insecure. The realities of family life were harsh, but Lefebvre practically lived for his intellectual and party life. He was evidently unprepared for family life (1989a: 296). In effect, he was forced into teaching by economic circumstances. After his military service, rather than go back to driving the streets, he took up a college post teaching philosophy in the Lycée de Privas, a high school or college.[10] He had always dreamed of a post in a Paris university but had to settle for a relatively marginal job instead. In 1930, he taught one course at the Sorbonne on Marxism – the first – at the request of students. This made Lefebvre one of the first in Europe to teach Marxist theory at the university level, but it got him no closer to a permanent position.

Attempting to remain as close as possible to Paris, he took up a position commuting to the Lycée de Montargis (1930) rather than risk being appointed to a provincial university far away from Paris. This extraordinary determination to stay in Paris reflects the centralised quality of French cultural and political life. Thus he commuted back and forth to his teaching job rather than take a better post in a provincial university. After joining the PCF, Lefebvre experimented with sociological fieldwork, conducting 'worker sociologies', which may have been published anonymously in *Pravda*,[11] writing on Lafarge Cement (see Hess 1988: 85), the silk industry in the Lyon region and the Paris telephone exchange (note the correlation with Henriette Valet's work). This work was part of the Stalinist programme of worker-researchers organised throughout Europe, the *rabcors*. Lefebvre was thus among the forerunners of a more professional industrial sociology, but the greatest significance of this work is that it represents Lefebvre's encounter with the problems of fieldwork methods and the holistic quality of specific localities, company towns and specific work envi-

9 Columbia University's Butler Library holds Guterman's papers, including Lefebvre's correspondence. The best sources that draw on this important resource are the doctoral research of Burkhardt and articles by Trebitsch. Lefebvre's handwriting, with its unjoined loops, offers an important insight into the gruelling conditions of the times and Lefebvre's pace. Many are undated and remain, at the time of writing, uncatalogued.

10 Under the French educational system, the *lycées* are the equivalent of North American senior high schools. Philosophy remains a required subject. At the time, few students would have proceeded on to university, instead graduating into the professional workforce at about the age of 17.

11 This is the claim of several biographers and of Lefebvre himself. There is the hint that they were published pseudonymously as others' work. However, this author can find no record of articles on such topics in *Pravda* or its magazine supplements (see *Current Digest of the Soviet Press 1949–1992* and *Letopis' Geztnykh Statei 1936–1993*). See Burkhardt 1986: 191 and footnote 16.

ronments. It also extended his preoccupation with a non-intellectual philosophy, partly in response to criticisms of abstraction and intellectualism (1989a: 432).

While doing his military service, some of the *Philosophes* formed *La Revue Marxiste* (1929–30),[12] with the mission of making the work of Marx and Engels more widely available (only five works had been translated into French by 1927). Focusing on the work of the young Marx, the *Revue* attacked the tendency to reduce socialism to economic logic and necessities. In the form of Stalinism, this was the *de facto* philosophy of the PCF. This ignored the cultural and political aspects that had motivated many who had supported the formation of socialist states. Unfortunately, *La Revue Marxiste* was as short-lived as its predecessor. Pierre Morhange was said to have gambled away money donated by Friedmann to finance the *Revue*, although there may also have been some involvement by the Communist Party to quash this independent and alternative voice of Marxism. Its ignominious collapse was followed by the break-up of the *Philosophes*.

During the 1930s, Lefebvre made several visits to the United States to keep in touch with Guterman and collaborate in their translating ventures, centred on the works of Marx, Lenin, Hegel and Nietzsche. Guterman's command of several languages allowed him to go on to become one of the most successful and important of American translators and an editor of *Monthly Review*, one of the most important progressive journals identified with the New York Left. His pursuit of the mystical revolution led him to his orthodox Jewish roots. Lefebvre lamented that he joined the Hassidim, but the two remained firm friends and collaborators, amassing an enormous correspondence until Guterman's death.[13]

Like his critiques of institutionalised religion, Lefebvre attempted to maintain a critical, anti-dogmatic stance throughout his association with the PCF. However, he sacrificed his integrity to attack the unorthodoxy or criticism of others so often that his claim cannot be regarded as credible. Nizan is a case in

12 One of these visits was made together with Henriette Valet (Burkhard 1986: 341 n 24, lending credence to his claims to have had a hand in the writing of her successful novel *Mauvais Temps* (1937). Lefebvre dates his involvement with the project to 1934 (Lefebvre 1975c: 51). However, during this time, Lefebvre's own literary projects, *Vie Comique de Jésus* and several plays were left uncompleted or abandoned 'to the gnawing critique of mice and dust' (Lefebvre 1989: 439; Burkhard 1986: 191). Lefebvre lived with Valet in Paris and commuted to Montargis, where he taught for a time and was a municipal councillor from 1935 to 1936 (see Trebitsch 1992: 71–2).

13 The Guterman papers are now in the collection of Columbia University's Butler Library. For a systematic treatment of the early decades of Lefebvre and Guterman's collaboration based on interviews with Norbert Guterman before his death, see Burkhard 1986; see also Trebitsch 1987a, 1987b, 1990a, 1990b, 1990c, 1992. Hess (1988), from a French perspective, treats Guterman as having 'withdrawn from the world'. In fact, Guterman's withdrawal was only from Europe, and from militant politics. His activities as a translator and his essays in *Partisan Review* mark him as an important New York left-wing intellectual.

point. Lefebvre was conscious of the contradiction, however, and discussed this with others:

> The opinion of . . . Lukács, with whom I spoke about these problems, was that to critique socialism, to see the weakness and contradictions was easy enough. 'One mustn't believe that we are incapable of a critical spirit', he said. 'We understand the defects of our socialism, but all critique will be used to hurt us. We are stuck in this contradiction'.
>
> (Lukács; cited in Lefebvre 1991: 24)

By the 1950s, his position had changed, and this was one of the main reasons for his expulsion. Indeed, his position was that one of the main reasons for the check of socialism was that it was unable to develop and learn from its own critique. One cause, he claimed, was the anti-modernity of the countries in which socialism first developed.

> The new relations of production preceded the growth of forces of production, in place of following their growth. They block the barriers to development, but from above rather than from the bottom-up. The superstructures created new social relations, in place of disengaging social relations already implicated in the growth of productive forces. The classic schema of Marx was inverted. From which the numerous consequences concerning the state. . . .
>
> (1959i: I, 69)

Rather than ending alienation, it was reinvented in support of a bureaucracy that attempted to maintain and exploit its monopoly over the accumulation of capital in order to develop an industrial economy. Despite the self-criticism – 'we crucified the sun!' – in his dialectically structured autobiography, *Le Somme et le reste* (1959i) – and his resolution never again to accept the party's imposition of silence, his interviewers were always too polite; they leave unexplained Lefebvre's actions over so many years. While the 1930s might have passed under the sign of common enemies and united fronts, and the early 1940s under the blanket of Occupation and Resistance, what of the late 1940s and, even more acutely, the 1950s? Hypocritical or strategic, did he too sacrifice the abstract ideals of a modernist public sphere for the close-knit 'tribe' (as Maffesoli would call it, 1996) of the political *gemeinschaft* that the Communist Parties offered (and continue to offer)? This leaves open the question of whether critique is overrated as a rallying cry for new revolutions and counter-revolutions. Or was intellectual critique and debate underrated and misunderstood as a crucial element of complex cultures? Nonetheless, he maintained that the problem of alienation was the core of Marxism and criticised the economism of the PCF. This humanistic position insisted on locating the person as the root of all meaning and thus the highest priority for any social change. However, this was always criticised by political economists, who feared the potentially subjective tendencies inherent in such a position. In place of the person, pure economic conditions of survival and social reproduction furnished the basis for a contrasting 'scientific Marxism', later championed by Louis Althusser in the 1960s and 1970s. Instead, Lefebvre was unorthodox, in favour of a populist, non-institutionalised form of socialism. Even under the yoke of party discipline, he maintained his own independence and intellectual freedom. Throughout the 1930s and 1940s, Lefebvre cooperated by submitting his works to party censorship and collaborated with party purges of his rival intellectuals, some even his past friends and colleagues. However, it is noteworthy that he maintained any independence at all during a time when Lukács, for example, had been forced to disown his *History and Class Consciousness* (1972). Similarly, Karl Korsch had been 'shoved to the periphery of German political and intellectual life. And Gramsci languished in a Fascist jail' (Burkhard 1986: 314). Walter Benjamin was eventually to commit suicide, while Adorno and Horkheimer exiled themselves to the United States to work on Allied wartime propaganda.

Lefebvre paid for his status as the most profound and original of France's Marxist thinkers with this total political subservience to the party. Thus, on the one hand he denounced his old colleagues Friedmann, Nizan and Politzer and later Sartre as one by one they left the ranks of the party faithful in disgust. Yet on the other hand he produced and was heavily criticised for his heretical anti-Stalinist works, which placed an emphasis on dialectical logic against any dogmatic 'dictatorship of the proletariat'. The relative autonomy of the 'truth' and of 'science' was to be defended against simplistic dismissals of bourgeois science. When the Soviets banned research on genetics and when starvation eventually followed from the misguided agricultural policies of Lysenko, which were based on Stalin's refusal to countenance wheat hybrids 'because they were undialectical', the protests of French intellectuals were smothered by the PCF (see The Birth of Rural Sociology, below).

This situation is revealing. On the one hand, French academic theorists managed to secure a position for themselves within party politics as 'defenders of the faith', whether right-wing or left. However, the cost of this toehold in the political structure was a paradoxical silence on key issues (of which colonial wars were the most controversial), on their collaboration in dubious policies by producing supporting arguments or rationalising ideological decisions, and being caught in conflicts of interest as they were asked to denounce colleagues who competed for the same academic jobs as them. Several of Lefebvre's texts were censored by party officials or their publication by Communist-sponsored publishing houses cancelled. The 1931 manuscript of a critique of philosophy and of intellectuality in general was not only censored but lost (probably destroyed) by the PCF (Hess 1988).[14] Meanwhile, Lefebvre encountered

14 This 'long denunciation of official philosophy was turned down by Jacques Robertface of Editions Rieder, since the pamphlet of Nizan, Politzer and Emmanuel Berl had already saturated

resistance at the Sorbonne to his thesis proposals, Brunschwicq refused left-oriented topics, including research on Hegel, probably because of their associated politics.

In 1932–33 left-wing refugees poured into Paris from Germany. The Frankfurt School, uneasily embracing internationalism, remained a source of pro-German inspiration. The German Communist Party (KPD), focusing on internationalism as a measure against the tide of German nationalism, succeeded only in being accused by other Germans of being a 'fifth column', funded by English interests (1991c: 45–6). For Lefebvre and Guterman, yet another new try at publishing a review, *Avant-Poste*, was begun in the summer of 1933. This review dedicated itself to leading a struggle against bourgeois culture, which disguised the problems of everyday life and the unhappiness of living under capitalism. Breton and Gide, old heroes from *Philosophies*, were critically demolished in snarling book reviews. Burkhard argues that the rhetorical violence of *Avant-poste* was a symptom of its efforts to set itself apart from the mainstream of both literary and political journals. However, the true importance of this short-lived journal was the publication of the concluding translations to the series begun in *La Revue Marxiste*, including the last section of Marx's 'Third Economic and Philosophical Manuscript' of 1844 and 'The Critique of Hegel's Dialectic and General Philosophy' (Marx 1975). Lefebvre and Guterman profited from a summer together in New York to work on a rigorous conception of Marxism. At the time, this was lacking among the political militants of the European communist parties.

Attacks on competing journals and rival circles of intellectual 'nonconformists' critical of the social status quo marked the break-up of the united 'cultural fronts' against imperialist wars such as the Spanish–Moroccan war and the fragmentation of what had been seen as a critical voice of youth against capitalism.[15] Lefebvre's polemical style of bashing other writers in the numerous book reviews and short comments published in the early 1930s was one sign of this break-up. The major disagreement was between those 'nonconformist' social critics who sought a spiritual or moral revolution on an individual, or 'personalist' basis (Morhange, Mounier, and others), and those who aligned themselves with Marxist critics and the PCF. Given Lefebvre's central geographical position in Paris and his leading role as a left-wing intellectual active in a number of attempts to come up with a unified left-wing front

the market. Then he completed reports on the cement and silk-weaving industries and turned them over to a Party official for pre-publication approval. The manuscripts were never returned to Lefebvre, but surfaced in *Pravda* some time later' (Burkhard 1986: 191).

15 Lefebvre was included in the new wave of dissenting youth asked to contribute to a collection of statements on the direction of youth for the 'Cahiers de Revendications' published in *Nouvelle Revue Française* in December 1932. The statements were summarised by Denis de Rougemont, who argued that the divergent statements, all rejecting the status quo, 'agreed at least about what they were breaking away from, and to some degree on what goals they sought' (Burkhard 1986: 193; see Winock 1975; Loubet del Bayle 1969).

against Fascism, it is significant that he came into only indirect contact with
Georges Bataille or with Walter Benjamin. Although similar themes appear in
the work of Bataille and the young Lefebvre, they were kept apart by Bataille's
critique of the Surrealists and of Hegel, whom he accused of merely elevating
negation to an idealist fetish without following it to its logical conclusion, and
by Bataille's allegiance to Durkheim's and Mauss' insights concerning the
sacred status of the group or collectivity. Benjamin was also a member of
Bataille's informal '*Collège de Sociologie*', but his allegiances were much closer to
Lefebvre's adherence to Marxism after 1928. Benjamin was one of the best-
known members of the Frankfurt School, who were developing a neo-Marxism
similar to Lefebvre's. Benjamin would commit suicide out of fear of being
caught by the Gestapo, and the other members of the Frankfurt School, such as
Adorno, Horkheimer and Marcuse, would be exiled to New York during the
Second World War. Walter Benjamin was a refugee in Paris from the late 1920s
until the early 1940s and, like Lefebvre, travelled to Marseille when Paris was
invaded. He read and enthusiastically annotated *La Conscience mystifiée*
(Benjamin 1993: 227; 767–8) in order to unravel the status of late nineteenth-
century French poets:

> In place of leaving one to believe . . . that it is necessary to lovingly
> follow the most sincere [person], one should know how to research
> the underbelly of every sincerity. But bourgeois culture and the
> democracy has too much need for this value! Democracy is a man
> with heart in hand; his heart is an excuse, a reason. . . . He is profes-
> sionally convincing, moving, such that he dispenses with being
> truthful.
> (Guterman and Lefebvre 1936: 151 cited in Benjamin 1989: 767–8)

While they must have been aware of Lefebvre, there is little record of
contact. Lefebvre's interest in Nietzsche makes such near misses glaring and
demands comment – there is more to tell than this book will have space for.
Lefebvre's telling of Bataille's importance – the Nietzschean tragic – runs as
follows:

> Bataille too sought . . . a junction between the space of inner experi-
> ence on the one hand, and, on the other, the space of physical
> nature . . . and social space (communication, speech). Like the surreal-
> ists – though not, like them, on the trail of an imagined synthesis –
> Bataille left his mark everywhere between real, infra-real and supra-real.
> His way was Nietzsche's – eruptive and disruptive. He accentuates
> divisions and widens gulfs . . . until that moment when the lightning
> flash of intuition/intention leaps from one side to the other, from
> earth to sun . . . and likewise from the logical to the heterological,
> from the normal to the heteronomic (which is at once far beyond and

25

far short of the anomic). In Bataille the entirety of space – mental
physical and social – is apprehended *tragically*.

(Lefebvre 1991d: 19–20)

Second World War *Resistant*

With the outbreak of the Second World War, he moved to another Lycée at
Saint-Etienne (1940) until his exclusion from teaching in 1941, when the arrest
of all members of the Communist Party was ordered by the Vichy government.
More than simply a Communist sympathiser, Lefebvre had become a municipal
councillor and had published a critique of Fascism, *Hitler au pouvoir, bilan de
cinq années de fascisme en Allemagne* (1938c). He fled first to Navarrenx, the
home of his maternal aunt, where he wrote to Guterman of his desperation and
worries about his children (letter, 27 March 1941), then to the Aix-en-
Provence/Marseille region, where he joined Tzara, the Resistance and, with
others, wrote reports on the French situation for the Third International. These
passed through the novelist Roger Vailland, who lived near the Swiss border.
The romanticism of Resistance, subterfuge and the risk of discovery are melded
together with Lefebvre's continuing adherence to Communism. It was a game
in which adventure novels became life. At this time, Lefebvre has argued in
interviews, three groups struggled for control in the 'red orchestra':

> Those who depended directly on the soviet army and who were infil-
> trated; those who depended on the Party; and finally, the Third
> International group, of which Lefebvre was a part. With the dissolu-
> tion of the International in 1943 [by Stalin], Lefebvre found himself
> 'down and out – out cold!'
>
> (Lefebvre interview BLS/L I,11; cited in Hess 1988: 110)

For a time, Marseille was the only free port in France. In this overcrowded
gateway for dissidents, persecuted Jews and intellectuals seeking a way out of
Europe, the atmosphere was charged with intellectual ferment and the personal
drama of refugees.

> We met three kilometres from the town . . . ten of us. Our reunions
> had a conspiratorial character; there were concrete actions, notably in
> relation to the railroads which were incredible. . . . These led to the
> execution of collaborators, the derailment of trains. . . . We also met in
> the cafés on Mirabeau where one could see many people, even suspect
> ones. . . . We worked also to give an ideology to the Resistance, which
> it really needed because the ideological offensive of Vichy was consid-
> erable. They had taken up the flag of the Revolution and the Empire.
>
> (1991c: 50)

Lefebvre's contacts diminished, however. He quarrelled with Aragon, whom he visited in Nice in 1941, over his extreme pro-Soviet position. By 1942, the German army had occupied Marseille and the atmosphere had hardened. In the Resistance, violent conversations broke out because Marxists were regarded as following German rather than French intellectual traditions. In 1943, Lefebvre, failing a spy mission, fled again. This time it was to Campan in the Pyrenees with Danielle,[16] the mother of his son Olivier, with whom he had been living in Marseille. Again, he worked with the Resistance. His health suffered. While organising and cataloguing the town archives in Campan, he began historical research into folklore, which would lead to his doctoral thesis (1954) and the publication of *La Vallée de Campan. Étude de sociologie rurale* (1963). During this period, Lefebvre continued to prepare economic reports but now sent them to the Allied general staff headquarters. Combined with ill-health, this meant that Lefebvre remained a loner, pursuing an isolated agenda even in the midst of a resistance movement.

Having developed contacts with the Resistance in Toulouse, at the end of the war, Lefebvre worked for a time as director of cultural affairs for Radio Toulouse until the withdrawal of the Communists from the government with the beginning of the Cold War. Meanwhile, in recognition of his wartime contributions to strategic understandings of the economy and sociology of Occupied France, he was invited to give occasional courses at the École de Guerre military academy in Paris. These extremely different pursuits give Lefebvre's postwar activities a polymathic quality, but he continued to be under pressure from the PCF to use his broadcasting position to disseminate Communist propaganda. Meanwhile, right-wing and centrist colleagues perceived him as too Communist already. His radio career was thus doomed to be short-lived.

In provincial France, remote from the centres of intellectual life, publishing and politics, Lefebvre had survived the treacheries of the war and the factional plots within the Resistance, but he was still plagued by weak health. Out of food and money, he wrote to Guterman: 'If I was in better health, more activities, an official post in Paris, I could take the lead' (letter to Guterman, 7 June 1945; cited in Trebitsch 1992: 81). However, his experiences in the Pyrenees during the war gave him a social basis for field research that finally led away not only from traditional philosophy but also away from equally abstract and intellectual debates and critiques of philosophy. His experience and background in rural France paid off when he was appointed as a researcher at the Centre National de la Recherche Scientifique (CNRS) in Paris by the well-known French sociologist Gurevitch. Before moving on to his postwar life, it is worth focusing specifically on the positions that Lefebvre developed in the mid-1930s

---

16 Lefebvre omits family names and maiden names in his correspondence and autobiography, *Le Somme et le reste* (1959i).

on alienation and everyday life. These are taken up again and again throughout his later life and provide a basis for understanding his positions on Existentialism, his final break with PCF dogma, and his role in the 1960s as mentor of the Situationists and the student revolt of May 1968.

3

FOUNDATION WORKS:
PHILOSOPHIES, HEGEL,
SURREALISM

Lefebvre was like an electric wire: he conducted ideas from movement to movement and generation to generation. The purpose of this chapter is to survey his early theoretical work, which introduces and reappears in his later work and thus the later thematic chapters that follow. This involves taking seriously his engagement with ideas and proposals generated by the artistic avant-gardes of the 1920s and his work on Hegel and dialectical materialism – a theoretical encounter chaperoned by Surrealists such as André Breton. His involvement with different movements stretched from attempts in the early 1920s to resolve the malaise of post-First World War society to working alongside bohemian poets and radically disenchanted artists such as the Dadaists and Surrealists. Even as an avowed Marxist, he joined forces with Existentialist philosophers and Situationist artists and sociologists; later, he aligned himself with the student counterculture of the 1960s and the urban planning movements of the 1970s. His ideas took on an international life of their own, inspiring the German Green Party, British anarchist punks, such as Class War (Home 1988), and both American postmodernists (Jameson 1984; see Chapter 8) and their Marxist opponents (Jameson 1991; Harvey 1989; 1991). He maintained links in Quebec, in Ottawa, in Central and South America, and above all in Eastern Europe, where he became a confidant of the Romanian dictator Ceaucescu. To understand Lefebvre's work fully, however, it is necessary to remember his Nietzschean and Surrealist roots. Can would-be Dadaists turn into Marxists? Yes – and no.

Without doubt, a radical left-wing agenda was his long-suffering allegiance. His obedience to the Parti Communiste Français (PCF) explains some of his written production. His work was often censured and some books withdrawn to survive in only a few manuscript copies. He bitterly remarked that he lost 25 years of free thought and reflection to the PCF (1989a: 443). But, as Michael Gardiner has commented 'Once freed from the Party's intellectual straight-jacket, Lefebvre never wavered from his aim of conjoining a critical utopianism with the analysis of everyday life' (1995: 97). His regional roots in the south and west of France – the Pyrenees and Occitaine – are important keys to Lefebvre's career in first rural, then urban sociology and his development of a theory of the social production of space. His interest in popular movements and his romantic addiction to popular revolution explain something of why he never fitted in with the bureaucratic PCF.

Philosophies and the avant-garde

Lefebvre's early work begins with his student days at the Sorbonne. This 1920s work appeared in a journal that he formed with a group of other *Philosophes*, notably Politzer, Nizan, Friedman and Guterman – all well-known names in the intellectual history of France's interwar generation of philosophers and novelists. In Chapter 2, *Philosophies* was argued to centre around the idea that it is possible to create one's life lucidly as an art work. What would this art work be like? A never-ending adventure in which ideas (and their implications) were lived out.

The relationship of philosophy to broader social life and the general historical moment was a central preoccupation of all those involved with the journal. At a time of the collapse of old philosophical keywords (God, absolute time and Cartesian space; historical authority and political order), the *Philosophies* group was noticed because it – almost accidentally – made the task of critical thinking central (see Chapter 2). Working through contemporary contradictions and critical ideas, the articles in *Philosophies* can be characterised as a proto-Existentialist and proto-phenomenological test-bed. These themes were carried further in the group members' interest in 'living out' their philosophies and in their concern with how to approach the material conditions of social life. This meant a 'hooligan style' from the lecture theatre to the library and the street. It meant absurdist gestures: 'philosophy with the fists' and attempts to provoke the relatively elderly, well-established philosophers – Brunschwicq, Bergson and Kojève – to respond in kind.

Tristan Tzara, one of the founders of Dadaism, made a lasting link with Lefebvre after the publication of Lefebvre's admiring expansion of Tzara's 'Sept manifestes dada' in the fourth issue of *Philosophies* (1924). Lefebvre met the Romanian, Tzara, through the mostly older Surrealists led by Max Jacob. Marcus comments that Lefebvre acted as if he had missed out on something big – and it was – something he regretted all his life: not being 'there', in Zurich, in the Cabaret Voltaire, which Dadaists such as Hülsenbeck, Hugo Ball and Tristan Tzara founded to present their absurdist and mocking poetry and music performances (see Chapter 5). Following them, Lefebvre explored the implications of attempting to 'live out' his philosophy (see 1925a). This presented two problems. On the one hand, he shared the problem of how to replace a reliance on God to justify moral decisions, reading both Pascal and Nietzsche to retrieve an ethics. This attempt to ground a situational ethics not in Aristotle but in Nietzsche has returned in the thematics of postmodernism and debates around alterity and ethics (Ilcan *et al.* 1997; Maffesoli 1996). But, unlike most of the others of his generation, Lefebvre was willing to replace his ideals entirely with the materialism of Marx and Hegel, which offered a more practical and action-oriented set of values and political guidelines. Lefebvre's precise concern became the search for what Marx had called *praxis* – the translation of abstract theory into revolutionary social action.

More prestigious intellectual periodicals, including *Nouvelle Revue Française* and *Nouvelles Littéraires*, took notice of *Philosophies*. Unexpectedly, it was reviewed in the staunchly Communist journal *Clarté* (Michael 1925: 230; cited in Hess 1988). The *Philosophes* fancied themselves to be 'radical' but were hardly Marxist or even 'Marxian' at this time. If *Philosophies* could be called left-leaning, this was limited by its religious rhetoric and romantic over-tones (Burkhard 1986: 41). Lefebvre credited Surrealist André Breton with introducing him to Hegel's *Logic* in 1925. He would only discover Marxism through reading Hegel in search of a solution to the *theological* and philosophical problem of how to move from a historical period of rationalistic theories in which people were alienated from themselves, from others and from the products of their labour to an unalienated period where there would be no split between mind and body – something that would amount to a life, and even a society, governed by intuition and not by Cartesian rationality. A time of 'spirit' and of 'joy'.[1] He once commented: 'At first we read [Marx] as a critique of religion, of Christianity as much as Judaism. We didn't discover his economic texts until after' (interview with Hess 1988: December 1987). A search for meaning led Lefebvre and his associates first to religion, then to championing the free, individual actor, and then to an attempt to remove the social barriers to meaningful individual action and self-actualisation. Later, alongside Existentialists and independent Marxists, he criticised the stifling effect of Stalinism and Communist Party dogma. All the while, he attempted to realise Marx's and Engel's dream of a society in which people were not oppressed by ideological or economic powers.

Throughout, Lefebvre retained a mystical position that only surfaces here and there in keywords such as 'moment' (see Chapter 4) and his references to 'love', 'joy', 'Law' and 'Spirit' (capitalised – see 1959i; Hess 1988), and 'presence' (1980a). These are indexes of the influence of Joachim de Flore, a Sicilian Catholic mystic whom Lefebvre studied during his days in Aix with Blondel. Joachim de Flore propounded a division of historical time into three key periods, which manifested the influence of the Father, the Son and the Holy Ghost (Spirit). Lefebvre equated these with law, faith and joy, respectively. Revolution is thus marked by the transition through this cycle towards 'joy'. Later, he was to propose that festivals might be moments from which this joyful throwing off of restrictions might begin. 'Joyous Revolution'?

---

1   If Lefebvre was already searching for a 'post-rationality' by the mid-1920s, he would only begin to solve this problem in the late 1940s with rigorous proposals for a dialectical logic that would do away with Cartesian concepts and formal logic (1947d).

31

These were certainly moments of total engagement in social life, moments when the husk of alienation was shed, displaced by the ripeness of mirth and fruits of collective activity.

> Between the moment of faith and that of joy there would be a place for the revolution. . . . Marxism . . . was a means to pass from the reign of faith to that of joy, or if one wishes, a passage from the reign of faith to the reign of Spirit.
>
> (interview with Lefebvre, December 1987; cited in Hess 1988: 55)

Lefebvre's early contributions to *Philosophies* were not directly mystical, but metaphysical, in that they postulated a system of belief rather than grounding that belief in a framework that could encompass the material, social conditions in which people found themselves. They emphasised the importance of realising freedom and meaningful action through actualising individual beliefs. This was critiqued extensively by Marxist reviewers. Although almost at the point of producing an original solution to the *inquiétude* of postwar culture, Lefebvre offered only the beginnings of a full social critique without a clear method. In *Clarté*, Michael dissected the inconsistencies of the young writer: consciousness was confused with action, and action itself buried by a retreat into talk about action and adventure instead of the practical application of theory, or *praxis*. Nonetheless, he concluded that

> When the editors of *Philosophies* better express and define themselves, the moment will arrive to expound on their optimism, which contrasts in such a singular fashion with the fundamental pessimism of the Surrealists.
>
> (1925: 86; cited in Burkhard 1986: 41)

May 1925 saw the last issue of *Philosophies*, which was again reviewed by Michael (1925: 38–9). Michael's review focused on Lefebvre's contribution 'Positions d'attaque et de défense du nouveau mysticisme' (1925). Lefebvre called for spontaneous metaphysical adventure lacking any grounding in the demands of everyday life (Burkhard 1986: 42). Self-definition could only be found through action and self-expression. This was not a matter of 'finding oneself' (as the countercultural movements of the 1960s espoused) but of 'being oneself' without compromise and regard for social norms, which stressed work and family responsibilities. But where was economic class, the reality of social relations for Marxists, in Lefebvre's existential dreaming? Michael concluded that the group members were, after all, merely blundering bourgeois. Significantly, however, the group had been noticed by the political Left – one cannot truly speak of self-consciously left-wing philosophers in France at this date – a positive change from the icy disdain with which *Philosophies* had originally been greeted.

The idea of the resolution of contradictions through action is probably derived from the work of Maurice Blondel. This is quite different from the abstraction of Hegel's original notion of *aufhebung*, the resolution or overcoming of historical tensions in a dialectical synthesis. Lefebvre was opposed to the traditional preoccupation of philosophy with intellectual concerns and its separation from life. His interest in the Surrealists was precisely because of their attempt to engage with social life and to disrupt the repetitiveness of daily routine through a kind of poetic guerrilla warfare. Central to Lefebvre's theoretical interests was the issue of Spirit. He wrote and talked about spontaneity, the importance of romantic attraction and of adventure. These indicate a romantic interest in individuality and the freedom of human beings as creative agents, which Lefebvre later pursued in his studies of Romanticism and writers such as Musset (1955f; reprinted 1970). Hess notes that for Lefebvre 'Spirit is the name of the reconciliation between spontaneity and analysis, between the vital' the lived 'and the discursive' or representational (1988: 65). Lefebvre's interest in the problem of faith might be traced to his childhood resistance to his mother's religious dogmatism. After *Philosophies*, practically the same group launched a new review to proclaim the uniqueness of life against the monotony of everyday existence under the title *L'Esprit*.[2] This lasted only two issues, but in it Lefebvre and the other *Philosophes* continued their polemic against traditional philosophical practices, which privileged representation over action. This marked a transitional phase of reassessment. The *Philosophes'* notion of 'adventure' or mysticism based on action had clearly failed to provide an ethical guide to action. Still, the search for a materialistic alternative to idealism centred on the individual body continued to be the goal. '*Se représenter l'être, c'est cesser d'être*' ('To represent Being, is to stop being') (Lefebvre 1926a: 23; cited in Hess 1988: 59):

> The consciousness which represents itself to itself with itself dies. To believe that one can hold the world in one's thought, to define and possess truth, is to represent truth as something which one finds once and for all. . . . It is not by forms that one enters the world but via the body. . . . The body lives in an evident world of contacts, of forces, of presences.
>
> (Lefebvre 1926a: 23)

Along with the rest of the *Philosophies* group, Lefebvre moved towards classical idealist philosophy. Out of this work, several translations were published.

---

2   Not to be confused with the journal *Esprit*, launched by Mounier slightly later.

Lefebvre provided a long 'Introduction' for Politzer's translation of Schelling's *Recherches sur l'essence de la liberté humaine* (1926; see also Schelling 1936; Lefebvre 1926b). Via his reading of Schelling's naturalism,[3] Lefebvre moved further away from an 'objective idealism' to materialism. For Schelling, 'the philosophical life is produced'; it is not something that arises out of nothing. It is both an innate need and an expansion of the senses by uniting and concentrating 'the diversity arrayed in space' by first perceiving the diversity of the world – a diversity that is at the same time Otherness and a profound identity (Lefebvre 1926b; cited in Hess 1988: 64–5). Influenced by his readings of Pascal and Nietzsche, he rejected Christianity in the form of institutionalised Catholicism, preferring to search for a mysticism unfettered by dogma. Much of the enormous output of this period was hastily written pieces that suffered from internal inconsistencies in the use of terms and confused argumentation. Their religious fervour resulted in a certain amount of embarrassment for Lefebvre (1927b).[4]

Hegel, Marx and the Surrealist consciousness

When Breton thrust a copy of Hegel's *Logic* in Lefebvre's face during the union talks between the Surrealists and the *Philosophes* in 1925, he dismissed him with 'Haven't you even read this?' (Breton; quoted in Lefebvre 1975c: 44–50).

However, the first real contact with Hegel may well have been through Jean Wahl's translation of a section of the *Phenomenology* in the first issue of *L'Esprit* (1926). Wahl published a commentary (1928) giving the *Phenomenology* distinctly religious overtones influenced by Hegel's early writings on theology (Burkhard 1986: 76), reading Hegel's master–slave dialectic as a metaphorical description of the relationship between God and man.[5] The encounter with Hegel marks the end of Lefebvre's idealism as he moved his focus onto Marx's works on Hegel.

Hegel and Schelling became bridges by which the *Philosophes* approached Marx. Their preoccupation with the abstracted universal consciousness was retained in a transformed shape as an analytic focus on social alienation, then a barely articulated or defined concept with the Marxist theoretical framework (Burkhard 1986: 76).

---

3 Schelling attempted to show the relation between the finite world of human beings and an eternal, Absolute divinity. He proposes Nature as the object form of the creative activity of this divine spirit – an Absolute that is also revealed in the creativity of art, the only place that the Absolute is consciously and wilfully manifested, attaining the status of intelligence and contributing to the progress of human freedom.

4 Lefebvre added a disclaimer stating that he had transcended the works, written in 1925, by the time they were actually printed in 1927.

5 The third person masculine singular is maintained as Wahl and other French authors would have and continue to use it, namely to indicate the abstracted individual, in all presentations of their ideas.

Although Marx and Engels looked forward to a utopian community in which alienation would end and in which equity would become the key principle guiding the division of wealth and labour in society, this could hardly be argued to be a utopia of 'joy' or 'Spirit'. This is a crucial difference between Marx's and Lefebvre's philosophical leanings. Even though he was one of the greatest champions of Marx, Lefebvre's own intuition drew him and his formulation of Marxism towards a more Nietzschean, Bakhtinian celebration of the unquashable character of 'joy' and 'life'. It is in this sense that Lefebvre is a philosophical romantic. Marx rages in favour of humanity, but under the sign of Reason – the 'crucified sun' of repressed spontaneity, energy and desire that Lefebvre had first revolted against (discussed in Chapter 2). It is also this difference that makes Lefebvre *more* radical than Marx and distinguishes him from the Frankfurt School and other neo-Marxists – especially the Althusserian 'scientific Marxists' obsessed by lifeless structures and laws. It is this that makes him important at the end of the twentieth century at a time when the old utopias of the Left have been abandoned in favour of a presentism of 'getting along and getting by'. Lefebvre gives us a late echo of youthful ideals and a formula for selecting the crucial elements out of the shambles of old prophets such as Marx – and out of Nietzsche, the Romantics and peasant forms of collective life.

Hegel and method

In the early and mid-1930s, Lefebvre and Guterman had a unique comprehension of what would come to be known as humanistic Marxism, together with a firm command of the work of Hegel. In France, a 1930s 'Hegel Renaissance' is usually associated with the Sorbonne lectures of Alexandre Kojève (1933–39). However, Lefebvre and Guterman were the first off the mark with an accessible translation that allowed an overview of Hegel's work, *Morceaux choisis de Hegel* (1938b). They emphasised the ambiguity of Hegel's legacy[6] while arguing for a

---

6   Within a year *Morceaux choisis de Hegel* went through three printings. Lefebvre and Guterman traced its success to the shared interest in Hegel by both Communists and Fascists, who both found theoretical origins in Hegel's dialectical method for the former and his work on the state and on power for the latter.

There is a reactionary Hegel – a liberal Hegel – a progressive and even revolutionary Hegel. But there is not, properly speaking, liberal, reactionary or revolutionary works or fragments. These three characteristics – expressed with more or less clarity or success – interpenetrate one another, traversing the entire organism of his *oeuvre* in a living disorder.

Liberal logic . . . emphasised the reabsorption of the contradictions into an abstracted unity, without reconciliation or negation. This liberal logic paralleled the political life found in parliamentary democracies . . . and served to legitimate the fragmentation of class interests in the name of the status quo. In the second or Fascist logic, the opposition and conflict of contradictions was given pre-eminence, resolved not in an abstracted

35

Marxist interpretation of dialectics against liberal and Fascist appropriations. 'Totality' was presented as Hegel's realist concept of the 'whole', not a metaphysical or religious 'Absolute' as Jean Wahl had once suggested in their old journal *Philosophies*. But Hegel abstracted knowledge from life by resolving all contradictions within an Absolute Idea or Spirit. Lefebvre and Guterman argued that because both consciousness and everyday life continued their historical development, the point at which such absolute knowledge was possible receded infinitely into the future. Such knowledge was not only impossible, but the conceptualisation of Hegel's understanding of the world in terms of absolutes was dogmatic. It was alienated from the dialectical movement of thought in which every truth is partial and relative (1938a: 61–2).

> Consciousness is . . . always limited, be it the consciousness of an individual, a class or an epoch. Within this limitation resides the possibility of ideological illusion and of error, of mystification. Yet this situation is . . . the most true condition of consciousness. Consciousness *becomes* true in triumphing over error, in moving from ignorance to truth.
>
> (Burkhard 1986: 239, paraphrasing
> Lefebvre and Guterman 1934a: 70–1)

The book on Hegel was accompanied by translations of and commentaries on selections from Lenin (1938a)[7] and Marx (1934b).[8] Tellingly for Lefebvre's

unity but in the subordination of antagonisms to some form of Absolute. For example, the Fascist synthesis left the isolated individual defenceless when confronted with subsuming categories like the National Spirit or the State. . . . Only the third, revolutionary logic could resolve the struggle of the contradictions not by eluding nor exasperating those contradictions but through overcoming them. True resolution lies in the negation of the negation, the dialectical supersession (*aufheben*) which simultaneously destroys, preserves and transcends contradictions.

(1938b: 'Introduction'; cited in Burkhard 1986: 229–30)

7   Long before Louis Althusser, Lefebvre and Guterman argued that 'we must read Lenin as he himself read Hegel', presenting Lenin as an example of the methodological characteristic of Marxism to develop and renew itself by applying dialectical materialism to new fields and new situations. In their introduction to Lenin's reading of Hegel's *Science of Logic*, they argue that Lenin uses this approach to seek and transcend the points at which Hegel reached his logic limits and to develop the remaining points (Burkhard 1986: 235).

8   The contacts with German Marxists have been little discussed. Lefebvre was aware of Lukács' work by 1935 but probably knew of his *History and Class Consciousness* (1972) even in the 1920s. Guterman would certainly have noted an article by Lukács in *Archiv Marksa-Engel'sa* 3, the issue from which they were translating the *1844 Manuscripts* into French for *Avant Poste* (1933g, 1934b). Trebitsch notes that contacts with German Marxists in Paris did exist, because the *Zeitschrift für Soczial Vorschung* was published by the Paris publisher Alcan. Judging from *Logique formelle, logique dialectique* (1947d), written before the war, in the late 1930s Lefebvre appears to have been aware of the work of Korsch, Horkheimer and Raphael (Trebitsch 1991: 41).

future problems within institutionalised Marxism, they concluded in their 'Introduction' to the Hegel reader: 'Neither Marx, nor Engels, nor their followers have yet provided a complete discussion of the dialectical method and the problems posed by the separation between this method and Hegelian idealism' (1938b: 11). Later, in *La Conscience mystifiée* they would accuse Marxists of simplifying and taking over the partial truths (i.e. historically contingent) available in Marx's economic writings without developing the philosophical methods essential to Marxism (Burkhard 1986: 250). Why was this important?

> At a time when Hegel was officially being cast as a forefather and Hegelian-Marxists within the Soviet Union forced into silence, Lefebvre and Guterman offered more than a partial rehabilitation. They claimed one could make valuable methodological extractions from Hegel's works, and tied Marx more directly to Hegel than was usually the case. Moreover, they assert that not only is Hegelian thought . . . open-ended, but that Marxism is equally – and as necessarily – incomplete and uncompletable.
>
> (Burkhard 1986: 232)

The method at the centre of Marxism hinges on alienation applied to political economy, which had led to Marx's analyses of capital, and critique of commodity fetishism (Burkhard 1986: 234). This method could be applied in other domains that Marx had not investigated – such as mystifications of everyday life:

> upon the basis of acts repeated billions of times (practical, technical and social acts, like the acts of buying and selling today), customs, ideological interpretations, cultures and lifestyles erect themselves. The materialist analysis of these styles has progressed very little.
>
> (1934b: 72)

4

FALSE AUTHENTICITY: THE
ROOTS OF FASCISM

> There is not *one* Marxism but rather many Marxist tendencies, schools,
> trends, and research projects. Marxism in France does not have the same
> orientation it has in Germany . . . there are also other expressions of
> intellectual life in France that one cannot disregard, such as surrealism,
> since they have intersected with Marxism.
>
> (Lefebvre: *Nietzsche*; cited in 1988e: 75–6)

Lefebvre's early association with avant-garde artists and poets such as Tristan
Tzara, the inventor of Dadaism, and Surrealists such as Max Jacob and André
Breton provides a basis for understanding his eccentric Marxism. Why call it
'eccentric'? For two reasons: Lefebvre fashioned his own Marxism by applying
Marx's *method* of dialectical materialism more systematically than Marx
himself. Also, Lefebvre was always an outsider. His path was an 'eccentric
orbit' around the institutionalised Marxism of the Stalinist-dominated
Communist Party. He compared himself with Heine, who 'used poetry as a
yardstick for revolution but, preferred justice to poetry,' even to the point of
preferring a future in which poetry might be put at risk (1995 [1962i]: 34).
Nonetheless, the dialectical model always remained at the core of Lefebvre's
work.

The Surrealists introduced Lefebvre to Hegel, and his dissatisfaction with
their personal and poetic revolt against everyday life led him to Marxism and
the Parti Communiste Français (PCF). For the rest of his life, however, he
continued to work on the themes of the Surrealists: the importance of everyday
life, the idea of constructing oneself as a 'work' or *oeuvre*, and the search for
moments of pure presence in which alienation was transcended.[1] Lefebvre never
accepted that a Soviet-style 'revolution' was truly revolutionary or would have
an outcome that was radical enough unless it affected the everyday conditions
and consciousness of life in communities. He went on to influence future gener-

---

1   Other authors would call these moments of 'flow' (Csikszentmihalyi 1990). See also the journal
    Space and Culture 1: 1 (Shields 1997).

ations, functioning as a conducting wire for these key themes, which he radicalised and transmitted to avant-garde groups such as the Situationists, who attempted to blend culture and politics.

Alienation

Kristin Ross comments that as France entered a period of rapid modernisation after the Second World War, 'Lefebvre progressively recoded his initial concept of "everyday life" into a range of spatial and urban categories'. As France changed from a nation of peasants whose highest value was self-sufficiency into a nation of urban commuters who dreamed of the latest appliances and a house in the suburbs, Lefebvre charted 'the emergence of a new image of society *as* a city – and thus the beginning of a whole new thematics of inside and outside, of inclusion in, and exclusion from, a positively valued modernity. Cities possess a centre and *banlieues*, and citizens, those on the interior, deciding who among the insiders should be expelled and whether or not to open their doors to those on the outside. . . . exploitation could not account for the vague, almost nameless anxieties. . . . Their problems fell more under the category of "alienation" ' (Ross 1996: 150). He watched with fascination as new towns were thrown up in rural areas of France, displacing peasant farmers into their monotonous suburbs. Lefebvre's importance was not only as the person who introduced dialectical materialism between the wars, but as a long-running reporter on modernisation and a diagnostician of the malaise of the new France of the 1950s and 1960s. His key category of alienation in retrospect provides the key to understanding the twisting path of modern culture. This 'humanistic Marxism' was to drive a wedge between his work and the position of the PCF, which focused instead on the economic issue of exploitation in its attempt to gain political power. The focus on worker exploitation was central to its influence over the union movement in France.

> [In] the postwar period a growing number of intellectuals began to formulate theories of everyday life that also took the theatre as a model of explanation. In France, Marxist historian Henry Lefebvre [*sic*] wrote his *Critique of Everyday Life* . . . which dealt philosophically with the problem of authenticity, concluding that life was better conceptualized through models of theatrical display than through appeals to human nature. In the United States, Erving Goffman's *The Presentation of Self in Everyday Life* [1969] . . . offered a by now classic sociological account of everyday communication as a series of theatrical stagings with people assuming a variety of roles on and off stage. Later . . . Raymond Williams argued that in the age of television, the dramatic form 'was built into the rhythms of everyday life'.
>
> (Williams 1989; cited in Spigel 1997: 223)

Marx had identified three forms of alienation, which is most easily under-stood as 'estrangement' (see Chapter 5). People could be alienated from their work and activities; they might be alienated from each other through excessive competitiveness, for example; and they might be alienated from their own essence, their 'species-being' or human-ness, which meant that they misunder-stood what it was that made them human (Marx 1975). Lefebvre located these all-pervasive forms of alienation not just in the workplace but in every aspect of life. Estranged from our activities, ourselves, and from each other, we still barely experience our lives, moving in a daze from obligation to obligation, programmed activity to programmed activity. Worse, Lefebvre and Guterman noted that this situation is 'mystified' (*mystifié*), or covered over with myths: people were actually convinced that they were living the 'good life'.

John Moore, the translator of *Critique de la vie quotidienne* into English, has noted that one contribution was to extend alienation from the domain of work in particular to everyday life in general. Lefebvre's 1958 'Preface' focuses on the realms of leisure and consumption. One reason that alienation is so central to Lefebvre's interpretation of Marx is his compression of Marx's various expres-sions – *Entfremdung, Verwirklichung, Verselbständigen, Entäusserung*, and *Vergänglichung*[2] – into the single word *alienation* (Moore 1991: 258n5). This has the effect of both amplifying the importance of alienation – the word appears again and again – while hiding nuanced aspects of alienation that it becomes necessary to 'rediscover'. Lefebvre later gives alienation a plural – 'alienations' – indicating its multiple character (1991: 42). However, he rarely follows up on the potential for either a deconstruction or a deepening of this analytical term. In translation, *Entfremdung*, foreignness or estrangement, is closest to the general English-language sense of 'alienation'. The remaining terms have different meanings – to materialise or embody inauthenticity (*Verwirklichung*); giving independence (*Verselbständigen*); renunciation or parting with an object (*Entäusserung*), and transitoriness (*Vergänglichung*), respectively.

It is Kristen Ross who hits on the key to Lefebvre's particular understanding of alienation – and it is worth making much more of this than she does. It is influenced by the effect of translating the term from German into French, with reference to its Latin origins, rather than focusing directly on Marx's diverse set of German terms (as is much more common in the English-speaking world, not to mention the Germanic one). Lefebvre's 'alienation' is a *spatial* concept refer-ring to displacement and distance. Like 'alien, it derives from the Latin *alienare*:

---

2   Moore (see Lefebvre 1991: 258–95), the translator of *Critique of Everyday Life* (Lefebvre 1991a) recommends the 'Glossary of Key Terms' in Marx's *Early Writings* (Penguin, Harmondsworth, 1975) for the standard English translations. Only unusual translations and interpretations by Guterman and Lefebvre are discussed specifically here. I owe a debt to the assistance of a number of students in the Culture and Communication Programme at Lancaster University for sorting out these distinctions.

to render foreign, other and further, from *alienus* or *alius*. And, from that, comes the French term *ailleurs*, elsewhere, and the equally English terms alias and alibi. Ross adds: 'Dilemmas of alienation highlight the twin poles of location and identity; to be alienated: to be displaced from oneself, to be foreign to oneself' (1996: 150). Henri Lefebvre would have imagined this statement in more than psychological terms of feelings of estrangement; he would have sensed the vividly material terms of a person being 'outside of themselves'. This describes a geography of consciousness that accompanies the individual's dialectic alternation between fully lived engagement and alienated withdrawal. This notion clearly sets the stage for studies of the absent-minded quality of everyday life as much as of its frenetic bustle, and for the mass movements from countryside to city as France modernised in the wake of the Second World War. These analyses remain valuable for research on contemporary problems of migration, urban poverty and development. Millions of peasants moved to 'new cities' such as Montargis, having internalised the dream of wage-labour, which would allow them to become commodity consumers, but having kept family ties to a not-forgotten rural identity. Even today, French city-dwellers will lay cheese on the table with the comment 'this comes from my native town – you can only get it from a farmer there'. In one stroke: cheese (fetish object), nostalgia (temporal alienation) and distance (spatial alienation) are wrapped together with an affirming identification (dis-alienation). Such complex and fluid dialectics of longing and identity fascinated Lefebvre and underpinned his precise analyses, which were so different from the thundering dogma that the Communist Party preferred to hear.

Alienation is defined by Lefebvre as the 'single yet dual movement of objectification and externalisation – or realisation and de-realisation' (1991: 72). On the one hand, objectification involves the freezing of phenomena so they can be treated as discrete objects, rather than, for example, as elements interacting in a larger situation. A 'cooling' of the world is effected so that it can be treated dispassionately and objectively. This process involves the unreflective perception of reality according to approved social norms of rationality. Out of several possible interpretations and out of many possible stances toward the world and others, only one is culturally approved under a given condition. Typically under modernity and capitalism, mystical and emotional attitudes are rejected in favour of a cool, reasoned attitude that emphasises the here and now. Although there are times and places such as holidays in leisure spaces set aside for alternative stances (Shields 1991), the objects that are 'realised' out of sense data are thus mute: they are merely physical forms and we do not allow them to 'speak to us' of the past, to remind us of good times (emotionalism), of our ancestors (historicism), of sacred forces (animism), or divine mysteries (mysticism). The metaphorical qualities of objects are also ignored in a general reduction of the meaningfulness of the world to a set of predefined and commodified advertising images. At the same time, this process is one of externalising oneself as also an object in the world and of casting out alternative perceptions. In so doing, we

41

reject the opportunity to realise ourselves as anything more than rational calcu-
lators. Unless, of course we think that no one is watching. And then this most
barren ground springs to life with the activity of the imagination.

Lefebvre's interpretation of Marxism sets his economic theory of capitalism
and sociology of classes arising from the division of labour within the overarching context of alienation as the human condition. Thus 'the alienation of the
worker by fragmented labour and machines is only one aspect of a larger – total
– alienation which as such is inherent in capitalist society and in man's exploitation of man' (1991: 37). Thus 'The *division of labour* is the economic
expression of the *social nature of labour* within estrangement' (Marx 1975: 369;
see Lefebvre 1991: 62). So concerned is he with this that he reproduces most of
Marx's famous passage on alienated labour from the *1844 Economic and
Philosophical Manuscripts* in his 'Foreword' to *Critique of Everyday Life* (1991:
59–61) and then provides an interpretation that restates Marx's argument in
point form to establish for the reader that 'Marx does not limit alienation to
exploitation'. The standard interpretation sets out three 'forms' of alienation,
but Lefebvre finds four:

1   the alienation of the worker who is treated like an object;
2   the alienation and annihilation of the creative and self-fulfilling aspect of
    labour itself, which is divided into repetitive and meaningless assembly-line
    tasks;
3   the alienation of people from their own 'human needs'[3] for self-
    actualisation through creative work; and
4   the alienation of people from their bodies and 'natural needs'.

Capitalism represents the perfection of a system of alienation that pervades
all aspects of life. Alienation is the distancing of subjects from the world, from
themselves and from others around them. The distance created between subject
(the person) and object (of thought) allows a rational analysis of the social
world to proceed along functional lines without being complicated by
emotional considerations or *a priori* moral principles. Only as a result of this
estrangement can people treat others like objects, compartmentalising concerns
for the welfare of people from concerns about them as workers. In popular
culture, the 'cool' attitude is a perverse celebration of this distancing. 'Be cool'
as the saying goes, and extract some of the benefits of this mode of relating to
others. Learn the 'tools of the masters' and use them against each other.

Lefebvre argues that Marx's economic analysis of capitalism as a mode of

---

3   In later sections of *Critique of Everyday Life* and in later works Lefebvre returns several times to
    the concept of 'needs' without much explanation of why. Here, his interest is made clear in light
    of the importance of both human needs and natural needs to a theory of alienation. Baudrillard,
    Lefebvre's assistant critiqued the concept of 'need' in an early essay (Baudrillard 1967).

production is built on these insights about alienation. It is the centrality of alienation – of the human condition – rather than economic exchange that makes Marx's work a sociology. The recognisably sociological aspects of his work such as class antagonism, the labour theory of value and ideological struggle are end results of the working through of a theory of alienation in practical, social terms. However, the sources of alienation lie outside of capitalism and capitalist society. They are an ongoing condition of daily life. Living is a complex mixture of wholehearted engagement, reconciliation and alienation. Thus, for example, people approach the world around them through the model of an alienated subject–object split. Self-consciousness requires reflection that is based on establishing a critical distance from the object of study. We recreate alienation both as a tool that allows dispassionate calculation about costs and benefits of action, and about the opportunities that exist in situations. Alienation is always created anew, and living is the process of engagement with the conditions of existence; *living is the practice of overcoming alienation* to reach a deeper level of understanding, of engagement and of reconciliation.

Let us fill in some of the details of this argument. Lefebvre argues that Marx's theory of alienation is primarily rooted in Hegel's systematic description of history as the ongoing resolution of contradictions. Hegel's model is of course the dialectic, in which syntheses are effected from contradiction (between theses and antitheses in logical terms, or more practically, between competing but exhausted political options). However, contradiction is rooted in an original alienation.

> In his system this alienation is the initial and absolute condition for development. The Idea leaves its self, becomes alienated, the dispersed *Other*, itself a constantly alienated existence, incapable of apprehending itself without entering into opposition with itself. . . . To know and to understand oneself, to reflect upon oneself, is to resolve contradictions while provoking new alienating contradictions. . . . Logic, which in Hegel appears at first to produce the world, is in truth only the human method for attaining the Idea (which is why it can rid itself of the Idea . . . in the Hegelian sense, and change course so as to enter Marxism).
>
> (1991a: 68)

The residue of irrationality in Hegel's attempt to produce the ultimate system of reason, which allowed the individual to dominate the universe by rational thought, is alienation. But in Marxism

> *alienation is no longer the absolute foundation of contradiction. On the contrary: alienation is defined as an aspect of contradiction* . . . Hegel explained contradiction by alienation, while Marx explains alienation by dialectical contradiction. This is what the well-known reversal

whereby the Hegelian dialectic has been 'set back on its feet' consists of. ... Marx wants to think of ... man as a being of nature in the process of self-transcendence, a being of nature struggling with nature in order to dominate it ... but doing so in such a way that in the very process of emerging from and dominating nature [our] roots are plunged ever more deeply therein.

(1991: 69–70, italics in original)

People have made their own history but have remained caught within Hegelian attitudes that attempt to forget and leave behind the original alienation of subject from object that makes rational calculation possible. While control over nature has been extended, this has only been through the technological process of objectifying ourselves by creating tools and objects that function like a second form of nature. They act on us, become addictive fetish objects and instill dependence. Technology is not used for the emancipation of people, or for enlightenment, but ends up both enslaving workers and dominating the lives of capitalists. Anyone who thinks themselves 'in control' need only reflect on their dependence on technology, on machines, on electricity for example, to conclude the frailty and utter vulnerability of the human being. This is the tragic paradox of enlightenment and of development. In short: 'if man has humanized himself, he has done so only by tearing himself apart, dividing himself, fragmenting himself: actions and products, powers and fetishes, growing consciousness and spontaneous lack of consciousness, organisation and revolt' (1991: 71).

'Mystification' and false authenticity: the rise of Fascism

All these ideas were applied in one of his first books, written with Guterman, on 'The Mystified Consciousness' – *La Conscience mystifiée*. They attempt to expand the understanding of alienation beyond the original concept (see Chapter 3). Burkhard argues:

La Conscience mystifiée is clearly a product of the specific times in which it was written. The aspirations of the Popular Front and the efforts to theoretically comprehend Fascism mark it as surely as the now-obscure debates Lefebvre and Guterman touched on in their text. But *La Conscience mystifiée* also belongs within a larger context from which it is often excluded, that of 'unorthodox' or 'Western' Marxism. ... George Lukács' *History and Class Consciousness* (1923), Karl Korsch's *Marxism and Philosophy* (1923), and Theodore Adorno and Max Horkheimer's *Dialectic of Enlightenment* (1944) all have striking resemblances to Lefebvre and Guterman's *La Conscience mystifiée*.

(1986: 259)

All of these texts were 'dialectical' in that they adhered to Marx's and Engel's dialectical materialism (see Chapter 6), with Adorno and Horkheimer the most pessimistic and more Kantian than Hegelian. But Lefebvre and Guterman had the advantage of drawing on Marx's early works, which were unavailable to other thinkers such as Karl Korsch and Georg Lukács. Lukács focus on class consciousness contrasts with Lefebvre's and Guterman's Hegelian stress on the inclusiveness of revolutionary consciousness. Lefebvre and Guterman also maintained a faith in the open-ended dialectic of mystification–demystification rather than Adorno's and Horkheimer's fatalism in the face of consumer culture.

Now, Lefebvre argued that a quest for absolute spirit was a dead end. He rejected his old idea of 'spiritual revolution' as conceived by Valéry, the *Philosophies* group and the Surrealists as leading to a withdrawal from the responsibilities of living in the world. Under the influence of mysticism, young intellectuals became a 'lumpenproletariat of thought' (1932: 804–5). Intellectuals also suffered from their arguments over their different abstractions. However, an abstract *esprit*, or grounding source of reality, characterised all the different versions of what Lefebvre and Guterman called 'bourgeois thought' such as the work of Bergson, Proust and the Surrealists (see 1933n: 91–2). All the competing theories were therefore the same at heart.

In their short-lived journal *Avant Poste*, Lefebvre and Guterman had offered the first definitions of the key analytical terms they were using: fetishism, alien-ation and mystification:

> First ... *fetishism*, borrowing directly from Marx to describe those confrontations of men with the products of labour in which the social labour process is not recognised and the products given an indepen-dent 'life' of their own. From this state of affairs derived *alienation*, the estrangement of man from man and from his own individuality. At that historical stage when a society becomes immobile, when changes cannot be made without rupturing the entire system and alienation stagnates, human consciousness becomes *mystified*. The true roots of the 'unhappy consciousness' ... lie in the projection of human desires ... into an unrealisable search from comfort in an Abstract [*esprit* or Spirit].
>
> (Lefebvre and Guterman 1933n: 106;
> paraphrased in Burkhard 1986: 202)

This was further clarified in the 'Introduction' to their *Morceaux choisis de Hegel* reader (1938b). Alienation occurred when consciousness reached its limits in comprehending a situation or understanding a problem. Because people aspire to transcend these limitations, their desires for knowledge could become subli-mated into artificial forms, such as magic, that 'explained' mysteries. Drawing directly on Marx and Hegel, desire is objectified and made 'alien' to its creators in the form of doctrinaire rituals or oppressive ideologies. By resolving problems and warding off paradoxes, 'pseudo-solutions' such as religion created a false sense of security that difficult questions had been resolved. Out of this false consensus, a sense of communion arose on which further social relations were then built. The end result was a 'mystified' social realm of fetishised and alienated institutions, practices and beliefs (1936a: 106–133). Because knowledge is always limited and consciousness is always partial, or contingent, Marxism's project of totality could never be achieved. There would always be room for the manipulation of consciousness and the mystification of everyday life. A dialectic of mystification and demystification would therefore always exist.

Mystification is a powerful reworking of the concept of 'false consciousness', which provides the true basis of Sartre's later concept of 'bad faith' (*mauvais foi*), sitting in a more theoretical relationship to notions of the subject, ideology and consumption than the English-language debate. Mystification is a reassuring overlay of consensual accommodations, where 'the worst' is adapted to and adopted until it has become accepted as 'the best'. We too easily succumb to delighting and showing off our accommodation to oppression and inequality, but this ironic complicity only masks our disinterest in, and alienation from, the social relations in which we are entangled and which ensnare us in a status quo that might almost be called 'dirty togetherness' (Podgórecki 1986). For example, the passion and treasures of the great collectors is taken as an achievement. Yet, as Benjamin noted from *Conscience mystifiée*, it rested on the repression of ancient taboos: the confiscation of collective resources; idolatry of objects; and the dependency of self-identity on fetish objects and signs. As he puts it in the *Passagenwerk* dossier on the collector:

> The collector brings to life latent, archaic representations of property. This could, in fact, be [understood] in relation to the taboo, as the following remark indicates: 'It . . . is . . . sure that the taboo is the primitive form of property. First, emotionally and fervently, then as common practice and law, taboos constitute title [to property]. To appropriate an object, is to render it sacred and off-limits for anyone other than self, to render it as a participant in oneself'.
>
> (Lefebvre and Guterman 1936a: 228; cited in Benjamin 1989: 227)

The clearest examples of what they called 'mystification' are those historical moments when all the preconditions for revolutionary change are present, but where the revolutionary momentum falters due to the ideological power of the dominant class (reminiscent of Gramsci's thinking at almost the same period) and due to insufficient self-consciousness on the part of the dominated sections of society. The turn to Fascism in Germany was a case in point. 'Mystification' is thus closely tied to the more familiar English terminology of 'false consciousness' and 'ideological hegemony' (Gramsci). It is however, more appropriately understood as 'false authenticity'. There is a less sustained analysis than in

Gramsci of how the 'ideas of the dominant class become the ruling ideas of an epoch'. Nonetheless, the economic reductionism and simplistic notion of 'false consciousness' is avoided. Lefebvre and Guterman are not just talking about a narrowly economic sense of class or of domination. This involved pioneering analytical critiques of possessive individualism whereby people define themselves through things. Why define mystification as false authenticity?

> The individual has above all a comfortable feeling. He is familiar with himself. He says: 'Me' like he says 'my feelings and my opinions', like he says 'my' house 'my' belly 'my' butt 'my' bed.
> (Lefebvre and Guterman 1933g: 2; translated in Burkhard 1986: 198)

Lefebvre and Guterman argued that efforts in psychology, sociology and biology to move beyond this definition of self-identity diverted attention away from class identity, remaining in the dead-end of the middle-class obsession with individualism, foundering in ideologies of 'race', or in vague concepts such as nation and society. Although they were unable to offer more than a schematic analysis of class consciousness, Lefebvre and Guterman argue that a socioeconomic class basis is necessary for the definition of a given individual's identity:

> Class is not an abstraction. It corresponds to the practical and daily life common to many others. It defines the conditions of this daily life. A proletarian has the daily life of a man belonging to a class deprived of the means of production. Individuals are not real each by himself, they are real in the ensemble of their reciprocal relations, by and in class. Conversely class is the reality of the ensemble of individuals that it envelops.
> (Lefebvre and Guterman 1933g: 4; translated in Burkhard 1986: 199)

One significance of *La Conscience mystifiée* is that it began to synthesise Lefebvre's and Guterman's different contributions to the critique of Fascism, with their theoretical understanding of alienation and dialectical materialism. This book was to be the first in a projected series of five essays on materialist philosophy, the third of which was to be his *Critique de la vie quotidienne* – subtitled *Volume 1 Introduction* when it was finally published after the Second World War (1947a) – revealing the continuity of Lefebvre's themes.[4] But it must be remarked that one fundamental shift in the relationship between

---

4 This series includes three volumes of *Critique of Everyday Life* and the fourth, *Eléments de Rhythmanalyse* (1992a) as well as a number of popularisations and introductions such as *Everyday Life in the Modern World* (1971h [1968]) and *Introduction to Modernity* (1995 [1962i]). The series is announced in the 'Preface' to *La Conscience mystifiée* (1936a; for a further discussion see also Poster 1975: 242–3; Trebitsch 1991).

democracy and everyday life is unmentioned and unanalysed by Lefebvre: women were given the vote in France in 1944 (one of the last European countries to do so). Lefebvre, dictating to his women typist-lovers, never grasped the importance of an equitable sexual politics, even though he provides a theoretical base that supports it. He is ultimately proposing to differentiate bodies, places, personalities, cultures – against what he sees as the homogenising and standard-ising tendencies of capitalist abstract space (1991d).

In general form, Lefebvre described this as a theory of bourgeois culture and ideology. Where the radical young thinkers of the Left had sneered at the 'death' of bourgeois thinking in the form of the apparent irrelevance of philos-ophy to resolving the 'inquiétude' of the 1920s, Lefebvre and Guterman argued that in the 1930s this changed into a question of the 'exacerbation' of bour-geois ideology in the form of right-wing politics (Lefebvre 1989: 453). While it had been mentioned since the time of *Philosophies*, a new engagement in the project of critiquing everyday life was formally introduced as the heart of this synthesis. On the one hand, the private consciousness (*la conscience privée*) of individuals is left to face abstract social forces and experience anomie and the loss of dignity. But the solution does not lie simply in the resuscitation of the individual, as suggested by non-conformist critiques of the time such as Emmanuel Mounier's *personnisme* (1949; 1960). By contrast, public conscious-ness (*la conscience du forum*) is sidetracked into nationalism; the mythos of the nation-state having once been a revolutionary and liberating concept is ossified into its opposite, an ideology in which false categories and ethnic identity are substituted for the reality of international relations of capitalism and then manipulated by Fascist demagogues (Burkhard 1986: 246). The rejection of the status quo by youth led to isolated revolts, superficial protests and more false promises by politicians of the Right. The project was thus to transcend the isolating humanism and false notions of the individual, community and concepts of 'bourgeois thought' and the abstracted concepts of philosophy into an alternative 'unifying authenticity', understood in terms derived from Nietzsche as the 'total person'.

In essence, Lefebvre succeeded in identifying the importance of the mysti-fied consciousness as a precondition of Fascism. Demands for revolutionary change in Weimar Germany were channelled away from a truly liberating social change into a revolution by, and in favour of, the state itself. In 'Nationalism against the Nation' – *Nationalisme contre le nation* (1937a, cf. 1933u), Lefebvre shows how class identity was converted into fervent nation-alism as part of this process (see Chapter 7). In 'Hitler to power: report on five years of Fascism in Germany' (*Hitler au pouvoir* (1938c)), he argued that exploited workers were brought to understand themselves as 'Germans' and even as an 'Aryan' master race.

L'homme total

Mark Poster has called Lefebvre 'by far the best interpreter of Marx in France' (1975: 56). He broadly supported the doctrine of the PCF until his exclusion from the party in the mid-1950s. Lefebvre's was a humanistic Marxism whose key critical principle was Marx's concept of 'total man' found in the *1844 Economic and Philosophical Manuscripts* (Marx 1975). 'Total man' or the 'complete person' transcended the partial images of people as purely economic beings (for example, as described by Adam Smith) or as first and foremost spiritual beings (as described in Christian doctrine). In a typical phrasing, Lefebvre answers his own rhetorical question: 'What is the total man? Not physical, physiological, psychological, historical, economic or social exclusively or unilaterally; it is all of these and more, especially the sum of these elements of aspects; it is their unity, their totality . . . ' (1968j: 157; see 1939b). It is the implication of, and the call to, this 'total person' instead of only the rational actor that Lefebvre finds attractive in the works of not only Marx, but also of Nietzsche, Fourier, the Romantic writers, the 1920s Surrealists and the student rebels of the 1960s (1975f: 11).

Lefebvre saw Marxism as fundamentally anti-reductionist, and Marx's later, so-called 'economic works' such as *Das Kapital* as a systematic application of the method of dialectical materialism and this original goal of the 'total person' against alienation in its most pernicious forms. Alienation was the key root of the 'mystification of consciousness' and of ideology, proclaimed Lefebvre in his seminal work *La Conscience mystifiée* (Lefebvre and Guterman 1936a). Without being aware of it, Lefebvre followed a line of argument pioneered by the young Lukács, which focused on the revelation of alienation as the central 'truth' of Marxism – a line of argument later recanted by Lukács in order to align himself with the Stalinists who took power in Eastern Europe after the Second World War. In France, Althusser was later commissioned by the PCF to produce an anti-humanist Marxism in the 1960s in order to throw off the influence of Lefebvre's anti-Stalinist stance.

In opposition to Calvez and other Catholic Marxists in France in the 1930s, Lefebvre, along with Maximilien Rubel and Kostas Axelos (1963), tried to answer the charge of economic reductionism. Marxism did not lead to 'economism' but allowed alienated spiritualism in the form of religion its own influences and distortions to relations between people. 'It was the special character of religious myths to have their own force, their own power, their own alienating effects' (Poster 1975: 56). Marx's great vision was to make people aware of the human foundation of nature in the long historical struggle to survive in the face of natural difficulties and climatic disasters. Alienation in the contemporary cultural arrangements of production did not linearly 'determine' alienation in other areas of life 'but all were reciprocally inter-related within the movement of historical totality' (Poster 1975: 57; see Lefebvre 1968j: 145–8; Lefebvre 1948f: 68), which is often referred to today as 'culture'.

Fundamentally, history was the introduction of human finality, human purposes, replacing chance and casual determinism in society and nature. To Lefebvre, the humanization of society and nature was at the same time the humanization of man: the conscious, human control of society and nature accompanied, *mutatis mutandis*, the coming into consciousness of human potentials. Thus, far from being a determinist philosophy, "Marxism is a practical philosophy of freedom".

(Lefebvre and Guterman 1934b: 12; in Poster 1975: 57)

By the 1960s and after his expulsion from the PCF, Lefebvre's position on alienation, one of his guiding concepts, had changed. Philosophy itself appeared as a special form of alienation, in which thought was disconnected from action. 'The alienation of philosophy was measurable by the degree to which it gave privilege to certain aspects of reality and devalued others' (Poster 1975: 242). A *Métaphilosophie* (1965e; 1967b) needed to be linked to not only practice but to mapping the phenomenon of alienation, for each region of social life contained its own types of alienation.[5] The problem was that philosophy made alienation into merely an ethical question of relationships, rather than something that could be studied empirically, by the social sciences, and remedied by action (see Chapter 7).

Critique of Fascism

The context of Lefebvre's critique was not only intellectual but personal. The years from 1932 on formed a long run-up to Lefebvre's activities during the occupation of France in the Second World War. Summer hiking and hostelling vacations in Germany introduced him to the ardour of the Hitler Youth and the bureaucratic rigidity of the German Communist Party, the KPD. While German intellectuals in exile and the KPD itself predicted that Fascism would be short-lived, he prepared for war. Lefebvre watched as Fascism rose by an unlikely route: 'The German workers allowed themselves to be seduced and won over by national-socialism, because the latter presented itself as socialist and revolu-tionary, more revolutionary in the national situation than the KPD' (Lefebvre 1989: 453). This was the point of departure for his work on a theory of mystifi-cation, presented together with Guterman under the title *La Conscience mystifiée* (1936a).[6] Was the working class, by nature, given to revolutionary ideology and action? This was one of Lefebvre's favourite texts, to which he was to return again and again.

5   Bourdieu makes a similar argument, adhering to Structuralist tenets but arguing for the relative autonomy of different areas of everyday activity (1971).

6   This was announced as the first of five volumes, also including: *La Conscience privée, Critique de la vie quotidienne, Science des idéologies* and *Matérialisme et culture*. These were never published, but Lefebvre continued the project throughout his career, using these titles sometimes for

With Guterman, Lefebvre wrote two of the first books on Fascism, *Le Nationalisme contre les nations* (1935) and *Hitler au pouvoir* (1938). These continued the theme of *La Conscience mystifiée*. The critique of Fascism provided Lefebvre with a much-needed focus around which his thought on alienation and mystification took on a more coherent form. Against the pure polemic and jeering tone of the earlier pieces, these critiques are marked by a sense of urgency. Fascism was presented as 'revolution' and nationalism hid imperialism (Lefebvre and Guterman 1933g; Burkhard 1986: 202).

> A revolution that denied Marxism led to the Right . . . and a denial of class conflict in the name of a spiritual renaissance ignored the real problems of economic and political domination. . . . Lefebvre connected the 'morale' revolution of *Esprit* to the 'humaine' revolution of *Revue Français* to the 'spiritual' revolution of von Papen . . . [in] his effective but crude assault on the [left] non-conformists as protofascists.
>
> (Burkhard 1986: 204, paraphrasing Lefebvre 1933: 68–71)

In the fight against Fascism in France, both a conservative critique and a Marxist critique could be found among younger radicals at a time before the political realities of the Second World War and the Occupation forced a clarification of intellectuals' positions for or against Fascism. While they provided an important running commentary, moral and philosophical arguments stood in for political programmes. The intellectuals had little impact on political policy. The significance of these arguments in the 1930s is that they establish the lines of left-wing versus right-wing moral debate in France for the postwar period.

Such was the focus on class and the Marxist framework of a workers' revolution that Lefebvre does not expand on the racial aspect of Fascism. Instead, he argues for a universal humanity, treating race as a category of bourgeois politics, an imposed distinction that keeps the exploited from identifying their common interests. Lefebvre and Guterman did not extend their harsh words for nationalism and patriotic self-identity to racist colonial wars of the time. While they were certainly against, for example, the Spanish–Moroccan War and would later campaign against the Algerian Civil War, they almost never note the racial, or even ethnic and religious, lines of these conflicts. Lefebvre provides a perfect example of the way in which 'race' tends to vanish in 'class' analysis, just as 'gender' and sexualities were all blurred together in the terminology of 'mankind'. There is little recognition of the growing importance of France's

---

complete books, at other times for sections within books and papers (e.g. 1959i Vol. 2, Part 4, Ch. 17 'Sur la livre annoncé et non publié: La Conscience privée': 555–8). Burkhard (1986: 242) argues that *La Conscience mystifiée* should be read as an early part of Lefebvre's *Critique de la vie quotidienne* (1947a) and its sequels (1962b, 1981).

immigration problems from the Algerian War on, its xenophobia and discrimination against outsiders, notably, North Africans. Yes class is essential, but the organising lines of motivation and desire cleave along the lines of racial stereotypes. In a sense, this reflects the Parisian context, with the prevailing cultural attitudes towards women and xenophobic arrogance towards other cultures, skin colours, hair types and obsession with 'perfecting' and protecting the French language from the lilt and drawl of regional accents. According to post-colonial critics (Bhabha 1989), this racial blind spot, however, continues in Marxian analyses of nationalism – for example, Benedict Anderson's *Imagined Communities* (1981). The result contributes towards the odd sense in which Lefebvre's 'working class' are only the descendants of the French peasantry, not the visibly exploited immigrants and guest labourers of a globalised proletariat.

Despite this shortcoming, Lefebvre and Guterman argued that the advantage of materialism was that previously separated elements were united in a totality. This was true in theory, if not in their application of the theory. They do not unify all the relevant aspects but leave out significant dimensions of not only racial and ethnically despised, but also non-heterosexually gendered, 'others' (see Blum and Nast 1996). By contrast, the 'bourgeois philosophy' of Bergson or Valéry reflected and responded to life in capitalist societies but diverted one from the underlying class conflicts concerning economic power. The end result was a form of alienation at the level of thought and value judgement. The values of 'bourgeois culture' in general 'mystified' or obfuscated the situation in such a manner that everything appeared as its opposite.

In his later years, he attempted to go back to his 1930s interest in everyday life and consciousness, expanding on his early theory of 'moments' of enlightenment. Lefebvre and Guterman had attempted to relate time, space, consciousness and production together (1986b). They stand at a midway point between Benjamin's vision of societies 'dreaming' their way into the future in the form of un-reflected-upon action that progressed from moment to moment much as the haphazard sequence of a dream might. Abandoning the primacy of narrative history, Benjamin proposed a method based on collecting and montage. Horkheimer and Adorno envisioned a 'dialectic of enlightenment' in which the elements of progressive enlightenment later become fetishised, enslaving traditions and technical objects. Between Benjamin's discontinuous montage and Horkheimer's and Adorno's smooth dialectic of enlightenment and disenlightenment, we can locate Lefebvre's idea of 'moments' of enlightenment and 'presence' bursting out of the most banal, alienated, and taken-for-granted aspects of everyday life (1980a; see Chapter 5). We therefore turn to the question of alienation and Lefebvre's vision of dis-alienation through 'moments of *presence*'.

5

MOMENTS OF PRESENCE

Neither Surrealism nor Dada

In the 1920s, Lefebvre was associated with the Surrealists and influenced by Tristan Tzara's Dadaism. From his first encounter, Lefebvre was taken with the radical potential of Dadaist poets' refusal to make sense and satisfy the expectations of their audience. Dada came to Paris from Zurich, where it had flourished briefly, having originated as a nonsense word to describe the absurd performances at the legendary Cabaret Voltaire. Along with Hugo Ball and Richard Hülsenbeck, Tristan Tzara was to emerge as one of the key figures of Dada, drawing on experiments in poetry and music. Hülsenbeck, Tzara and others performed pieces intended to shock the audience with their outrageousness and anti-rationalism. But before it became a well-known movement, Dada was simply one of many nihilistic art-for-arts-sake acts that fancied themselves the heirs of Nietzsche. Dada has been described as 'nonsense with a straight face', or an 'absurd negation that wants no consequences' (Marcus 1989: 193, 199). Dadaists placed disintegration in the midst of their works. By stringing vowels together into meaningless sound poetry, or by attempting to shock, frighten or disgust its audience, Dada's moral disorder pioneered the series of twentieth-century avant-garde movements that led to the Situationists, May 1968, punk and anarchism. In November 1915, Hugo Ball had predicted:

> In an age like ours, when people are assaulted daily by the most monstrous things without being able to keep account of their impressions, aesthetic production becomes a prescribed course. But all living art will be irrational, primitive and complex; it will speak a secret language and leave behind documents not of edification but of paradox.
> (Diary, Hugo Ball, 25 November 1915; cited in Marcus 1989: 196)

The Cabaret Voltaire flourished for five short months in Zurich from its launch in February 1916. In the midst of the First World War, it counterposed Nietzschean aphorisms, collage, mysticism and sound poetry in performances intended to provoke and shock its audience of students and artists. On the one side, it was a response to the chaos of war-torn Europe, pitting meaningless 'sound poetry' against the mindless slaughter of trench warfare. On the other, it was the original exposure of 'negative dialectics': long before Horkheimer's and Adorno's famous critique, the Dadaists presented the reversal of Enlightenment into barbarism, of scientific progress into horror and the advance of reason into immorality. A number of artists who later became well-known figures in the abstract art movement were involved. They included the Alsatian artist, Jean Arp (later known for his oversized sculptures based on everyday objects ('Swiss Cheese and Pitchfork' sits outside the Fondation Maeght near Nice; the Metropolitan Museum of Modern Art holds other works); Tristan Tzara; Marcel Janco, a poet and artist from Romania; and Hugo Ball, Emmy Hennings and Richard Hülsenbeck, a German playwright, singer and poet, respectively. Taking over a pub, the Hollandische Meierei, Arp reported:

> On the stage of a gaudy, motley, overcrowded tavern are several weird and peculiar figures representing Tzara, Janco, Ball, Hülsenbeck, Madame Hennings, and your humble servant. Total pandemonium. The people around us are shouting, laughing, and gesticulating. Our replies are sighs of love, volleys of hiccups, poems, moos, and the miaowing of medieval *Bruitists*.[1] Tzara is wiggling his behind like the belly of an Oriental dancer. Janco is playing an invisible violin and bowing and scraping. Madame Hennings, with a Madonna face, is doing the splits. Hülsenbeck is banging away nonstop at the great drum, with Ball accompanying him on the piano, pale as a chalky ghost.
>
> (Jean Arp; cited in Marcus 1989: 193)

Lefebvre's inheritance was Dada's all-out attack on traditions and sources of legitimacy and authority. In New York, Man Ray and Marcel Duchamp became some of the best-known artists who took up the Dada label. Man Ray produced collaged photographs, drawing the latent similarities between objects out into the open. Thus, in one famous image, a woman's back was turned into a violin by simply adding the scrolls of fretwork. Duchamp exhibited a urinal as a fountain and mounted an exhibition in which twine was strung from side to side of the room making it an impossible-to-enter thicket of string. The young Lefebvre was transfixed by the potential of surprise, shock and humour for thinking of not only artistic images but of everyday life in new ways. By

---

1   'Bruitism' is noise with imitative effects – animal sounds, bird calls and parodic imitations – as well as chanted vowels and phonemes (*Omm* is the best-known meditative sound), which at different times were held to have occult effects by inducing trance states. 'Bruitism is life itself, it cannot be judged like a book, but rather it is a part of our personality, which attacks us, pursues us and tears us to pieces' (Ball; cited in Marcus 1989: 225).

focusing on such aspects as nonsense sounds and poetry composed of words with no referent, 'art for art's sake' removed the rational elements of traditional art. By not representing objects, people or emotions they rejected the prevailing idea that art should serve a social purpose. By showing how everyday objects could be exhibited as 'art', the Dadaists challenged the dividing line between high and low culture, that is, between art and everyday life. The idea that a simple object might be appreciated as 'art' and even framed and exhibited is now, almost 85 years later, well-understood by many: it has lost its shock value, making the outrageous and daringly prankish quality of Dada hard to grasp. In Zurich though, Dada was pure rage. Marcus labels it 'a voice of teeth ground down to points, more suited to manifestos and hit singles than to poems, a near-absolute loathing of one's time and place, the note held until disgust turns into glee' (1989: 195). Lefebvre's interest was in the way in which such works forced one to concentrate on the structure of meaning itself – it grabbed one's attention in ways that one never forgot. By the following year, the group had gone their own ways, back to Berlin cabarets, moved to New York, where it was the sort of prank that was the artists' prerogative, and transplanted to Paris, where Dada became an artistic *scandale* with philosophical pretensions – and the root of a long line of radical demands.

Lefebvre and Dada

Dada was transposed to Paris in the person of Tristan Tzara, but André Breton was its primary booster. As the darling of the Surrealists, Tristan Tzara represented art that mixed up the boundaries between art and life by creating situations in which theatre audiences were confused. Breton had written to Tzara over a period of a few years encouraging him to come to Paris. Lefebvre had started to associate with Breton's fledgling group of Surrealists, who greeted Tzara as the Surrealist messiah. With completely overblown expectations, there were soon disagreements about the direction the 'movement' should take. Breton's interest in founding a new dogma clashed with Lefebvre's fascination with the unalienated, un-rule-bound person and Tzara's inclination to anarchy. The Surrealists were concerned with careers as avant-garde artists, not merely a five-month infamy. For this basic reason, Lefebvre was more sympathetic to Dada than the staged *scandales* of the Surrealists: inciting bar brawls, insulting famous artists in letters that appeared on the editorial pages of Paris newspapers, or pranks trying to steal the limelight by denouncing Charlie Chaplin at his own Paris press conference for the opening of a film.

Unlike Lefebvre, the Surrealists sought to transcend rather than banish alienation. In this strange manner, their response to alienation was a secularised version of a religious experience. In this, transcendence was reconstructed as an intensely individual, private experience. Surrealism's impulse to abolish tedium through art became enclosed within the very structure of individualism, which was the cultural basis for the rational worker of industrial capitalism. Their art was so intensely individualised that there was little chance of organising groups on the basis of such private revelations. Surrealism was a predictable symptom of what has been called the 'sovereign individual of capitalism' (Abercrombie 1986; MacPherson 1962). Yet, despite his criticisms, Lefebvre's lasting admiration for the Surrealists as adventurers comes through in a interview from 1990:

> In this group, Eluard is one of the personalities who had most impressed me. I had excellent relations with him. He wasn't content to write poems, but tried to live the poetry. At one point, he had disappeared, in the Orient. Someone told us that they had met him in a road in a native quarter of Singapore or Jakarta. He would explore. . . . For sure he was the image of Rimbaud. But Rimbaud had renounced writing poetry while Eluard and Tzara found a source of inspiration there. This was a profound difference. For them, the bourgeoisie had abandoned poetry even while taking inspiration from it . . . even in using it.
>
> (1991c: 37)

The Surrealists invited Tzara to Paris to learn from Dadaism. Even though the leader of the Surrealist movement, André Breton, had introduced Lefebvre and the *Philosophes* to Hegel, and therefore to dialectics, the rapprochement between the *Philosophes* group and Surrealism was as short-lived as many of the Surrealists' memberships in the Parti Communiste Français (PCF). Why? Marxism approached the resolution of alienation through a reconstruction of class relations. Economic classes are based on people's positions in the production of goods, their relation to the means of production. In all of Marxism, the fundamental source of contemporary alienation is held to be alienation from work. But to change the class-based social relations between groups of people is a quite different response to alienation than the Surrealist's advice that each person end their own personal alienation through art and a 'poetic revolution'. Greil Marcus, looking back on what Lefebvre had said about Dada, commented:

> Yes, Lefebvre had said, he preferred dada . . . dada at least reached for an absolute: 'the end of the world'. But it was a puerile absolute, 'solely the spirit-that-says-no', 'vainly proclaiming the sovereignty of the instant', a 'pseudo-society': 'As Dada moves to escape all definitions, its negation defines itself all too powerfully as its own negation'. As philosophy, dada was . . . your basic Sophistry 1-A: everything I say is a lie.
>
> (Lefebvre 1924g; cited in Marcus 1989: 191)

For Lefebvre, Dada fluctuated between absolute affirmation of life and absolute negation of everything that had gone before. Each cancelled out the other. But either way, the absolute was made present: the boredom and meaninglessness of day-to-day existence was smashed by Dada's nihilistic spirit in these 'moments of presence'. This idea of a transcendent moment remained Lefebvre's fascination all his life. It kept him from ever being simply a Marxist. Instead, he continued to ask how Marxism could make a difference in everyday life in no matter what kind of society – capitalist or communist. His notion of the 'impossible–possible' and the need to aim for the ultimate in order to achieve the least (see Chapters 3 and 4) was an attempt to renovate Dadaism as a political project. As Henry Miller wrote at the time:

> 'They give us a lot of piffle about the revolution – first the revolution of the word, now the revolution in the street'. . . . Dada was 'more entertaining. They had humour at least. The Surrealists are too conscious of what they are doing. It's fascinating to read about their intentions, but when are they going to pull it off?'
>
> (Miller 1939: 159–60; 163; cited in Plant 1992: 53)

When he encountered Dada in 1924, Lefebvre saw in it a solution to the postwar malaise. In his 'Sept manifestes dada' (1924g), he argued that Dada had fragmented the structures that perpetuated the trivialisation of the lives of people. Every time they met, Tzara mocked 'Have you finished picking up the pieces?' 'No,' said Lefebvre with a quip that became famous, 'I'm going to finish smashing them.'

Dada challenged the invulnerability and reliability of meaning. The Swiss linguist Ferdinand de Saussure had given lectures in which he argued that meaning did not lie in the words *per se* but was just associated with them by convention. Words were arbitrary, just convenient sounds; a society could invent a new word to replace any existing one. Instead of 'dog', one could say 'chien' or even invent a new word, provided listeners agreed on what it referred to. This provided the basis for modern linguistics, but at the time such insights appeared like blowing out the flame of a candle. To the artists and writers of the time, the result seemed to be empty words: a radical emptiness at the centre of words that they had once taken for granted as encapsulating all that they held dear.

These ideas found ready sympathy with Lefebvre. For example, they implied that there could be no one interpretation of Marxism. Ideas and concepts could also be destabilised: they too were ambiguous, fluid. And, Dada fitted with Lefebvre's interest in Romanticism. Dada was the prototype of the 'modern sublime' (Bürger 1984), that is, a mixture of awe and terror as our imagination and concepts fail to grasp an experience. Classically, this had always been a goal of art. Kant gave the examples of a beautiful sunrise or looking over the waves across an expanse of ocean. A popular nineteenth-century example of this 'classical sublime' was Niagara Falls, which instilled a kind of terror and amazement in its viewers. Many fainted, overcome by the vertiginous feeling. Two very different twentieth-century examples are the unspeakable horror of the Holocaust (Lyotard 1990), or the fragile-looking smallness of Earth from space. Significantly, all such experiences are held to be indescribable. The sublime is a phenomenon in which one is 'lost for words'. This sense of 'losing one's feet' conceptually fits with the descriptions of Dada, and with Lefebvre's naming of these as 'moments of presence'.

Moments

Moments are those instants that we would each, according to our own personal criteria, categorise as 'authentic' moments that break through the dulling monotony of the 'taken for granted'. Moments outflank the pretensions of wordy theories, rules and laws, and challenge the limits of everyday living. Few have paid attention to either the short interjections or even the book-length works by Lefebvre on this topic. Although we can read his puzzlement between the lines, to his credit the Marxist geographer David Harvey is one of the only English-language writers to take notice in print.[2] Moments are 'revelatory of the totality of possibilities contained in daily existence. Such movements', and surely he meant *moments*, 'were ephemeral and would pass instantaneously into oblivion, but during their passage all manner of possibilities – often decisive and sometimes revolutionary – stood to be both uncovered and achieved' (Harvey 1991: 429). Moments are those times when one recognises or has a sudden insight into a situation or an experience beyond the merely empirical routine of some activity. A moment is a flash of the wider significance of some 'thing' or event – its relation to the whole, and by extension, our relation to totality.

Lefebvre used this concept to understand the euphoria of revolutionary fervour, as during the Paris Commune or the experience of being in love (1961j: 341–357; 1962i; 1965f). In a 1959 article, 'Justice et vérité' (Justice and Truth), Lefebvre described history as the overcoming of a series of spheres of limited emancipation, from the cosmic and divine through the philosophical, political, economic, to art. While this last sphere offered poetic freedom in the manner that the Surrealists had always dreamed of, Lefebvre argued that in defining the human experience through exceptional moments, external to everyday life, artistic freedom itself needed to be transcended in the search for a sphere of total liberty (1959a). This would bring a revolution into the mundane

---

2 However, a number of other writers, such as Ed Soja and Mark Gottdiener, are aware of these aspects of Lefebvre's work. It is because of the professional interest of those who have been most responsible for bringing Lefebvre to the attention of an English-speaking audience that major foci of Lefebvre's *oeuvre* such as the Theory of Moments appear to his English readers as fringe elements. Lefebvre has been much more assimilated as a geographer/political economist and even semiotician than as a philosopher of dialectics with one of the greatest ranges of all twentieth-century theorists.

and trivial details of everyday life, attacking alienation from banal tasks at their root.

Lefebvre formulated his idea of 'moments' as an objection to Bergson's notion of time.[3] For Bergson, time was conceived of as linear duration (*durée*) or 'becoming', as an arrow of progress, or as a series of separate instances. It took little account of personal insight or feeling. A moment is not an instant, but it is opposed to a stress on simply the passage of time. By 'moment', Lefebvre means that the experience of time passing is variable. One does not feel that time has 'stopped' or that one is outside of time. In the moment, one does not feel the passage of time – it is, in a sense 'timeless'. Instead of time travelling in an arrow-straight line (*conceptual time*), we need to think of *lived time* qualitatively. It is *involuted* (Lefebvre 1989a: 234). One possible metaphor is a river current, full of swirls and eddies; at one level it goes faster here and slower there. But Lefebvre is more interested in another aspect: lived time can be broad (collective) or narrow (individual); above all, this sort of temporality is repetitive and reversible. It is full of anticipations, insights into the future and of *déjà vu*, the sensation that one has already been through the moment one is now living. The theory of moments dates back to one of Lefebvre's earliest published papers, 'La Pensée et l'esprit' (1926a, written in 1925), in which he attempted to specify the link between the body and consciousness in terms of presence rather than possession, abstraction or pure concept.

In 'La Pensée et l'esprit', Lefebvre proposes that we think of moments as having a concrete existence that transcends and unites the subjectivity and objectivity of traditional philosophy. Moments are results and summaries of the entire development of the human being as such. Spirit is thus brought nearer through the spoken word more than through writing, through poetry more than through knowledge (Lefebvre 1926a: 55, 67), through the body more than through classical spirituality. Spirit is conceived of as natural life metamorphosed through the deployment of creative force of nature itself, seized in its 'being' and not through a manifestation such as *durée* or fluidity as in Bergson (Hess 1988: 61).

Years later, echoing his youthful mysticism, Lefebvre concludes in a hardly materialist tone: 'Thus the consciousness and the life of the conscious being reproduces in this theory the great cosmic movement which creates and reproduces distinct beings in carrying them along in its immense becoming' (1989a: 234). Nonetheless, he argues that lived time can be thought of as having 'substance'. Lived time is not a thing, yet it has a certain tangible quality: it is

---

3 Lefebvre explicitly denies that he is using the term 'moment' in any Hegelian sense, such as 'moment of inertia' or a moment in the progress of civilisation. Nor does Lefebvre mean a psychological or existential experience, although he admits that some sort of subjective experience is involved (1989a: 234).

recollected as a thing. Materialists and realists would object that he is confusing the relational matrix of time with events (which are causally more important). A similar critique has been made of Lefebvre's handling of space (see Chapter 8). It is what happens that counts, not the temporal qualities of our experience of events.

Lefebvre is not explicit, but he may mean that lived time is a 'form', which can be conceived of as a thing quite separate from its contents.[4] Moments are themselves essential forms in which everyday contents are arranged in recognisable patterns. As such, they are experiences of detachment from the everyday flow of time, or *durée*. Thus he defines 'moments' as 'modalities of presence', which are in themselves but glimpses: 'Partial totalities, I see them as "points of view" reflecting totality' (1989a: 234–5). Totality is defined as the entirety of existence, plus all that can potentially exist in the future as a result. Neither just one instant, nor an absolute revelation, they link the particular to the universal because each moment is a fragment of totality. Totality is thus the sum of these fragments. Lefebvre describes this as a dialectical situation, but it is without a simple synthesis, always in 'Heraclitean flux': 'I would introduce into becoming . . . a structure at the same time intelligible and practical, both real and normative, without cutting up into absolute discontinuities' (1989a: 235).

Presence

Experiences of totality are experiences of what he calls 'presence'. This 'Theory of Moments' provides a manner of conceptualising 'presence' that rejects a single vision of totality that would throw out all other viewpoints. Such views would form a gigantic 'absence'. If the banal frame of mind and trivial activities of everyday life are rejected by saying that people are not really living or are ignorant of Being, such an absence is created.[5] Lefebvre is also critical of the banality of everyday life, especially as it results from capitalism, but he refuses to give up on everyday life. Moments of presence are themselves within everyday life. They puncture the 'everydayness' or banality of repetitive tasks like a ray of

---

4   Lefebvre commented that in the 1940s and 1950s he wrote dozens of pages on a theory of moments, none of which were published. Some, however, may survive in the collection of correspondence that Lefebvre sent to Norbert Guterman, now in the Butler Library, Columbia University.

5   Lefebvre is criticising Heidegger, who in *Being and Time* argues that life or 'being' (small 'b') has become trivialised, and the presence of 'Being' (capital 'B') is 'taken for granted'. As a result, we are spiritually dulled. The route to recovering our consciousness is through philosophy and metaphysics (see discussion, Chapter 1). Lefebvre is also criticising Bergsonian 'vitalism', a favourite target, for making a similar argument: people neglect the process of 'becoming' and miss the potential and 'vitality' of the moment because they are caught up in the unreflective passage of time. The prescription for this malaise is again philosophy. The result of these two theories is that the realm of everyday life is rejected and scorned.

sunshine through clouds. Banality is broken up or divided by 'moments'. In effect, these 'moments' are what redeems everyday life for Lefebvre:

$$\textit{Everyday Life} = \textit{Banality} \div \textit{Moments of Presence}$$

This division, puncturing, is of course a dialectic, but Lefebvre would have enjoyed the equation, a form he also uses, for example in titling his dialectical autobiography, 'The Sum and the Remainder' (*Le Somme et le reste* 1959i). He writes of a 'bouquet of "moments" mixed into the banality of everyday life' (1989a: 235; see also 1961j: 340–57). The everyday, then, is an undifferentiated space of the mundane interrupted by a primordial form of time, the 'moment'. Gardiner points out the similarity between this and Bloch's concept of the *novum* (1995: 118 n9) and there are, indeed, striking parallels to Benjamin's notion of the 'optical unconscious'. Presence, a pure exception in the undifferentiated, is temporalisation, and this is a remarkable indication of the centrality of time in Lefebvre's thought on space. We might label his life-project as one that involves bringing meaning to the banal and the spatial. For him, *praxis* is the means of maintaining within oneself the fluid potentiality of 'becoming' while at the same time creating a stable world. We will return to this in Chapter 10, but briefly, for Lefebvre, revolution is only one political form of this *praxis*. It stands beside involution, dissolution and evolution. A completed theory of moments would correct the overly simple periodisation of modes of production and the fetishism of a linear historicity of progress found in Marx (1989a: 236). However, like his other ideas, this one was rejected out of hand by the PCF.

Such a philosophical theory appears too emotional; it deals with things that are too ephemeral for the hard-boiled Marxist, and so Harvey, for example, mentions it but brings his readers back to geography, our feet back on the ground. But Greil Marcus, reaching for an understanding of the links between cultural avant-gardes, searching for the connections and the 'secret history' of fringe movements and critical artists such as the Paris Commune, the Situationists and 1980s Punk, exposes the central importance of the theory of moments. Marcus, popularising Lefebvre, has put it in terms of individual experience:

> Instead of examining institutions and classes, structures of economic production and social control one had to think about 'moments' – moments of love, hate, poetry, frustration, action, surrender, delight, humiliation, justice, cruelty, resignation, surprise, disgust, resentment, self-loathing, pity, fury, peace of mind – those tiny epiphanies, Lefebvre said, in which the absolute possibilities and temporal limits of anyone's existence were revealed. The richness or poverty of any social formation could be judged only on the terms of these evanescences; they passed out of consciousness as if they had never been, but in their instants they contained the whole of life.
>
> (Marcus 1989: 144)

Yet Lefebvre, the sociologist-philosopher, would not have allowed his readers to go away with an overly individualistic or psychological idea of such moments. However, it is true that he does describe them in a manner that is easy to misinterpret. Take the following comment on being in love:

> 'Love is a moment.' By this I mean first the permanent temptation of the absolute. Love tends toward the absolute; if not it does not exist. However, the absolute is impossible, unlivable, untenable, absurd. In its neighbourhood lurks madness: the alienation of one's feelings and passions [*l'alienation passionnel*], that of solitude, or of the renunciation of that which is not it. It slyly seizes, takes hold of you. . . . And you use cunning with it to retake yourself.
> (Lefebvre 1958: 343; cited in Hess 1988: 28–29)

'Love' is usually portrayed as a 'mystery', as a miracle, but Lefebvre manages to re-establish the centrality of agency at the heart of being in love: it happens perhaps not rationally but with people's complicity. 'The moment of love is situated at the intersection of the impossible absolute and of the everyday, which it also makes impossible. It is a moment lived in the mode of contradiction' (Hess 1988: 29). In other words, it is the 'impossible–possible'.

Lefebvre always tries to connect personal 'moments' with social totality. This is what makes Lefebvre's theory *radical*, in every sense. In addition to this, he criticises twentieth-century life for making such connections difficult and obscuring or (as he puts it) 'mystifying' them. As a result, we do not appreciate that such experiences may link us to others' experiences at other times and in other places. Instead, we are trapped in our own psychological appreciations. Thus we are divided rather than brought together (1961j: 342). If the experience of 'moments' is one thing that makes us human, capitalist modernity has found a way to make this something that separates rather than allows us to share and brings us together.

Lefebvre is a humanist who believes that such sentiments are cultural universals.[6] In contrast to current positions that unveil the socially constructed nature of nearly everything, Lefebvre had complete, and even naive faith in the primacy of authentic experience. The postmodernist debate on authenticity, on how one recognises 'the real thing', has never reached closure. Lefebvre's work is a placeholder, a bookmark in the unfinished debate. Lefebvre would compare the life of a peasant in Meiji Japan with one in postwar France, or the grind of a clerical worker in late twentieth-century Los Angeles with the life of a minor func-

---

6 In this, Lefebvre takes a similar position to Lévi-Strauss (Kurzweil 1980: 59), believing in people's spontaneity, their wish to raise themselves 'to the highest degree of existence'. The result is that individual volition is more central than in forms of Marxism of the Althusserian type and in Structuralism itself, which focused on the social systemic level of analysis.

tionary in ninth-century China on their attitude towards such moments and the quality of the society's response to experiences of authenticity. Are 'moments' dismissed but then commercialised and sold back to alienated people as commodified experiences? Thus Lefebvre argues that it is possible to compare the displacement of direct experience of 'moments' under personal control by the *consumption* of commodities, of entertainment, and of experiences (such as tourism). Against all forms of falsity, all signs of consumption compensating for alienation and starvation for authenticity, Lefebvre counterposed moments of presence and his ideal: the 'total person', *l'homme total*.

In all this, we have not yet defined 'presence' itself as a philosophical concept. Throughout Lefebvre's work, the most mysterious asides concern presence. For example, in *La Production de l'espace*, (*The Production of Space*) (1991d), this statement is lodged in a discussion of production: 'Modernity is a dialectic of presence and absence' (see Shields 1992). In *La Presence et l'absence* (1980a), Lefebvre surveys the various aspects of the question. He also describes the link between consciousness and the body in terms of presence rather than possession. Rather than thinking of the body as the private property of the mind (a capitalist metaphor), we might theorise subjectivity in terms of a presence. A similar example is the case of the Sign, which makes an abstract idea 'present' by giving it the concrete form of the sign such as a word or logo. All such concepts are 'concrete abstractions' in which the abstract becomes concrete, or in which the absent is made present. Any meaning of 'presence' of course has to do with nearness (and thus spatial location: here!) and with the present (location in time: now!). 'Presence' is thus central to philosophical debates about ontology because 'what exists' is distinguished by its ability to be present. 'Presence' also has much to do with questions of epistemology, because 'what is true' is often a judgement based on the witness of one's senses. 'Seeing is believing' and 'out of sight is out of mind' are popular sayings that indicate the importance of the concept of presence in common sense. A youthful Lefebvre once commented that 'One loves a presence. . . . Thus speaks the thought which wishes to determine the object of love' (1926: 48).

> If one pretends that love has a cause or reason, one returns from the object to the subject and inversely, because the subject and the object are that which thought thinks of love, which remains without reason: a moment which abolishes . . . all such separation [distance]. . . . it operates through the encounter [meeting].
>
> (1926: 50–1; cited in Hess 1988: 28)

Does being in love have a cause? An alternative to a theory of cause and effect is to consider love dialectically, as an encounter or a coming-together that abolishes the distinctions between causes and effects, one and the other. Hence its ineluctable, fascinating character. The advantage of analysing such experiences in terms of presence and absence is that they allow one to seize events and experiences in their phenomenological flow rather than by imposing a predefined grid of categories. Presence and absence capture social processes 'on the hoof', as it were, as they come and go *between* categories, for example, as experiences of oppression overflow concepts such as race or ethnicity to take on class and gender dimensions – all at once, but not precisely one *form* of oppression or another.

6

THE CRITIQUE OF EVERYDAY
LIFE: MARX AND NIETZSCHE

The search for everyday life

'Against the shining progress of technology and commerce,' Lefebvre said 'everyday life was "a backward sector" in the modern world' – 'a colonised sector' argued his student, Guy Debord: 'an affective Third World in the heart of the First' (cited in Marcus 1989: 145). Marx had set in motion the complete critique of the economic form of capitalism and its social consequences. Lefebvre believed that by applying Marx's method – dialectical materialism – to the social and the cultural itself, a critique of the way that people lived and approached living collectively could be launched. As Marcus points out: 'It was in the realm of the trivial that any critique of everyday life, and therefore any critique of social reality, began (1989: 145).

Lefebvre was one of the first social theorists to pay attention to the details of everyday life outside of macro-social structures, such as kinship patterns, employment and status, that can be generalised from person to person and society to society. Lefebvre's interest in the everyday was originally a critique of philosophical responses to the perceived banality of post-First World War life. Across social classes, Europeans perceived a loss of meaning and an increase in repetition in their lives. Lefebvre moved from a philosophical response towards sociological investigations of this banality, or 'everydayness' (*quotidiennété*) as it is referred to. At the same time, he developed his philosophical analyses of alienation. This chapter presents both of these parallel streams of thought, arguing that it is impossible to understand Lefebvre's critiques of everyday life without some comprehension of the thoroughness of his philosophical investigations of alienation and fetishism, spontaneity, desire, subjectivity, spectacle.

Modernisation wrought rapid changes in the patterns and routines of daily life and highlighted the loss of individual control and sense of community with the acquisition of a materialistic lifestyle. This was particularly apparent after the First World War, and again after the Second.

Contrasting the French experience to the slow, steady 'rational' modernisation of American society that transpired throughout the twentieth century, Lefebvre evoked the almost cargo-cult-like, sudden descent of large appliances into war-torn French households and streets in the wake of the Marshall Plan. Before the war, it seemed, no one had a refrigerator; after the war, it seemed, everyone did.

(Ross 1996: 5)

The populace was seized with enthusiasm for the new riches, for *modernisation* and the culture of the 'new and improved', when everyday objects suddenly shone with the transformative power of the sublime (1961j: 84–91). Kristin Ross comments that Lefebvre 'attributes his whole discovery of the concept of "everyday life" to his wife's tone of voice, one day in their apartment, when she praised a particular brand of laundry soap' (1966: 73). But the deadening experience of banality – of the taken-for-grantedness of everyday life – is presumed to be the same for everyone. This is not just Lefebvre's phallocentrism. Even contemporary commentators miss the opportunity to disaggregate and examine the unevenness and unequal features of everyday life – and even in the midst of books on just that topic.

It is from the Surrealists that Lefebvre drew this central concept of *le quotidien*, the everyday. At heart this was a notion of the banal, trivial and repetitive quality of life under capitalism (see Chapter 4). This idea of 'the everyday' and of 'everydayness' is thus not the same as simply 'everyday life' or 'daily life' (*la vie quotidienne*). These terms were more often used to refer to the uncatalogued, habitual and routine nature of day-to-day living rather than used critically to refer specifically to the alienated, dry 'everydayness' of daily life. In true Nietzschean fashion, Lefebvre attempts to realign the common French phrase 'daily life' (*la vie quotidienne*) with the *critical* concept of an alienated life summed up in the term *le quotidien* (see Chapter 5; Lefebvre 1991a [1947a]).[1]

In *La Conscience mystifiée*, everyday life was merely the tedious and banal reality of daily living to be replaced by a revolutionary, involved and unalienated social life. Over almost forty years in his series *Critique of Everyday Life*, everyday life emerged as the ground of resistance and renewal, which was essential to the 'moments' and flashes of unalienated presence that punctured it (see Chapter 4). In Chapter 4, the important difference between 'everyday life', understood as 'daily life', and 'the everyday' (*Alltäglichkeit, le quotidien*) – by which theorists such as Lukács, Heidegger and Lefebvre mean 'triviality' or 'banality' – was noted. Here we go further. To criticise everyday life is to begin to theorise the complaint that 'life is boring'. What does this mean and what are the implications of a boredom so deeply seated that we drift off in our own

---

1   There is thus a big difference between Lefebvre's comment that *la vie est quotidienne* ('life is banal') and the French phrase *la vie quotidienne* (daily life), which is too often lost in English translations of Lefebvre's work.

fantasies? As people say, we 'go on autopilot', 'not really thinking', 'doing nothing' and 'walking around in a daze'. All these idioms express a felt distance between consciousness and body, and thus between subjectivity and identity. This 'distancing' and estrangement amounts to an insidious form of alienation that is often 'mystified' (Lefebvre and Guterman 1936a; see Chapter 4) – that is, denied or explained away. Not only is this self-alienation but the alienation of mind from body. Lefebvre argues that this is a symptom of more than conditioned docility (for example, assembly line workers who force themselves to be automata until the end of their shift). It indicates a domination of areas of human activity and relationships whose richness, if revealed, could become the basis for a reconstruction of human society.

The concept of everyday life (triviality) goes back to the book that Lefebvre wrote with Norbert Guterman, *La Conscience mystifiée* (drafted 1933–4, published 1936a) which takes up themes of alienation developed in *Avant Poste*.[2] Lefebvre later and very explicitly linked his *Critique of Everyday Life* (1947a; 1961j; 1981a; 1992a) back to these works as part of his lifelong project of 'establishing Marxism as critical theory, i.e. as both philosophy and the supersession of philosophy.' To ' "rediscover authentic Marxism" was to discover "the critical knowledge of everyday life"' (Trebitsch 1991: xiv–xv). This critique parallels George Lukács' separate work from 10–15 years earlier in his book on the birth of tragedy; his seminal book on the question of everyday life, the sphere of trivial and repeated activities, was published in 1911. He was heavily influenced by the German sociologist Georg Simmel, whose 1909–10 seminar he attended in Berlin (see Arato and Brienes 1979: 13–15). In these lectures on alienation and on money, Simmel argued that currency, as an abstract system of equivalences into which the value of any thing could be translated, levelled entirely different spheres and kinds of value into one system of exchange. Lefebvre and his circle (Guterman, Politzer, Nizan, Morhange, Friedmann) drew the notion of everyday from Heidegger's *Alltäglichkeit*. Heidegger had, in turn, taken this from Lukács *Metaphysik der Tragödie* (1911). There, Lukács had pointed out the trivial life of human beings, indistinguishable from the world of objects. Heidegger followed by contrasting mechanical repetition with 'authentic life' or Being (*Dasein*). Lefebvre and Guterman argued that

> The idea of escaping from the combination of elements of the past – of repetition – was an idea that was at once poetic, subversive and audacious. It already implied that this was a project with a difference [and of Lefebvre's search for a politics of difference]. It isn't easy to invent new pleasures, or new ways of making love . . . a utopian idea – but not really – since, effectively, we lived, we created a new situation, that of

---

2 For example, the analysis of Fascism as ideology, defined as a 'mystification' of the potential of revolution (see 1933a; 1933n; and the first three issues of *Avant Poste*).

exuberance in friendship, that of the subversive or revolutionary microsociety in the very heart of a society which, moreover, ignores it (Lefebvre 1975c: 157–60; cited in Marcus 1989: 146).

Heidegger graces Lukács' work by taking over his terminology of *Alltäglichkeit* or 'triviality' and *Erlebniswirklichkeit*. He argued that, in the ordinary 'world of experience', people's creations and even their lives appeared to them as 'things' that were impossible to change. This process of 'thing-ification' (*Versachlichung*) was based on Lukács' study of reification: 'everything, once it appears in the world, takes on an existence entirely independent of its creator and purpose.' (1914: 321; cited in Arato and Brienes 1979: 15). Lefebvre and Guterman make no mention of Heidegger. Guterman claimed that they were unaware of his work (Jacoby 1981: 182 n22), but Lefebvre was introduced to the notion of 'everyday life' in Heidegger's *Being and Time* by André Breton and Tristan Tzara. He reacted violently against Heidegger and proposed several unsuccessful thesis topics that aimed to reassert the politics of 'everyday life' against Heidegger's philosophical usage. Lefebvre may well have been aware of the origins of the term and the concern with everyday life, even if not with Lukács' work written in Hungarian, which would have been inaccessible to him at the time.[3]

Lefebvre's critique of the 'everydayness' of daily life was always underpinned by his early collaboration with Norbert Guterman in translating Marx's early works on alienation (*1844 Manuscripts*, see Marx 1975) and their book *La Conscience mystifiée* (1936a), which developed the concept of mystification and alienation. In *La Conscience mystifiée*, Guterman and Lefebvre searched for a Marxist critique of bourgeois ideology: 'How are we to proceed...? By starting with the portrait of the most prosaic of men in his daily life' (1936a: 69–70). They argued that individualism as a form of self-consciousness cannot be explained by itself, or by digging deeply into psychological theory or into developing a metaphysics to 'ground' modern individualism (at root a critique of Bergson, and of Heidegger's historical ontology). Such an approach merely reproduces the commodity form in which objects become 'other than themselves' by appearing as things that they are not and by hiding their real nature as products – artefacts – of human labour. Both Heidegger and Bergson separated individual consciousness from the body and experience. In this philosophical

---

3   Burkhard (1986: 354 n44), to whose in-depth research I am indebted, suggests that they may even have read Lukács' contributions to *Archiv Marksa-Engel'sa* 3, the issue from which they translated the *1844 Manuscripts* into French beginning in 1929. Indeed, Lefebvre claimed that they were aware of Lukács' censure by the Hungarian Communist Party and hence omitted him in line with party policy. As has been mentioned, Lefebvre often played a dubious and ambiguous role, simultaneously colluding in the censorship and intellectual demolition of other unorthodox Marxists while proceeding with his own similar research and being censured himself.

approach, the body becomes an object over against the subject, the situation of modern individualism. In this situation, fetishism and alienation are not only economic but also lie in the inability to comprehend this Other, the body, and all others. Split off from ourselves, we are unable to comprehend totality. Bourgeois life is thus distanced from the real and fragmented. This artificial, constructed quality of life makes 'mystification' possible. Thus 'mystification' derives from our alienated situation.

One significance of Lefebvre's approach to reification is to conceive it in terms that are at once spatial and embodied, or 'lived'. His reification and its attendant alienation are strongly marked, as noted in earlier chapters, by the French sense of 'alien' as the 'foreign' and distant. For example, Lefebvre refers to Paris as his passion, yet also as his alienation from his homeland in the Bearn in the French Pyrenees.

Dialectic of banality and presence

Everyday life is a collection of things and activities that are repetitive and banal. They were the more strikingly ordinary in the first half of the twentieth century because common, everyday activities were generally ignored by both philosophers and social theorists. The focus was on great events or institutions. We can thus locate Lefebvre with Fernand Braudel and the *Annales* school of historians in the broad French interest in reinstating the micro-scale texture of typical activities in social and historical research instead of focusing only on unusual or grand-scale events or activities.

It is worth distinguishing carefully between everyday life and the concept 'the everyday' in order to clarify its meaning. The term 'everyday life' in Lefebvre's books means 'banal and meaningless life', not daily life. In French, there is a certain interchangeability between this idea of banal activities and daily tasks. While 'everyday life' in the sense of daily tasks is an amorphous set of more or less usual and unremarkable activities 'the everyday' always means the ordinary, banal and repetitive. In contrast to Lefebvre, Agnes Heller approaches everyday life in a different manner. She takes a phenomenological stance, investigating everyday life as an arena of practical ethics and ontological authenticity. Lefebvre foregrounds the lack of authenticity and the pervasive domination of daily life by alienation, which turns daily life from a set of creative and self-actualising experiences into the boring and repetitive 'everyday'. For Heller, daily life is the 'particular' and the immediate. It is the dimension of survival. This set of activities is dominated by analogy, and the repetition of ways of doing things that are learned or copied from others. 'The way things are done' is unquestioning and ethically passive (Heller 1984: 313). People not only describe but also justify these aspects of life as 'the way things have always been done'. Tradition and repetition simply override any ethical considerations or the need for change. Conformism, repetition and habit are the typical forms of action in daily life, while generalisation, uncritical ethical passivity, technical reason and analogy are the typical forms of knowledge. Heller's critique of daily life is thus based on the tendency for it to become a sphere of practical reason of 'knowing how'. 'Knowing what' to do, freely setting goals and examining options become extraordinary activities that are the preserve of specialists.

One would have expected Lefebvre to declare numinous 'moments' of presence or revelation to be outside the everyday (see Chapter 4). However, he does not make this clear distinction, arguing instead that trivial and repetitive activities are also occasions for moments when people can experience themselves and their activities in an unalienated manner. Lefebvre refuses to make a Cartesian division, because this classification would result in two solitudes, where the everyday was condemned to perpetual alienation, with perplexed academics debating the efficacy of strategies for transforming elements of the everyday into elements of an unalienated extraordinary set of 'moments'. Instead of two distinct sets – one alienated, bad, everyday; the other special, good, unalienated 'moments' – Lefebvre proposes two overlapping sets. Each element of the alienated everyday is also potentially an element of the unalienated extraordinary set. This overlap means that each and every activity must be rethought as a dialectic of presence and 'absence' (a word that Lefebvre uses as a synonym for alienation and mystification; see 1980a). Each activity is simultaneously an opportunity for alienation and for dis-alienation. Furthermore, Lefebvre recognised that alienation and disinterest always set in once activities have become routine or once skills have been mastered. Thus he described not only the negative quality of alienation but also its dialectical entwinement with dis-alienation and wholehearted involvement.

In contrast to the Surrealists, Lefebvre and Guterman held to their commitment to public change rather than trying to resolve alienation by developing the private emotions or consciences of individuals (hence Lefebvre's later critique of Sartre; see Chapters 4 and 7).

> For us, the solution was in the direction of the horizon. We were those who scrutinised the horizon. We looked towards forward not backward. To the question 'What is thinking?' we didn't respond with Being [like Heidegger] but with the possible.
>
> (interview with Lefebvre, February 1988; cited in Hess 1988: 54)

By introducing the idea of 'everyday life', Lefebvre hoped to short-circuit the traditional philosophical obsession with origins: 'From where does this come?' Lefebvre's question is 'Where to go?' The intention of the phrase and of his series of books on everyday life was to foreground the importance of transforming consciousness by changing the everyday routines and material elements of daily life, as opposed to the Surrealists' more conceptual approach, which stressed a personal 'romantic' revolution. The significance of daily life was that 'it alone was a measure of the balance between human realisation as "*l'homme total*' and its dialectical antithesis, alienation' (Poster 1975: 244). Lefebvre contrasted modern life with the 'festival' of everyday life as he perceived it in its Dionysian form, in ancient Athens and in medieval festivals, when norms were periodically inverted or suspended (see Shields 1991: Ch. 2).

> Championing a world of incessant flux and becoming which under-scores but is nevertheless dominated by reason's insistence on the stability of being, Nietzsche saw an endless movement of becoming, difference, chance, and chaos washing against the categories of reason to power a recurring threat.
>
> (Plant 1992: 109)

Nietzsche and everydayness

The sphere of everyday life is a dynamic arena of practice. The person of this everyday life (*l'homme quotidien*) is both the subject and object of becoming. Lefebvre thus portrays a person who unites all aspects of himself to become what he called the 'total person'. This Marxist appropriation of Nietzsche's 'Overman' is conceived of as the unity of the socially formed individual and the person as 'natural' body. This is thus a unity of the general and of the particular characteristics of the human in a particular historical moment. Lefebvre's 'total person' reconciled thought and life, mind and body, by living life as an *oeuvre*, a work of art that required the full investment and reconciliation of both body and mind. Thus, 'whereas a *work* has something irreplaceable and unique about it, a *product* can be reproduced exactly, and is in fact the result of repetitive acts and gestures.' In a moment of naturalistic pantheism, echoing Schelling – which appears odd only twenty years later given the impact of biotechnology – he continues:

> Nature creates and does not produce. . . . Nature does not labor. . . . Nature knows nothing of these creations. A tree, a flower or a fruit is not a 'product' – even if it is in a garden. A rose has no why or where-fore; it blooms because it blooms. . . . The beings it creates are works . . . to say natural is to say spontaneous.
>
> (1991d: 70)

Life was an adventure, Lefebvre had said early on. It had to be lived to the fullest, rejecting all the compromises, refusing boredom and taking full respon-sibility for the outcome (1925a). The key was to make living into a practice of unalienated production, which Lefebvre understood according to Marxist theo-ries of labour and authentic use value. He had operationalised Nietzsche's portraits of the Overman by developing a model of the everyday practice of what Nietzsche had called *Überwinden* – 'overcoming'. 'Overcoming' was a critical alternative to Hegel's model of the dialectic in which oppositions were sublimated (*Aufhebung*) through a process of synthesis.[4] Nietzsche stressed the ongoing and reversible character of this 'synthesis'. Unlike Hegel's model, which Marx adopted as a model of historical progress, the traits of the original ingredients – the thesis and antithesis – were never lost or perfectly blended in the synthesis. Syntheses were always falling back or apart. Hence they were reversible. History too could thus be reversible, falling back as much as following an arrow-like course of progress. In Nietzsche's time, this brought angry responses from most European thinkers, who were committed to a vision of perpetual progress and evolution.

Lefebvre at first criticised Nietzsche for falling back from Marx's and Hegel's dialectical philosophy (1939a) but finally accepted the importance of reversibility and instability in everyday life (1975a). This is much closer to contemporary Hegelian scholarship on the sense of *Aufhebung* or sublimation. Yet one important element that Lefebvre contributed was to turn attention away from a simplistic idea of the dialectic as a temporal succession from contradiction to synthesis (see Chapter 8). On the level of daily activities, outcomes were never guaranteed to be progressive, and constant effort was required – continually 'overcoming' – because of the fragmentary quality of social life. Hence the strategy employed in issuing a series of books on the *Critique of Everyday Life* over four or more decades: updates on an inconclusive struggle. Thus, societies are always changeable (and hence open to creative 'projects' as Sartre called them, or 'works' (*oeuvres*) as Lefebvre called them) and always incomplete. This presents the opportunity not only for political agency and human creativity but also the possibility of an ongoing social revolution in which people collectively and continually resolve to overturn 'everydayness', the alienating conditions and meaninglessness of daily life. *L'homme total* constantly overcame the dialectical opposition between mind and body, between self and other, and thus overcame alienation. They had a better grasp of totality because of this unalienated outlook and the refusal of 'mystifications' of bourgeois

---

4 Nietzsche presents his ideas through poetry, allegory and theatre. Oversimplifying, he can be begun to be understood as a critic of Hegel's dialectic. Steeped in studies of the Greek classics and focused on discovering archetypal cultural traits that had been preserved in German culture, Nietzsche worked in the philological tradition. His presentation of the idea of the Overman is thus intended as a demonstration of the importance of the ethical attitude towards life in which constant struggle is required. The key principle, a kind of life force, is the 'in-process' quality of life. It, we, are constantly developing and engaging in effort. Life is in Heraclitean flux. Against the principle of entropy, that all things die (formulated in the natural sciences as the tendency of materials to fall to their lowest energy state), and against the tendency of society to maintain static, reified artefacts as expressions of the Apollonian power of humans, Nietzsche asserted the importance of the Dionysiac. Dionysos is a metaphoric figure of desire and eternal becoming, always dying or being fragmented only to be reborn whole. On the Dionysiac, compare Michel Maffesoli's *L'Ombre de Dionysos*, translated as *The Shadow of Dionysos* (1995), who broke with Lefebvre's foregrounding of Marxist theory to present a more clearly Nietzschean base to social theory.

ideologies of the middle-class culture of capitalism. To understand totality meant understanding the relationship between what was possible in the future – projective reason – and the existing conditions of everyday life. This grasp of totality is thus the precondition for effective agency.

Lefebvre's *l'homme total* conceals the humanistic aspirations that are hidden in this concept. It is not for nothing that he is called a humanistic Marxist. While wishing to attack the fragmented quality of individual life, Lefebvre held to a unified conception of the human psyche. Divisions and splits within the individual were symptoms of alienation. He later admitted that alienation was almost a natural condition, setting in again after every unalienated 'moment'. However, he continued to posit a state of mind and body in which there was no differentiation between thought and action. This Freudian stress on the internal consistency of the person, who is thought of as a monad, is at odds with the more fluid model of subjectivity that he sought to import from the Romantics, from Dada and the Situationists.

His interest in a radicalised romanticism surfaces again and again throughout Lefebvre's life. However, it is clearest only in his few books on literature: *Rabelais* (1955g); *Musset* (1955f) and *Pignon* (1956f), and *Contribution à l'esthetique* (1953c). These were each respectable studies but are more an interpretation of each author from a Marxist perspective and a presentation of selected readings than in-depth studies. By comparison with Lucien Goldmann or Lukács, Lefebvre has been much less influential as a literary theorist. His interest in romanticism is the crucial tie between all these works, which must be understood as part of a wider attempt to disengage the progressive potential of romanticism. Furthermore, Lefebvre's reading of Marx, which stressed alienation, relied on a notion of Marx as a fundamentally romantic writer. Similarly, Nietzsche's notion of 'the tragic' could be argued to be linked to a romantic *esprit du temps*. Romanticism often degenerated into sentimentality and nostalgia for a lost golden age. Nonetheless, as a latent critique of status quo conditions, it was a form of utopian yearning with revolutionary potential. Lefebvre therefore has roots in the tragic and the Romantics' horror at the gap between signifiers and reality. In this, he is perhaps at his closest to Walter Benjamin. The metamorphoses and instabilities of language hint at the impossibility of fully controlling nature and life. As the Surrealists argued, renaming could itself accomplish a type of empirical change to the world by altering perceptions and understandings (Hess 1989: 57, 211; Lefebvre 1957h). Hence the importance of a *dialectical* understanding of the flux of empirical life, which could grasp the indeterminacy and changing nature of life itself rather than a *formal* understanding of processes frozen as 'things' (see Chapter 6).

Lefebvre draws on Dada, on Surrealism and on the Romantics' fascination with a total unification of all aspects of experience, which would unite the rational and the subjective together. Areas of human identity that exceed normative standards of the self would be integrated. Thus, the fluidity, changeability and formlessness of humanity would be acknowledged. Lefebvre based some of his strongest critiques of Foucault on this insight. The body exceeds clinical categories (1971d). However, he nonetheless avoids discussions of the undefined, the formless or what the Romantics called 'the monstrous'. On the one hand, he condemns the overly rationalised, machine-like person, which he calls the '*cybernanthrope*' (1971e; see Chapter 4). This is not Haraway's 'cyborg' – the human body extended and enhanced technologically, whether by dental fillings, implants or other devices. Lefebvre is referring to a technological and rational attitude. On the other hand, the formless and monstrous appear only implicitly in Lefebvre's work as forms of lack and alienation. Only when defined as ambiguity and 'becoming' in the case of the *oeuvre*, or as the 'impossible–possible', which he and Sartre identify with utopia, or 'spaces of representation' (often translated as 'representational spaces'), does he move beyond rational calculation. He never lets himself get carried away – even when one expects it. Thus he appears to reduce 'moments' back to logic, and love to instrumental calculation.

This tension – the way he cannot quite break with an old language of formal reason and methodology – is precisely one of the significant and productive aspects of Lefebvre's work. He is the dividing line between the achievements of European philosophy and the complex forms of indeterminate 'fuzzy' logic, complexity theory and methods based purely on probability rather than truth and falsity. By attempting a synthesis of Nietzsche, Marx and Hegel (1975a), he tried to create a set of tools that could grapple with this 'realm of shadows', as he called it. However, he remained committed to a formal and logical approach to social action. He saw theory as an instrument for calculating political projects, even when he was attempting to consider the 'explosion' of energy during May 1968, or the unpredictability of moments of presence. In the end, he leaves us with something like the scissors-and-rock game played in school-yards and seems almost to shrug, saying 'events overturn theory' (1968h: 1).

Critique of everyday life

Unlike the long tradition of criticising the banality of everyday life in the name of transcendent truths and more profound activities, Lefebvre criticises everyday life from within. The tradition of disdain – of the body, of mundane activities – was the work of exceptional thinkers but concealed its own contradictions and ideology. Past ideologies attempted to solve the problem of alienation and of the relationship of the individual and the social but only displaced it. For example, organised religion projected the moment and possibility of reconcilia-tion and unity outside both the individual and the social, into an afterlife of the dead, while reinscribing an inner division bringing alienation into the centre of the formation of the individual. Good and evil, sin and salvation, eroded the unity of the person to produce a self-policing and self-objectifying individual oppressed from within as well as without.

The criticism of everyday life was the preoccupation of a social class whose pursuit of the exceptional and extraordinary 'was in fact a criticism of other classes, and for the most part found its expression in contempt for productive labour' (1991: 29). Lefebvre's work replaces this with a critique of everyday life that analyses ' "life", as it is, without making an obscure entity of it' (*ibid.*: 66). Lefebvre is asking 'What is socialism exactly? How does it intervene in everyday life? What does it change?' (*ibid.*: 47). He admits that the answer is unclear; however, there is no better guide to reading his various works on everyday life than these questions, which explain his interest in the everyday, and make the stakes clear. Especially in the period 1945–1958, Lefebvre risked his position for this attack on party dogma and was ridiculed for questioning the primacy of the state as the only objective and prize of Marxist struggle.[5]

In 1946, 1961 and again in 1981, Lefebvre issued volumes under the title *Critique of Everyday Life*. The first was merely an 'Introduction', the second 'a Sociology of Everyday Life' and the third a 'Metaphilosophy of the Everyday' in which he tried to apply his more Nietzschean position to his old topic. Lefebvre's periodic return to this personal version of the longitudinal survey shows the consistency of his position, which remained critical even while evolving to incorporate new elements. Looking back in 1958, he found the first book 'inadequately substantiated' (1991: 4, originally published as 1947a). Perhaps that inspired him to write the second book under the same title to make up for the shortcomings he saw as:

> In the first place, it should have formulated and attempted to resolve the problem posed by the concept of alienation. It should also have explained what a Marxist sociology . . . could be. . . .
>
> Today we are only just beginning to glimpse the complexity of the questions the theory of alienation poses. . . . *Historically*, we must discover what role this concept played in the development of Marxism. . . . *Theoretically*, we must determine what becomes of the *philosophical* concept. . . .
>
> Finally, the problem *philosophically* is of knowing what meanings and (critical or constructive) importance should be given at the

---

5   Looking back on the reception of the first volume of *Critique of Everyday Life*, Lefebvre attacked his Stalinist critics:

> The Marxists who imported this Stalinist interpretation into France – not merely uncriti-cally, but actually shooting down the slightest hint of criticism as though it were treason . . . could not accept sociology as a science, or the philosophical concept of alien-ation. . . . So dogmatic was their attitude that all they could see in the *Critique of Everyday Life* was an attempt to analyse certain aspects of bourgeois society *sociologically*, without actually making a stand against it . . . (Sectarian and dogmatic Marxist criticism frequently begins by isolating texts from their context, and then from the author's other works, in order to pin down some 'formula' or other.) . . . (Sectarian Marxists have nothing much to say – and everything they have to say they say over and over again.)
>
> (1991: 53)

present moment to the concept of alienation. To what extent should a philosopher take it up again . . . and put it at the centre of his thinking?

(1991: 4)

The first volume is an essay-length tour of everyday situations and a survey of the problem of politically changing the style and quality of everyday life rather than changing the government. The second was a full-length study of contemporary life in the early 1960s. The third outlined what had changed and what appeared to remain the same in the conditions of daily life after almost forty years. At a time when few wrote in such terms as 'modernity', Lefebvre pointed to the emergence of a reflexive conception of the 'time of modern life' identified not so much by its politics as the changes that had taken place within everyday life. In this book, he spoke of the crisis of modernity, anticipating the postmodern argument that postulated a qualitative change in the tenor of life.

His work, however, is transcended by the trenchant activism of the Situationists, who carried the critique of everyday banality to new levels while Lefebvre moved on to new areas. They agreed on the importance of moments of dis-alienation (discussed at length in Chapter 7).

Who can gauge the striking power of an impassioned daydream, the pleasure taken in love, of a nascent desire, of a rush of sympathy? Everyone seeks spontaneously to extend such brief moments of real life; everyone wants basically to make something out of their everyday life.

(Vaneigem 1979: 187)

Lefebvre would place the experience of the body at the centre of attempts to reground theory – 'The body, at the very heart of space and of the discourse of power is irreducible and subversive. It is the body which is the point of return' (1976e: 89). The Situationists maintained their focus on the slightly decentred but shared banality of the everyday: 'We still have to place the Everyday at the centre of everything' (Debord in *International Situationist Anthology* 1986: 69). However, they agreed that 'under what we have called "the colonization of everyday life," the only possible changes are . . . fragmentary.' As Gregory concludes, the rhetoric of 'colonisation' is an important element in Lefebvre's entire understanding of the development of contemporary, capitalism – not just in its globalised extent, but in its penetration into everyday life, into the worlds of images and dreams, to become what Lyotard once referred to as 'hypercapitalism':

Everyday life replaced the colonies. Unable to maintain the old imperialism . . . and having decided to bid on the internal market, capitalist leaders treated the everyday as they had treated colonial territories.

(cited in Gregory 1994: 403)

Lefebvre likens this turn to 'an inverse shock wave' by which 'decolonization acts upon the industrialized ... the centres of decision-making. ... Paradoxically, neo-capitalist exploitation has come to include internal colonization. The double exploitation of producer and consumer carries the colonial experience into the midst of the erstwhile colonizing people.' Twenty years before the explosion of interest in the contradictions of global cities such as Los Angeles and New York (Sassen 1991; King 1990; Soja 1996), Lefebvre observed that 'the population in the metropolis is regrouped into ghettos (suburbs, foreigners, factories, students), and the new cities are to some extent reminiscent of colonial cities' (1969d: 92–3). Sadie Plant summarises the scene from the Situationist side:

> Vaneigem argued that even the tiniest of gestures – opening a door, holding a teacup, a facial expression – and the most private and individual actions – coming home, making tea, arguing with a lover – have always already been represented and shown to us within the spectacle.
>
> (1992: 67)

The spectacle and visuality: metaphor, metonymy and legibility

With all meaningfulness confiscated, turned into spectacular forms, everyday life is 'devoid of its glamour representation, experience becomes almost embarrassing, something of which one feels ashamed; an event without a camera', uncool (Plant 1992: 67). The *spectacle* is the ultimate alienation, in which not only one's own handiwork has to be bought back from a store at the end of a working day but also one's identity and dreams have been commodified, turned into spectacular, generalised lifestyles and images and sold back to one. The spectacle is thus the triumph of media transformed into commodity. Drawing again on Sadie Plant's excellent study: 'images and commodities ... effectively represent their lives to them, people experience reality as second-hand. Everything has been seen and done before. ... "My dears," said Debord in one of his films, "adventure is dead," confirming the death of Lefebvre's youthful romanticism of adventure' (Debord in *International Situationist Anthology* 1986: 37; cited in Plant 1992: 10).

Lefebvre shares this vision but at the same time regards everyday life as the plane of immanence in which moments of enlightenment emerge and flash, like sparkles of light on a field of snow. While everyday life is colonised, and even while he adopts the terminology of 'banality' or everydayness to describe it, Lefebvre maintains that everyday life is also the site of the authentic experience of self, of the body and of engagement with others. In effect, he presents a *dialectical* notion of everyday life which involves a double essentialism – everyday life is both, by definition, alienated and, in essence, also unalienated or authentic material. When this material is recognised for what it is, when it is broken free of the contradicting and mystifying veils of the spectacle and false authenticity, the everyday is suddenly synthesised as unalienated experience, brought to consciousness as the truly authentic. The 'taken for granted' is broken down and an individual attains – even if only momentarily – that status of the 'total person'. The project was thus

> to conceive everyday life in such a way as to retrieve it from its modern state of colonization by the commodity form and other modes of reification. A critique of the everyday can be generated only by a kind of alienation effect, insofar as it is put into contact with its own radical *other*, such as an eradicated past . . . or an imagined future.
>
> (Ball 1987: 30)

The notion of spectacle is the ultimate return of fetish to haunt the soul of the subject; it also relies on a visual image of the exhibition, display or cinematic event. It is as if the concept of spectacle itself is not direct but alienated, rooted through visual and media metaphors. Both Lefebvre and the Situationists utilise a visual metaphor, but the former explicitly theorises the importance of 'ways of seeing' in the optical construction of modern, capitalist, understandings of property, space, the person and use-value.

Derek Gregory focuses on the importance of vision for Lefebvre's later work on social space. In what ways is the development of visual regimes of signification, valuing (evaluation) and knowledge related to the colonisation of everyday life? Not only is the spectacle central, but Lefebvre develops an extended theory of the alienation of vision, stretching over a dozen texts and running as many years. We see but cannot understand, look but cannot comprehend. Lefebvre's prescription is, as argued above, a return to the body, a theme developed by his one-time student Michel Maffesoli in terms of the importance of tactile social interactions (1996).

> Lefebvre describes the advance of visualization in a language of menace. It is at once 'an intense onslaught' and 'a threatening gambit', whose victim is the human body. Lefebvre argues that this strategy of visualization achieved a decisive victory with the installation of a *logical space* that had its origins, or so he believes, in the discovery of linear perspective during the European Renaissance. The production of *perspectival space* involved the construction of symmetrical visual pyramids, the apex of one, the 'vanishing point' in the painting, the apex of the other the (single) eye of the painter or viewer. The geometricization of knowledge that this implies was focal to Renaissance humanism as a whole.
>
> (Lefebvre 1991d: 261; cited in Gregory 1994: 388–9)

This visuality is a regime not only of signification but of perception, such that 'the eyes' underwrite 'the dominant form of space' (1991d: 99). Power, which Lefebvre refers to as 'phallocratic', is conveyed visually by verticality and height. But the mechanisms involved hark back to Lefebvre's semiotic studies: a process of metonymy involves an ongoing 'to and fro movement . . . between the part and the whole, whereby great wholes (the size or façade of an apartment building) substitute for the pitiful 'pathetically small size' of each person's living quarters. 'The bodies of "users" . . . are caught up not only in the [metonymic] toils of parcellized space, but also in the web of what philosophers call "analogons"':

> the web of images, signs and symbols. These bodies are transported out of themselves, transferred and emptied out, as it were, via the eyes: every kind of appeal, incitement and seduction is mobilized to tempt them with doubles of themselves.
>
> (Lefebvre 1991d: 98)

Space itself comes to be seen as strictly a visual medium – the line of sight, field of vision, vista and painterly landscape – a notion that is duly codified in architecture and urban planning from the earliest origins of modernity. As he comments of the great architectural historians, Siegfried Giedeon and Bruno Zevi:

> Zevi considers that the visual conception of space rests upon a bodily (gestural) component which the trained eye of the expert observer must take into account. Zevi's book brings this 'lived' aspect of spatial experience, which thanks to its corporal nature has the capacity to 'incarnate', into the realm of knowledge, and hence of 'consciousness', without ever entertaining the idea that such a bodily component of optical (geometric–visual) space might put the priority of conscious-ness itself into question.
>
> (Lefebvre 1991d: 127; see Zevi 1974; Giedeon 1941; 1962)

Thus façades, landscapes, views of the city become the *sine qua non* of the mastery exercised by sovereigns, the state and planning professionals. But these visions, as De Certeau points out, mask the lived reality and everyday (re)constitution of the city as a space of difference. They code micro-terrains (one walks on the sidewalk, thereby actualising it as a specifically pedestrian space, rather than driving on it, and so treating it as a roadway). Everyday performativity undergirds the self-assurance of the 'view from above'. The aerial view is constructed and rendered 'readable' by codes of perspective, which Lefebvre treats as strategies for the mimetic translation of three-dimensionality into the flattened, abstract space of the plan, and of power. This 'legibility' is to be distrusted and constitutes a third aspect of the alienation of vision. For example, monuments, constructed to represent, to be legible, mask as much as they may present. Their selective representation of history is a direct translation of ideology and temporality into material and spatial culture. Monumentality, the façade, the perspectival vista, the map: Lefebvre distrusts them all for their imposition of coded representation on space itself (for a brilliant critique of the conventions of the UK Ordnance Survey see Bonnett 1996).

In comments that summarise my own critique of architecture – a profession without a theoretical measure of architectural success, let alone beauty or space – Lefebvre notes that Zevi 'does not appear to understand the implications of his findings . . . beyond the education of connoisseurs. . . . ' The historians 'do not take the tasks that still await the history of space proper: to show up the growing ascendancy of the abstract and the visual, as well as the internal connection between them; and to expose the genesis and meaning of the "logic of the visual" – that is, to expose the *strategy* implied in such a "logic" in light of the fact that any particular logic of this kind is always merely a deceptive name for a strategy' (Lefebvre 1991d: 128). The purpose of that strategy is to colonise, to subjugate through displacement of objects of desire (metaphor) and substitution of legibility and coded exchange for tactility, total engagement and interaction (metonymy).

7

POSTWAR INTELLECTUAL

The dilemma of the Communist intellectuals

The rocky relationship with the Parti Communiste Français (PCF) became more and more difficult in the postwar years until Lefebvre's suspension in 1957. With Lefebvre, being a Marxist has been described as a high-wire balancing act. Although loyal to the party, he was unable to abandon philosophical principles to the expediency of politics that attempted to turn the philosophy of dialectical materialism into a programme of social change. However, the denunciations of and aggressive attacks on Sartre and other intellectuals are testimony to Lefebvre's adhesion to party doctrine and his acceptance of the necessity of party discipline. In addition to philosophical engagement, Lefebvre's political commitment to Marxism is clear. After the war, the party hierarchy began to worry about the influence of leading thinkers, including Lefebvre and Sartre. Independent thought and political dogma were a contradiction in terms. Against the rise of progressive thinkers of international significance, progressive political forces in France paradoxically tightened a noose of demands for conformity and silence. They attempted to demolish the dangerous theoretical freedom that these intellectuals had. The Occupation

> ended with a bang and the explosion caused fits of creative agitation, in theatres, publishing houses, magazine offices, night clubs and cafés. The strait-jacket had been turned inside-out, and an entire populace was free again. . . . The chief representative of this new energy in artistic circles was a writer, Jean-Paul Sartre, and his headquarters were in a café. . . . Many of the eminent pre-war figures were still active . . . the world's attention was no longer on their grand salons, however, but on the downstairs room at the Café de Flore, on the corner of the Boulevard St-Germain and Rue St-Benoit. . . . Next to the Flore, forming a corner with the ancient Place St-Germain, was another café the Deux Magots. Between them, these two constituted the base-camp of the post-war Parisian avant-garde.

Among Sartre's inner circle . . . were Camus, Jean Genet, Raymond Aron, the singer and actor Mouloudji, Boris Vian, and Maurice Merleau-Ponty, editor-in-chief of *Les Temps Modernes*. . . . Talent existed in such abundance and variety in this group . . . that the *Temps Modernes* circle became a tourist attraction in itself.

(Campbell 1995:8–9)

Sartre, especially, had pushed the limits of dogma beyond what the Stalinist PCF would tolerate. His visibility and pronouncements on widely reported political issues made him a powerful and unpredictable force. A barrage of theoretical critiques were ordered in an attempt to discredit him. The attack on Sartre was an abrupt change from the unity of the Resistance:

Communist intellectuals in late 1944 began viciously attacking Sartre. Everything and everyone associated with Sartre was open for criticism: existentialism, *Les Temps Modernes*, Simone de Beauvoir, Albert Camus, and, to a lesser degree, Maurice Merleau-Ponty, who had close Communist friends (Courtade, Hervé, and Desanti). Henri Lefebvre began with a stinging rebuke of Sartre's article in *Action*. To Lefebvre, Sartre's existentialism had nothing to do with Marxism, but was part of the 'war machine' against Communism, an effort to enchant and mystify the youth of France, like old Socrates, with its 'pathological narcissistic consciousness'.

(Lefebvre 1945: 8; cited in Poster 1975: 110)[1]

Looking back on the mid-1970s, Mark Poster argued that 'while the existentialists of Sartre's circle were feverishly learning Marxism and hesitantly making syntheses of their thought with that of the Communists, the latter were condemning existentialism outright' (1975: 112).[2] In retrospect, this was unfair to Lefebvre. He had long been engaged with the ideas of Existentialism, if not with the official theory canonised by Sartre under that title. True, Lefebvre's *L'Existentialisme* (1946) was an attempt to catch up with and get back on board the Existentialist train he had avoided since his conversion to the PCF. However, he also tried to re-route it back into practical politics. Existentialism had all the problems of the 'adventurism' of the *Philosophes* and the Surrealists: criticising rationality yet offering only the alternative of a poetic, privatised consciousness, a 'neurosis of interiority, a schizophrenia'. Existential philosophy,

---

1 Lefebvre is here responding to Sartre's defence of *Being and Nothingness* (1958 [1943]) in 'Existentialisme et Marxisme' (Sartre 1944).

2 Poster notes 'Communists wrote full studies of *Being and Nothingness* to show its anti-progressive, idealist nature: Henri Lefebvre, *L'Existentialisme* in 1946; Henri Mougin, *La Sainte famille existentialiste* in 1947 . . . and Georges Lukács, *Existentialisme ou Marxisme?* in 1948, a book that was important in the French debate' (1975: 112).

disconnected from political issues, offered an 'abstract culture, its isolation, its disdain for the practical, its separation from life, its mediocre and vague social position' (Lefebvre 1946: 21).

> The 'boring', 'abstract', 'esoteric' existentialism of the 1940s was only a repetition of the original existentialism of Henri Lefebvre [and the *Philosophes*]. In one stroke Lefebvre gave himself credit as the first existentialist, relegating Sartre to the position of a mere latecomer, and presented a self-criticism in which existentialism was exposed as juvenile.
>
> (Poster 1975: 115)

Lefebvre acted inconsistently by violently attacking other non-conformist intellectuals such as Sartre (Lefebvre 1945). In so doing, he violated his own anti-dogmatic stance. How did Lefebvre come to subordinate his own values and arguments to the party bureaucracy? Such Faustian pacts were being made by intellectuals all over postwar Europe as dissidents were dismissed, and in other countries purged, exiled or executed. In an atmosphere in which collaborators and Nazi officials were being prosecuted, dismissed, and lynched or executed, it was easy to prefer left-wing orthodoxy to unprotected independence. Caught up in the fray, the reasons for this feud were partly personal, and not just an intellectual assassination obediently carried out for the PCF as Poster implies (1975). Lefebvre resented being neglected by the exclusive camp of Parisian intellectuals. As Trebitsch remarks, it is revealing that his postwar contacts with universities were nil. While Lefebvre saw himself as the originator of Existentialism, he was ignored. He was even denied a place as a precursor of Existentialism. His mid-1920s essays published in *Philosophies* anticipate many of the arguments made by Sartre – who was also involved with the *Philosophes*. Lefebvre's 1940s critique of Existentialism remains one of the most original and thoughtful of the PCF's organised attack. And those criticisms were later to contribute to the development of Existentialism and the emergence of Existential Marxism (see Chapter 9) as Sartre attempted a reconciliation with Marxism beginning in 1944 and finally acknowledged Lefebvre's importance at the end of the 1950s.

Autocritiques and Romantics

Lefebvre was one of the first to write an 'autocritique' of his own works, a *pro forma* statement of orthodoxy that Communist Parties all over Europe were demanding from their writers and thinkers (1949e). Lefebvre responded to Jean Grenier's accusation that he was more a neo-Hegelian than an orthodox Marxist of the stripe preferred by the PCF – old criticisms dredged up from the 1930s, old debates rekindled from his youth. Lefebvre, committed to the ongoing effort to install a Communist government in France, apologised, retracted and genuflected.

'It is precisely in her stomach that Paris has recovered the least,' wrote the correspondent for the *New Yorker*, Janet Flanner (May 1946; cited in Campbell 1995: 7). In the late 1940s, in and mostly out of work, Lefebvre, who had been on and off the brink of starvation throughout the decade, continued to plead with Guterman in New York for money, help and work (letter to Guterman 1945). He wrote introductions, edited popular books – anything to make money to support his many children and himself. Poster observes that 'a glance at his long publication list reveals that Lefebvre retreated to the relatively uncontroversial sphere of literary criticism' (1975: 238). With his female partners, Lefebvre dictated his way through at least two book-length manuscripts and half a dozen journal articles per year. These were unusual liaisons – half romance, half business. They were referred to, ironically, as 'the dictator' and 'the typewriter'. Dictating gave his books their question-and-answer quality. Sketching out a series of key issues and questions, Lefebvre would simply answer one a day out loud while his partner typed. This raises again the essential, but ignored, role that women played in his work. Lefebvre claimed to have escaped the trap of heterosexual marriage, but he remained a patriarch and circumscribed his notions of love within the boundaries of the traditions of male–female desire. As time went on and feminist ideas took hold, at least the question of women's participation was more frankly acknowledged, with some of his last works being co-authored with his last wife and intellectual partner, Catherine Régulier-Lefebvre.

Not only was Lefebvre not silent; he was also continuing from prewar commentaries and books on key thinkers. It is important not to overlook his earlier commercial works on both philosophers (*Nietzsche* (1939a) and *Descartes* (1947c), not to mention Marx, Engels and Hegel (1938a; 1938b; 1947b; 1948f; 1948g)) and writers, written to generate income and help to feed his children from his marriage. These books are also one of the trademarks of Lefebvre's intellectual stance. All the many 'Everyman's Library'-style anthologies and edited collections of works by important French thinkers included 'Introductions' with his own dialectical interpretation of the writers' works. He played such an important role in translating and disseminating Marx's work in part because his 'outreach' to the world at large was not only the academic monograph or participation in a protest march but also the interpretation or commentary destined for a popular audience – a short 'intro' to a popular writer – and written in clear and simple language.

Besides literary figures, three volumes were written on historical philosophers out of over twenty works on other authors: the last volume on *Diderot* (1949d); *Pascal* (two volumes: 1949f; 1954c); *Pour connaître la pensée de Lenine* (published as 1957e). His political and economic commentary was limited to journal articles, while his serious thought went into his doctoral thesis on the *Val de Campan* (1963f; see also 1949c; 1951a; 1953a; 1956d;

1956h; 1965h). Lefebvre's wartime experiences in the Pyrenees exposed him to the ruins of mountain villages and Cathar traditions of independent thought dating back at least as far as the Cathar heresy and the Dominican inquisition. Lefebvre's heresy was his hybridity. He attempted to be both an independent intellectual for whom critical thought was the highest value and an activist who obeyed the orders of the PCF leaders.

Between 1948 and 1961, Lefebvre held research positions at the CNRS, where he was responsible for studying the changing social conditions of rural France. But his political problems continued: in the summer of 1953 he was promoted by the administration and immediately suspended from the CNRS by the Ministry of Education for his militant Communist links. It is said that this action was in response to Lefebvre's attacks on 'America, American sociology and the ideology of Americanism' (Hess 1988: 153). The Thèse-d'État, on the *Peasant Communities of the Pyrenees*[3] was finally defended in the summer of 1954 (1963f). After a year back teaching in lycées, Lefebvre was reinstated at CNRS in October 1954.

With trouble from the state on one side, Lefebvre chaffed at the intellectual restrictions imposed by the PCF on the other. As one of the creators of an in-depth and historically informed sociology of rural transitions – a study written with one eye on the potential for popular resistance and dissent – one of the major lines of irritation between the PCF and Lefebvre was his insistence on the importance of agricultural policy and the role of the rural peasantry in state socioeconomic development. In Russia, Stalinist purges and Leninist policy had not so much solved the problem of the peasantry and agricultural self-sufficiency as transformed it into one of consumption and the international agribusiness of bilateral grain exports. The Soviets were consistently forced to buy grain from abroad because of low harvests, partly due to dissatisfied rural peasants and alienated farm workers. Ironically, argued Lefebvre, rather than escaping capitalism, the Soviet state had become one of the best consumers of its essential products, and in so becoming was tied to a system of capitalist exchange. Later, beginning in the early 1960s, Lefebvre was one of the first Marxist analysts to take seriously such global markets and global circuits of capital (see 'Urban and Global Spaces of Capital', Chapter 10).

Lefebvre consistently criticised Lysenkoism – the Stalinist disavowal of genetics and wheat hybrids as an 'undialectical' capitalist plot – and the over-simplification of agricultural policy by French Communists. This was an important subtext in Lefebvre's theoretical work as well as in his applied research on rural sociology. One can discern a critique of Stalinism if one reads between the lines of his *Logique formelle, logique dialectique* (1947d). Years

---

3 The Thèse d'État is no longer given in France. It was a form of mid-career doctorate for academics, on the German model, awarded for in-depth and prolonged research.

later, Lefebvre commented that the Soviet and Eastern European states had developed a form of modernity in which the scientific revolution was left out. Thus the Soviets could be technologically modern in one sense but illogically dismiss genetics and many other aspects of biology simply on the basis of the decree of a leader. Logic, the work ethic and democracy as meta-principles were missing in a group of paradoxical societies that were modern in many senses and that stressed production, but which were dominated by an almost feudal state. In retrospect, there was a disjunction between technology and culturally specific labour practices, which included relations of trust and interdependence that were not taken into account in, for example, the policies and the minutiae of the practices of collectivisation. In this 'superficial modernity', a capitalist class was replaced by a party bureaucracy and the individual freedoms associated with Western European and North American modernity were lacking.

Rebel without a party

Any move to publish philosophical work that introduced new developments and political arguments to the party brought him into continual conflict with mainstream PCF intellectuals and activists such as Roger Garaudy (1960). Inside the PCF, Lefebvre was part of an internal opposition that pushed for greater PCF support for the Algerian independence movement. He signed the 'Petition of 121' calling on the party for concrete action regardless of the fact that all such action had been declared illegal by the French government. This petition called for clandestine action. As a result, arrests followed, and the PCF itself engaged in a campaign of internal trials and exclusions, which ultimately led to Lefebvre leaving. While the party focused on internal struggles, de Gaulle and the right-of-centre Gaullistes came to power.

It is significant that Lefebvre recorded few comments on the Soviet crushing of either the 'Prague Spring' of 1968 or the Hungarian Uprising, which was the Hungarian break for more freedom from Russian domination in the wake of the 'Khrushchev Report' in 1956. The sudden destruction of the personality cult of Stalin by Nikita Khrushchev brought Lefebvre's forward-thinking anti-Stalinism into fashion if not in France then in Germany and the Eastern bloc states. In Communist-ruled East Germany, Lefebvre was fêted and applauded by members of the ruling Party Central Committee for his argument that the great German thinkers such as Goethe and Hegel, rather than being censored as reactionary thinkers, offered the route to a renaissance of Marxism. Via Germany, Lefebvre had access to the report, which the French Communist Party censored. While tanks rolled over Hungary, party discipline held in France. In France, the implications of the Khrushchev Report on the Stalinist purges were little appreciated by most. For a long time, the report was believed to be a simple propaganda exercise consisting of lies. In contrast, in East Germany the question of a new Marxism was already being posed, perhaps as a route to a more independent economic policy (1975c: 94–7). But in the atmosphere of internal bickering, inquisitions and confessional 'autocritiques' in Paris, Lefebvre was accused of dissent from the PCF's continuing Stalinist doctrine and placed on internal trial. Suspended in 1957, he chose to quit. He was formally excluded in 1958. As a militant he left the PCF 'by the left, While many others had quit [the party] by the right' (Lefebvre 1975c: 100). In effect, Lefebvre parted company with the PCF but not with Marxism, finally liberating his thought from dutiful obeisance.

'It is hard for most of us to understand what it might mean to be excluded from an organisation to which one has belonged for some thirty years. The French Communist Party was not only a political party by the hub of its members' social and daily life (It has sometimes been likened to an extended and very close-knit family structure)' (Harvey 1991: 4280). Throughout 1956 and 1957, Lefebvre concentrated on rural sociology and great thinkers. The only break appeared in 1958 in his newspaper essay on Stalin and Marxism (1958f; see also Tort and Lefebvre 1986f). Lefebvre took the opportunity to reflect on his career by writing a 'dialectical' autobiography, Le Somme et le reste (The Sum and the Remainder), which won the 'Prix des Critiques' (1959i). If Le Somme et le reste marked Lefebvre's authorial break with official PCF allegiance and control, it did not mark any abandonment of commitment to the original philosophy of Hegel, Marx and Engels. But, while well-received by the non-Communist Left (i.e. what was now the extreme Left in France), its philosophical critique of dogmatism was the topic of ad hominem critique from a Leninist perspective for the PCF by Lucien Sève in his La Différence (1960). One of the principal criticisms was of Lefebvre's argument that the Parti needed a programme to accomplish social change, not simply marching orders by which it attempted to impose a dogma on progressive thinkers and activists. This suggestion in the direction of a sociotechnical[4] examination of the feasibility of socialism and the possibilities for meaningful social change (1957d; 1958b; 1962g) earned him and other members of the Arguments group years of ridicule before the PCF finally adopted exactly such an approach in the 1970s. For his critics, the autobiography was the evidence that Lefebvre, the petit bourgeois, had never been a serious Marxist and had understood nothing of Marxism. Even in the mid-1960s, party officials and intellectuals continued to write of Lefebvre as a 'petit bourgeois' who was an intellectual arriviste, a parvenu who had contributed nothing but only timidly looked on. While staging a public debate on whether or not the dialectic was a law of nature (which, incredibly, drew an audience of 6,000) Sartre was invited and Lefebvre deliberately excluded despite being a key figure in that debate (1947d; 1962g).[5]

---

4 'Sociotechnical' is here meant in the sense of attempts to socially engineer and plan social change. On this praxiological perspective see Podgórecki, Alexander and Shields 1996.

5 Engels' position had become the Zhdanovist orthodoxy within Communism: the dialectic was the law of all natural change and development.

Even in 1964, Maurice Thorez, who had long been one of the organisational talents and intellectual hatchet-men of the Left,[6]) wrote that Lefebvre was among 'the worst sort of renegades and adventurers, of degenerate elements, of revisionists chased from the ranks of communists because of their antimarxist points of view' (Thorez 1964, in *Pravda*; cited in Ferenczi 1988).

In 1958, Lefebvre reflected in *Le Somme et le reste*:

> How many pages under the Sign of the Crucified Sun? Since that time, I have not stopped thinking about myths. On the one hand, I think that reason drives away myths. It sends them off to ethnography, sociology, sometimes history.... The sign which gave me the flash to discovery was nothing but the sign of my own alienation....
>
> Myths? They cannot be completely eliminated. As long as I believed so, I obeyed dogmatism. In the clarity of the Crucified Sun I read Nietzsche....
>
> (1989a: 255–6, 257)

The sense of loss of what had been his motivating cause and raison d'être for nearly thirty years marked Lefebvre's subsequent years (see 1989a: 290). Nonetheless, he remained committed to Marx's analysis of alienation. He might have been characterised as a Hegelian Marxist – which he denied vehemently (1989a: 257) – because of his stress on dialectical materialism, but he had also been highly critical of Hegel's abstract philosophical categories. Lefebvre was therefore clearly a Marxist. What he was not was a Stalinist: he endorsed Rosa Luxemburg's argument that direct democracy must become a part of Communism if one was to avoid personality cults and the dictatorship of party bureaucracies (Lefebvre, interviewed in Latour and Combes 1991: 30). While Lefebvre remained a Marxist, what he could no longer believe in was the arrogance of a party that expected to be the natural leadership of a popular revolution.

Why was Lefebvre – thirty-five or so years later almost forgotten – so

---

6 Thorez had, for example, led the attack on Paul Nizan, who had left the PCF in disgust at the signing of the Nazi–Soviet Pact in 1939. The campaign began almost immediately but after his death – in battle – in 1940 it intensified with attacks by Aragon and Lefebvre, who claimed 'Paul Nizan had few friends and we could ask what was his secret. Today we know: all his books turn around the idea of treason.... He came from reactionary, and even fascist, milieux. Perhaps he was still a member even while pretending to spy on them,' for the Resistance (1946: 17–58). He was only to be partially reinstated by Sartre, Merleau-Ponty and others, who demanded 'We should not forget that this was a writer, who died in combat and it is our duty as writers to defend his memory. We address ourselves therefore to Lefebvre ... "When you say that Nizan was a traitor, do you simply mean that he left the Parti Communiste in 1939? In this case, say so clearly.... Or do you want to insinuate that he, even before the war, accepted money to inform the anticommunist government on our Parti? In this case, prove it"'. (*Le Figaro littéraire*, 29 March 1947; cited in Sirinelli 1990: 254).

important a figure to attack for so long? Gusdorf has argued that for Lefebvre, leaving the PCF was 'yet another manner of saving this truth which the Parti had falsified, and of defending Truth against the Parti' (1991; cited in Hess 1988: 156) The expulsion of key intellectuals and radicals discouraged young activists critical of the social order from entering the ranks of the PCF. The result was that, by default, a new Left intelligentsia was created in France. The PCF was alienated not only from grassroots politics but also from new political initiatives launched by intellectuals and students. It is difficult to appreciate the importance of the 1960s student intelligentsia, which was defined by its political and moral potential rather than its irrelevance to politics (as is the case now in many Western countries). Students are now more than ever contained within the limited world of universities (they are truly ivory towers for students, even while they provide a more engaged institutional base for some academics). By contrast, this well-educated and committed section of France's 1960s population was looked to for political innovation and moral leadership by the French populace.

The ideological and personal critiques made by PCF insiders appear to be the source of later assessments of Lefebvre as a mere witness (cf. Boschetti 1985: 218) rather than as either an actor and philosophical innovator in his own right or as a sort of Ariadne's thread connecting the artistic radicals of the 1920s to the Marxist-Existentialists of the 1950s and so on. For, like an electric wire Lefebvre (even unwittingly) conducted ideas from generation to generation and movement to movement. Excluded from PCF politics, he sought a new engagement with political change based on his prewar experience of Surrealism and the intellectual independence of the *Philosophies* group. The 1920s interest in spontaneity and identity returned. One article proclaimed that Marxism was *the* spiritual event of the century (1961c). His 1962 books *L'Introduction à la modernité* (*Introduction to Modernity*) and the second volume or sequel to *Critique of Everyday Life* (1947, English translation 1991) announced his political programme. This new engagement was to be through uninstitutionalised political movements that would bring a 'new wave' of philosophical critique directly into the spheres of political and social action (1959g). The process of forced exclusion from party politics and the rediscovery of the important role that they could take as an intelligentsia laid the basis for both the *Situationnistes'* attempts to revive a Dadaist-style political avant-garde of artist-activists at the beginning of the 1960s, and the unexpected impact of student revolts at the end of that decade.

The Situationists in Strasbourg

Let everyday life become a work of art! Let every technical means be employed for the transformation of everyday life!

(Lefebvre 1971: 204)

Still outside the Parisian inner circle of such figures as Sartre and Merleau-Ponty, Lefebvre took up a post in 1961 as Professor of Sociology at Strasbourg, where he developed an applied approach to sociology. Graduate students animated a centre that carried out research for the public good. For example, doctoral students conducted empirical research for the benefit of unions and community groups. This provided the first blueprints for his later approach at the Institute of Sociology, which he headed at Nanterre (in suburban Paris), from the founding of the university there in 1965. The research conducted for unions and public organisations reflects Lefebvre's interest in the application of theory to social issues and ongoing attempts to change society for the better. Just as in his writings, where he insisted on the centrality of dialectical materialism as a method that Marx had only begun to apply – and only in an initial sector, the economy – Lefebvre appears as a type of methodologist. While he maintained that Marx's inspiration was the problem of alienation (the focus of the early works of Marx), he is what we might call a 'methodological Marxist' in that he argues that one of the most enduring contributions of Marx's work was to provide the method of dialectical materialism, which could be applied in many more places than he had had time to. Hence, Lefebvre's ventures into unexplored areas such as spatiality and his attempt to develop dialectical materialism itself beyond Marx into more complex forms, such as what Soja (1996) refers to as his 'trialectics' of social space. This commitment is also paralleled in Lefebvre's continuing output of works on Marx intended for students and lay audiences.

Disenchanted with the dogmatic and bureaucratic aspects of party activism, Lefebvre turned to smaller groups on the model of the Surrealists. In Strasbourg, he came into contact with the Situationists and Maoist activists. His work was brought to their attention by Dotremont in the late 1950s. Students approached Lefebvre for his support in organising a French peasant uprising in support of the Algerian independence movement. He scoffed at their naivety: they did not take into account that 1950s France was not post-First World War Russia: agricultural reform had changed the status of the French peasantry, who could not be regarded as mere proletarians. Yet it appears that Lefebvre was impressed by their spirit and willingness to risk all in an idealistic adventure-in-revolution, exactly the sort of project in which a younger, 1920s Lefebvre might have become embroiled. Even in the late 1980s, he could remark that 'adventure' was '*ce que advient. Le retournement du sens vient du fait que l'aventure signifie de "que l'on invente"*' – 'It is, "that which comes". The reversal of the meaning comes from the fact that adventure means "that which one invents"' (Interview with Lefebvre, February 1988; cited in Hess 1989: 88).

Those students and hangers-on, in particular Guy Debord (who was introduced into Lefebvre's seminar group by Michele Bernstein – more evidence of the largely unrecorded importance of networks through women on the French Left) formed the core of the politically avant-garde grouping of artists, writers and architects who came to be the *Situationniste Internationale* (SI) after the succession of international movements to export the Russian revolution, which were called the first, second, or later '*Internationale*'. Debord used the Surrealists' tactics, which he learned in part from Lefebvre and from the artistic inheritors of Tristan Tzara's mantle of avant-garde outrageousness, Isidore Isou's group 'Lettriste Internationale'. Debord's *Situationnistes* (or Situationists) were a radical and more political breakaway section of the Lettristes. Situationist tactics included outrageous media stunts, thought-provoking graffiti ('Think Globally, Act Locally' is one of theirs), and radicalising pamphlets to make people rethink their lifestyles. Their first success was in Strasbourg, where Lefebvre was Professor of Sociology, when they succeeded in organising student strikes and in issuing a scandalous political pamphlet that called for mass insurrection. When Lefebvre moved to Paris, their second success was in preparing the ground for the 1968 student occupations started by Lefebvre's students of the university buildings at Nanterre on the outskirts of Paris, then the Sorbonne, and then spreading through Paris and out into workers' factory occupations and sit-down strikes (see Marcus 1989).

Both Lefebvre and the Situationists ('Situs' for short) agreed that

> everyday life is the very realm over which we should have control, yet it is experienced as mundane and dull in its ubiquity. On the escape from the fragmentation and mediocrity of our own experi-ence, we run blindly towards the promises of wholeness, fulfilment, and unity implicit in the world of the abundant commodity. And it is in the hopelessness of this scramble that the disjunction between the possibilities of life and the impoverished realities of survival are most keenly felt; it is here that the revolution becomes a living and immediate possibility.
>
> (Plant 1992: 64)

The Situs began to explore past grassroots revolutions with Lefebvre (see Chapter 7). These included the Paris Commune (1871). While it lasted only a short time and was marred by political indecision, behind the famous barricades of the streets of Paris, the Commune championed the original ideals of the French Revolution and was marked by an outbreak of carnivalesque celebration. A new social and moral order was proclaimed and initially took the form of an ongoing festival. Intrigued, Lefebvre and the Situs explored the similarities with the experience of Dada and the Surrealist demand for a poetic revolution. The strategy of May 1968 was set: Lefebvre, always churning out books, proposed the model of the 'festive revolution' in his *Proclamation de la Commune*.

This little book caused an uproar. Lefebvre published what were really the results of collective discussions among the Situationists and was abruptly excluded. While they advocated the elimination of copyright and glorified the practice of stolen works with the excuse of 'artistic license', Lefebvre became one of the few justified targets in an endless round of in-fighting and exclusions (Plant 1990; 1992: 63–4).

Nonetheless, the work on the Commune remained disconnected from an analysis of more recent historical attempts that might support his proposal for a 'festive revolution', such as the uprising in Hungary in 1956. Such blind spots are testaments to the focus of the French intelligentsia on developments at home – a sort of withdrawal to the domestic after the loss of the Algerian War of Independence – and the effectiveness of Soviet management of information and news.

Politics and revolution: the Situationist legacy

In Lefebvre's own *Groupe de recherche sur la vie quotidienne* at the CNRS, Guy Debord signed on to the project of critiquing the banality of everyday life. But he went further, arguing that everyday life was 'colonised', that its alienation was not intrinsic but the result of a social organisation of the everyday. For Lefebvre, daily life was always coming in and out of banality. It was full of boring routine on the one hand and engaging opportunities for creative work on the other. The problem was that capitalism closed down the possibilities for engagement and for self-fulfilment. However, by the end of the 1950s, after the stress of being thrown out of the PCF, some of the fire had gone out of Lefebvre's invective. Debord re-ignited it, arguing for a direct assault at the level of daily life. There was to be no alienation, no routine in daily life. Lefebvre was caught off guard by the brief political success but lasting cultural influence of 1968 because, by the end of the 1950s, the shortcomings of polit- ical revolution as a way out of 'everydayness' or repetitive monotony became increasingly clear:

> Do they really imagine that one fine day or one decisive evening people will look at each other and say 'Enough! We're fed up with work and boredom! Let's put an end to them!' and that they will then proceed to the eternal Festival and the creation of situations?
>
> (Lefebvre; cited in Plant 1992: 96)

The slide from Leninism to Stalinism and the focus on internal party disci- pline rather than outreach with projects of liberation had thoroughly 'alienated' Lefebvre from the mainstream Communist movement. He had become more radical by abandoning institutional political activity. In 1958, Marcus argues, Lefebvre was 'a communist in name only and a situationist lacking only the name' (1989: 146). In *Le Somme et le reste*, published the next year, Lefebvre even more clearly broke with the PCF by criticising the Marxist project of state revolution:

Political revolution, in the cases where it has taken place, would not resolve all the problems of individual life, of love, of happiness. Moreover, would it realise the practical (social) conditions in which the individual might more liberally pose these problems and resolve them? What is the immediate and necessary link between the collective ownership of the means of production and the blossoming of the individual?

(1959a: 468)

Such doubts about the promised revolution were heresies and remained so for most committed Marxists into the 1980s. Nonetheless, Lefebvre continued to seek a social form that would allow the exploration of alienation in everyday life. He is not so much a romantic revolutionary as a Marxist, without the reassurance of a future revolution. He thus reproduced an earlier comment from his 1939 study *Nietzsche*:

Socialism doesn't resolve all the problems of man; but it does inaugurate the epoch in which man can pose in true terms (without mixing in social preconceptions of the human problems of understanding, of love and of death. . . . A true culture is at the same time a way of life of thought and action. It is a sentiment of life incorporated into a human community. It involves a relationship between man himself and the world. The great culture to come should integrate the cosmic with the human, instinct with knowledge. It will be the culture of total man.

(Lefebvre 1939a; cited and italicised in 1959a: 473)

This critical orientation leads us to Lefebvre's own conclusion that 'There is not *one* Marxism but rather many Marxist tendencies, schools, trends, and research projects. Marxism in France does not have the same orientation it has in Germany. . . . there are also other expressions of intellectual life in France that one cannot disregard, such as surrealism, since they have intersected with Marxism' (Lefebvre 1988e: 75–6).[7] The fidelity of this argument to the lines of his very early essay 'Positions d'attaque et de défense du nouveau mysticisme' ('Positions for and against the new mysticism') on understanding is remarkable (1925a). Lefebvre takes a consistent position over many years (1925a, 1939a, 1959a). All are based on his thesis proposal on the philosophy of consciousness, which was to have examined identity and consciousness (but which was rejected). The argument runs: the key to action lies in privileged 'moments'

---

7 Lefebvre presents this as a quotation from his earlier book *Nietzsche* (1939a, written 1937–8) but it is the sole self-citation in *La Somme et le reste* without source page numbers. Lefebvre rarely bothered to reference or give citation details in his texts, but on this occasion all other quotations from *Nietzsche* gave page numbers.

when a dialectical mysticism provides insight into the spirit. A 'total act' (Nietzsche, Schelling) unifies the individual and the spiritual. Ceaseless 'adventure' based on faith in one's choices creatively transforms the isolated individual.

Modernity

Because of his critique of everyday life as well as capitalism, Lefebvre stands as one of the great theorists of 'modernity', a concept generated by turning 'the modern' – a term that is really an adjective used to describe a style of life or accomplishments – into a historical period. At the turn of the century, 'modernists' in architecture and the arts saw themselves as part of a 'modern movement' that rejected the traditional role of art as a form of decoration. Instead, art and architecture were to accomplish by other means what had traditionally been done by social revolutions. By the late 1920s, this led to the Dadaist and Surrealist demand for a poetic revolution (see Chapter 5). Lefebvre surveyed the scene and declared a new social reality had been born out of the wars, the imperialism, the technological developments and the new forms of alienation of the twentieth century – the age of 'modernity'. He is one of the first to show how 'modernity' could be used as a critical classification for social theory, distinct from architectural or art history, or Nietzsche's philosophical discussions. In a Nietzschean fashion, 'modernity' builds a critical edge into a common expression – 'the modern'. Lefebvre cast 'modern times' as something with a beginning, middle and end. Rather than 'being modern' or having a 'modern' character, people are 'in modernity' – a social condition of consumer capitalism working at a planetary scale and supported by complex systems of mystification, spectacle, and national and international government. Some trends were in line with Marx's and Engels' assessment of capitalism back in the 1850s and Lenin's First World War studies of imperial expansion as a geographical 'fix' to the contradictions of capitalism: society was becoming more and more closely governed, capitalism had expanded through colonialism around the world, and wealth had been steadily concentrated into the hands of the bourgeoisie (1962i; 1968i/1971h). In this, Lefebvre noted the importance of the planetary integration of cultures and economies, making him, in the 1960s, an important precursor of 1990s theorists of 'globalisation' (King 1990; Featherstone 1995).

There were distinct differences from Marx's time: capitalism had changed, the nature of ideology had changed, and the working classes had changed. For over two decades, Lefebvre argued for a Marxism of the moment that would recognise and respond to these shifts, beginning in *Introduction à la modernité* (1962i); in *Position: Contre les Technocrates*; in *Everyday Life in the Modern World* (1968i/1971h: 68ff); and again in *La Revolution n'est plus que c'était* (1978a) and *De la modernité au modernisme* (1981b). Poster summarises these and is worth quoting at length:

Monopoly capitalism had replaced competitive capitalism; superstructure and base interpenetrated each other and lost their distinct
outlines; old social classes had been transformed; new ideological
structures and modes of alienation had arisen. . . . The old proletariat,
no longer immediately revolutionary in any sense, was being progressively depoliticised; its economic demands had lost their political
character . . . workers sought stability of employment first; their needs
resembled, more and more those of the petty bourgeoisie. With new
abundance of material goods, new scarcities – of space and of desire –
emerged, and 'the centre of interest' had been displaced from work
toward leisure and the family. New groups, bearing new forms of alienation, had emerged – white-collar workers, women, young people –
who might become part of a new radical force, though they did not
constitute social classes.

(1975: 244–5)

Echoing Gramsci, the chief tool of these changes had been the state (1976a;
1976b; 1977; 1978b), which everywhere had the same effect of alienation and
control: 'the bureaucratic society of controlled consumption' (1968i/1971h:
68). Nonetheless, the proletariat retained its potential force, and a new working
class could be found, leaving hope for the future. Sounding conservative, 1960s
'modernity' lacked direction, social coherence and a defining 'style' of the age
because of the lack of common reference points and culture despite the high
level of social coordination and socialisation. The concept of *la vie quotidienne*
allowed Lefebvre to focus on the conditions of life under advanced capitalism:
alienation, consumption and privatisation around the home and couple and
tedious homogeneity. Thus everyday life was structured by spatial routines and
temporal rhythms. People suffered the 'constrained time' of commuting,
frequent periods of waiting or transition – appointments – that broke up the
day and that specific commodities such as the magazine were used to fill (Ross
1996: 143; Lefebvre 1961j). As *Rhythmanalyse*, written with his second wife,
Catherine Régulier-Lefebvre, argues, shifts in time were as significant as shifts in
spatiality (1992a). Capitalist societies replaced the cyclical time of nature, and
the body's rhythmic 'lived time' with a linear time based on the demands of
production and work schedules or the false cycles of commodities. Linear time
allowed the control and discipline of populations on a modern capitalist model.
Yet the requirement of reproduction – the presence of children and the
different rhythms of the life-cycle, expressed in family life – permanently
exempted everyday life from total colonisation by the regulatory framework of
linear time: this provided a natural starting point from which the traditional,
humanistic time could be expanded. The antithesis of industrialised temporality
was spontaneity and renewal – summed up once again with a twinkle in his eye,
but never fully explained, as the 'moment' (see Chapter 5; 1968i/1971h:
182). Spontaneous moments in everyday living, no matter how alienated or

misunderstood, were a potentially fertile ground for revolutionary change outside work because they escaped the structures of linear time. However, the shift from work to non-work would require a fundamental reworking of Marxist notions of revolution.

Leisure and everyday life

In France after the First World War, factory work was reorganised by rationalising production and streamlining workplace activities. Everyday life was affected by a similar impetus towards rationalisation and efficiency. One example that Lefebvre noted was the scientific redesign of the kitchen and the large-scale intervention in housework by corporations. Advertising discourses of rationality appealed to 'science', to time management and to efficiency understood as the reduction of effort. Ironically, at the same time, new tasks became expected parts of household labour, thus consuming all the time that was freed by, for example, self-stoking coal furnaces or gas cooking stoves, which replaced wood-fired appliances, which had to be tended. The everyday life of the nuclear family became the norm as mothers were portrayed single-handedly managing the household to high standards of care, nutrition and hygiene while husbands worked for wages elsewhere. This new form of the household was marked by its isolation and non-cooperation with other kin or nearby families. It did without the combined effort of the traditional extended family, who had once shared the same roof. The elderly in particular were pushed into enforced 'leisure', institutional care. Above all, they no longer participated in either household or waged labour. The result was a day-to-day experience that was more technologically dependent and hence materially richer in appliances but impoverished in human contact and poorly integrated into the social life of a once close-knit community.

It is remarkable that Lefebvre did not seize upon the experience of women as the archetype of 'everyday life' in his *Critique of Everyday Life*. In retrospect, he could have followed up the unequal impact of these changes in daily life better on people of different ages and genders. Unfortunately, Lefebvre's theoretical insights and the analytical tools that his work provided have not been pursued as rigorously by most contemporary researchers who have focused on these questions. With the exception of rare conference papers (Nash 1994), there is much room for further critique and investigation. For example, Lefebvre's perspective on everyday life has been poorly integrated into feminist sociology in favour of theoretical criticisms of Lefebvre's use of Lacanian psychoanalysis with its focus on phallic symbolism and male discourse. Instead, by continuing the patriarchal and patrist tradition of focusing on male experience, everyday life appeared to many as a residual and marginal category made up of what was excluded from productive labour in the workplace and male participation in family life. This category was thus portrayed as commuting, coffee breaks, non-productive moments of bored half-attentive television viewing, and so on.

One defence might be that this was the common lacuna of practically all researchers throughout the first three quarters of the twentieth century. However, Lefebvre – inspired by his female typist-'muse' (his term) – the 'dictateur' and the 'dactylo' (my term and Lefebvre's term, respectively), makes the unusual feint of apparently publishing an award-winning novel under the name of his wife, Henriette Valet, critical of women's working conditions in the telephone industry: *Les Mauvais temps*. With all due respect, it is difficult to say with assurance whether Lefebvre was the author, a co-author, or whether or not Valet produced the book. She certainly typed the manuscript and inspired the novel, as she worked as a telephone operator. It was her links with the populist factions of the PCF[8] that sustained Lefebvre's unorthodoxy. He published other literary works, including poetry and plays. Although he was no playwright, and Debord dismissed the poetry as 'traditional', heavy and backward-looking, the case of *Les Mauvais temps* highlights the restrictions that French intellectuals were under. At the time, he wrote to Guterman of his embarrassment at dabbling in a popular genre and the scorn that he expected if it was published under his own name (undated letter to Guterman). On the one hand, women's everyday life was not an acceptable, orthodox topic; on the other hand, the novel was a genre that retained the frivolous, disreputable status that it had had since its inception.

The experience at work was the same: ever more rationalisation, ever stricter controls over what activities people performed. From agrarian and craft organisation, the French were propelled into a late industrial revolution. Lefebvre documented these changes in his doctoral research, which was one of the first rural sociologies.[9] It was finally published as *La Vallée de Campan* (1963f). Capitalism began to organise all of social life. The architectural projects of modernists such as Le Corbusier emphasised the re-formation of everyday life through the rational redesign of not only buildings and objects but also the way people lived. By contrast, the *Philosophes* (mis)understood the Russian Revolution as an end to excessive rationalism and repetitive, alienated work. The way out of the monotony of the everyday was through revolution: 'We thought of the revolution as a never-ending popular festival. From 1925, we wrote many things about the end of work. At this time, we saw that transformation of work as the revolutionary stake' (interview with Lefebvre, February 1988; cited in Hess 1988: 52–3).

8 These were the result of Henriette Valet's contacts in the union movement as a telephone operator and activist, and Lefebvre's *rabcors* research on working conditions in the silk, cement and steel industries. This fieldwork represents a precursor of industrial ethnography and sociological studies of work and organisations.

9 Lefebvre concentrated primarily on rural sociology in the early 1950s. However, other works, particularly on everyday life, also include comments on rural conditions. On rural sociology, see 1949c; 1950b; 1951a; 1953a; 1953b; 1956d; 1956h; 1957g; 1963f.

Leisure time provides a paradoxical example of alienation within the pursuit of emancipation and the attempt to dis-alienate oneself. Leisure time in the form of 'time off' and vacations is also both extraordinary and separate from everyday life but fully anchored within the everyday. As Lefebvre puts it:

> The worker craves a sharp break with his work, a compensation. He looks for this in leisure seen as entertainment or distraction.
>
> In this way leisure appears as the non-everyday in the everyday.
>
> We cannot step beyond the everyday. The marvellous can only continue to exist in fiction and the illusions that people share. There is no escape. And yet we wish to have the illusion of escape. . . . An illusion not entirely illusory, but constituting a 'world' both apparent and real (the reality of appearances and the apparently real) quite different from the everyday world yet as open-ended and as closely dovetailed into the everyday as possible. So we work to earn our leisure, and leisure has only one meaning: to get away from work. A vicious circle.
>
> (1991a: 40)

A critical leisure studies thus begins with the recognition of leisure as a practice that holds within itself a spontaneous critique of the banality of daily life. The 'impossible–possible' is buried within even the most commodified forms of everyday life. Leisure activities '*are* that critique in so far as they are *other* than everyday life, and yet they are *in everyday life*, they are *alienation*' (1991a: 40). This paradox that the most negative is the basis of the most positive is what fascinated Lefebvre. As a dialectical system of engagement and flight, work and non-work, leisure presents the subversive paradox of a reversible, Nietzschean dialectic between three terms: not just thesis and antithesis (work versus non-work) but also between each of these elements and their synthesis, play or 'creative work'.

Where once leisure was a clearly demarcated *time* within the community – think of Hallowe'en – the time of festival is now a *place* or even a space: a space of leisure, archetypally the Mediterranean or Caribbean basins. Hallowe'en (in its commodified/degenerate spelling) no longer represents any sort of successful compensatory mechanism for Capital. But in the spaces of leisure, resistance through folly and unproductiveness, escape and denial are normalised in a perpetual Mardi Gras of beach front 'red light districts', where the socially illicit and repressed becomes the commodified norm; in football stadia, where spectators indulge in ritual violence; in holiday villages, where one 'gets away from it all' (e.g. Club Med); in theme parks, which are simulacra of 'real' space – often 'mock Nature' in its splendid (but air-conditioned) savagery (cf. Busch Gardens, Tampa, Florida); and entire ensembles of countries and regions (to repeat, the Mediterranean in general, Florida in total (where even economic

98

activity from citrus agriculture to the Kennedy Space Centre is turned into a tourist object)).

Lefebvre considered the concept of everyday life to be his key contribution to social theory. In effect, he operationalizes Marx's critique of alienation by directing critical attention to all forms of taken-for-grantedness or of 'everyday-ness' in day-to-day life. By transposing the philosophical critique of alienation into a sociological critique of the arrangements of daily life, he allowed Marx's notion of alienation to be brought to the forefront of a distinctive political project: no longer simply a demand for economic change but a demand for meaningful lives for all. This clearly moved Lefebvre away from the political mainstream of the PCF and closer to the projects of artistic avant-gardes and radical reformers.

Writing in his seventies, in a book-length monograph, *Présence et l'Absence*, Lefebvre did not retract a word. He underscored his radical position by expanding on his ideas about presence. One of Lefebvre's key interests was ideology. How could a representation, such as a slogan or a sign, mask the absence of meaning? And inversely, how could representations make something as abstract as ideology into something felt, experienced and almost tangible (1980a: 210ff)? Representations mediate between presence and absence. Lefebvre cannot resist making representation into a pun on presence: re-present-ation. He renders what might appear to be a dualism into a three-part dialectic of the whole representation, the absent or illusory ideas or images being represented and the sign or performance making these 'present' by doing the representing.[10]

> The moment of the representation encloses a transition (something transitory, something which 'traverses'), thus a negation in the dialectical sense: to surpass, more or less destroy, but to take up [the essential elements] by surmounting that which is uncertain, slippery, or superficial in the relation 'representation–represented–representing'.
>
> (1991a: 213)

In the poetic act, presence is the given. Lefebvre intends 'poetic' to cover

---

10 The three-part dialectic occurs again and again in Lefebvre's work – a three-part dialectic of space, for example: (1) the lived experience of space; (2) the representations of space (architecture, urban planning); and (3) the imaginary preconceptions of spatiality (our set of spatial expectations, which artists such as Escher, Magritte and the Surrealists violated to surprise their audiences). The motif of three elements can be traced back to Lefebvre's early theological studies with Maurice Blondel, when he became particularly interested in the work of the Sicilian mystic Joachim de Flore's division of the Father, Son and Holy Ghost. At the time, he interpreted these as a universally applicable division between the rule of Law, of Experience and of Spirit (see Chapters 3 and 10).

unalienated production – the Greek *poësis* – as he explained in *Production of Space* (1974) and elsewhere. He does not mean 'creativity', which he denounces as a bourgeois parody of poetic action. Presence and *poësis* stand outside social relations of production. Flashes of inspiration, moments when one feels 'all together' and 'in touch', are not determined by economic relations and cannot be prevented, even in a prison camp. They are free to all. Taking these to be cultural universals common to all people, Lefebvre's argument allows him to make 'presence' the basis for what he calls a 'meta-analysis' (1980a: 212). With characteristic insight, one of the best sociologists of twentieth-century utopian thought, Michael Gardiner, highlights the extent to which this is a new departure for Marxism, which

> with its stress on concrete social practices . . . was an indispensable tool . . . failed to understand the everyday in all its complexity and rich-ness. . . . Lefebvre is adamant that Marxism's failure is more deep-rooted . . . orthodox Marxism is burdened with a 'metaphysics of labor.' This renders it blind to the vast range of human experiences external to the productive process *per se*, regardless of the fact that the 'problematization' of everyday life can be linked to particular sociohis-torical conditions. For instance, Lefebvre argues human *praxis* is not restricted to the utilitarian transformation of external nature through repetitive instrumental action [production]. It also involves love, sensuality, the body, affect – a plethora of creative, emotive and imagi-native practices . . . *poësis*.
>
> (1995: 98)

This shift is essential to any revitalisation of critical thought. This is a critique drawing on both the Surrealists and the Situationists – and not just a critique of the class relations of production but of repression and enslavement in all its forms. Lefebvre thus privileges the creation of 'works' (likened to artworks) instead of products or commodities. These 'works' or *oeuvres* are an antidote to alienation because they too are representations that make an abstract possibility, or even an impossible utopia, 'present' for the audience and creator. Craft work, interior decoration, community pageants and so on could all be analysed using Lefebvre's concept of *oeuvre*. These works are not necessarily artistic masterpieces, but they provide good examples of what Lefebvre is talking about.

> In contrast to the philosopher, the creator of works [*oeuvres*] doesn't distance himself from or bracket [*époché*] everyday life in a mania for the paradoxical . . . concepts, ideas, ideologies. In disengaging from the everyday and from social practice, he enters into another practice, his

own, *poetic action*, There he is in a relation with other works – earlier or made at the same time – with other creators of artistic work.

$$(1980a: 214)^{11}$$

But the most important *oeuvres* are the city and landscapes formed by human cultivation over centuries. To such works, there is an intrinsic human right – the creators' prerogative not to ownership but to its enjoyment and possession in the deepest sense: it is a totality assembling difference, characterised by formal simultaneity where all parts refer to the whole and vice versa (Kofman and Lebas 1996: 20; Lefebvre 1968b). The importance of the *oeuvre* is its character of being a totality, an indivisible whole, from which something is always lost if it is separated into component parts. Even though they can be commodified, and thus trivialised, they are always a potential occasion for 'moments of presence' when their internal qualities are recognised. Although people can be stirred into action by moments, the problem is the unpredictability of such experiences. Yet there can be no retreat from the complexity of such 'concrete abstractions': to insist on 'keeping our feet on the ground' is to refuse Lefebvre's method of projecting the 'impossible–possible' of utopia in order to inspire small achievements in our own lives. To refuse the challenge of presence is to be less than human – a kind of emotional cyborg, the 'cybernanthrope' he called it (1971e). It is fascinating to compare this with Haraway's cyborg (1991), better known to English-language readers:

> The *cybernanthrope* deplores human weakness and its own weaknesses. It knows its imperfections. It disavows the human, the human quality. It disqualifies humanism, in thought and in action. It hunts down the illusions of subjectivity: creation, happiness, passion, as empty as forgetting. It aspires to function, that is, to be nothing but a function. Behind the illusions of subjectivity, what is there? Neurosis. The robot does not possess an unconscious; it has no need of the psychoanalyst.
>
> To be precise, The *cybernanthrope* is no automaton. It is the person who . . . understands himself [*sic*] thanks to the automaton. It lives in symbiosis with the machine. In it he has found his double in reality. To find himself there, he has disavowed the double illusions of subjectivity and objectivity, of conscience and *oeuvres*.
>
> (1971d: 194)

Is Lefebvre's gendered language intentional as he switches between the neuter 'it' and the masculine 'he'? The *cybernanthrope* is not a machine; 'he' is a person who has given up something of 'his' humanity by thinking of 'himself' as a machine, as an 'it'. Haraway points out the technologically enhanced

---

11 Gendered terms as in the French original.

quality of the cyborg and notes that we are all in some sense 'cyborgised' in the manner in which we are dependent on machines, implants, prostheses and aids of all kinds. However, Haraway recodes her telling of the 'cyborg' as a feminist myth of emancipation in which people exploit the ambiguous line between technology and the human to challenge this process of 'cyborgisation' using its own logic of hybridity. Breaking down the categories of natural and artificial and showing how they routinely intersect has the potential to revolutionise political action by directing attention to the areas of science, technology, the body and the family (Haraway 1991). However, many argue that there is nothing intrinsically wrong with this. For its critical impact, Haraway's argument, first published in the mid-1970s, depends on Lefebvre's. Why? Lefebvre identifies what one risks losing if one treats oneself, and by implication, others, as machines. This is all the more relevant because the accomplishments of genetics tend to be taken as heralding the replacement of the subjective human with the machine-body experiencing chemically induced emotions honed through evolutionary trial and error. Yet the pundits are surprisingly silent on the precise, evolutionary function of emotions such as the anguish of loss and nostalgia for the past.

In the shadowy world of ideology, of half-formed ideas, there can be no question of truth or falsity: all is ambiguity. The artist plays with these illusions, linking them to the concrete and fixed elements of everyday life. The *oeuvre* contains both represented ideas made present and ambiguous elements open to interpretation that rest on implicit ideas that remain absences until they are made explicit through an act of interpretation or clarification. Works thus embody and contain moments of a dialectic that Lefebvre labels 'presence–absence'. These moments may be utopian, may be critical (i.e. provoke a crisis in everyday life).

The concept of presence, or more properly *presence-absence*, provides the philosophical underpinning for Lefebvre's sociological analyses of everyday life, of space as a cultural artefact, and of ideology, as well as the importance of the *oeuvre*, or unalienated production for the elimination of the current regime of alienating labour (see 1975b; 1976a; 1976b; 1977; 1978b).

> The abolition of labour . . . has the greatest importance and makes the greatest amount of sense. In effect state-capitalism and its alter-ego, state-socialism, maintain and will maintain labour and labourers as long as possible in order to dominate them politically as much as to exploit them economically. . . .
>
> What to do in non-labour? . . . The passage from labour to non-labour supposes a displacement of social interest from the product to the *oeuvre*, from productive labour to poetic action, and by consequence from the quantitative to the qualitative, from exchange value to

102

use value. A difficult movement, which will not take place without detours or reversals.

(1980a: 217)

The Situationists' critique of moments

Together with the politicised and radical artists and intellectuals who assembled in Strasbourg in the late 1950s as Situationists, Lefebvre sought to apply his theory of moments to the Paris Commune, an 1871 rebellion of Parisian workers and intellectuals who proclaimed their independence from a France reeling from defeat in the Franco-Prussian war. The Commune was short-lived but marked by an extraordinary outpouring of art, revolutionary fervour and symbolic, ritualised acts that attacked the legitimacy of the state (see Ross 1988). Lefebvre published his conclusions – which had resulted from their joint study – separately from the Situationists, leading to accusations of plagiarism (1962h; 1965f; see also Chapters 2 and 8). The association with the Situationists was over; they became bitter enemies. However, the study of the Commune allowed Lefebvre's idea of an ecstatic moment in which totality was experienced in a manner that was fully authentic to be linked firmly to the idea of revolutionary fervour. Thus the notion of the 'revolutionary festival': if presence could be experienced during the disorder of carnivalesque festivals and Mardi Gras, why not also during parades, demonstrations, riots and mass occupations? The stage was set for the student occupations of May 1968.

Both Lefebvre and the Situationists developed their theories with reference to each other. Debord participated in Lefebvre's seminars and was in turn introduced to Raoul Vaneigem and Gerard Lebovichi, the other key members of the Situationists.[12] The influence of Debord on Lefebvre and of Lefebvre on the Situationists is clear from the manner in which they formulate their arguments. The theory of moments, which would unite the affectual content of everyday life, bypassing oppositions between serious and frivolous, between love and hate, is refined in *Situationniste Internationale* 4 (June 1960: 10–11) and can be connected with their definition of the 'situation', which rather than remaining in the abstractions of an emotional moment, concretises the affect within a social context. To Debord, Lefebvre's theory of moments was 'the science fiction of revolutionary thought'. While Lefebvre spoke philosophically of a utopian future in which even the most alienated moments would be delivered from drudgery, for the Situationists the subversion of society was not a utopian question but a practical question of the highest order (*Situationniste Internationale* 3: 4–6; see Chapter 5).

---

12 See Sadie Plant, *The Most Radical Gesture* (1992).

Guy Debord and other Situationists criticised the theory of moments and refined it in crucial ways. Debord's *Society of the Spectacle* (1977) warned of state-sponsored spectacles that produced a false sense of presence. In effect, Lefebvre's idea could easily be – and had always been – hijacked by carnival promoters and ideologists alike. 'Bread and Circuses,' Karl Marx had said. Lefebvre recognised the danger of simulations of presence (1980: 225). His assistant, Jean Baudrillard, pointed out the impossibility of establishing the purely authentic (1983). Nonetheless, in Lefebvre's theory and discussions, there is no built-in method of determining 'real' moments from staged moments.[13] Lefebvre's roots were in the tragic (hubris and 'sin', see 1961j) more than spectacle (pathos and horror), the key term of the Situationists. Thus, unlike Baudrillard, Lefebvre preserved a notion of the real that could be an object of struggle. Its spectacular forms in the consumption of commodities as signs of social status and identity, and the hyper-real world of the media (if it is seen on television, it must have really happened), could be resisted.

For the Situs, Lefebvre's theory of moments was too abstract. It mixed existential experience with essentialist concepts of, for example, 'love'. Moments were in danger of being an abstraction, a muddled mixture of desires, perceptions and emotional reactions. The Situs stressed the conjunctural and existential quality of love as a lived experience that was different in different situations (going one better than Lefebvre in his arguments for the importance of lived, everyday experience). They argued that moments were not simply ruptures in everyday temporality but a different experience of temporality that amounted to a unique *type* of time:

> The *moment* is mainly temporal, it is part of not a pure, but a dominant, realm of temporality. The situation, narrowly articulated in a site is thoroughly spatio-temporal. Moments made into *situations* could be considered as moments of rapture, of acceleration, *revolutions in the individual daily life.*
>
> (*Situationniste Internationale*; 4 cited in Hess 1988: 216)

The creation of *situations* (situations yes, but the connotation is of 'happenings') that disturbed the blasé attitude of urbanites and norms of everyday life was to form the aesthetic medium for the *Situationnistes'* plans. Debord describes these situations as 'the concrete construction of momentary ambi-

---

13 MacCannell (1992) and Urry (1990; 1996) speak of 'staged authenticity' put on by local inhabitants of places exotic to the European or North American tourist. While the tourist may understand that he or she is essentially involved in a game, they nonetheless do not usually experience the 'truth' of the native's lifeworld. Instead, they are paraded through simulated 'native villages' and taken to staged folk dances and lunar festivals, which are put on every day of the tourist season to attract dollars.

ences of life and their transformation into a superior passional quality' (Debord 1957: 1). The plan was to invent new ways of using the city for non-productive, non-rational purposes through the shock tactic of staging surreal events. This was to be their *praxis*:

> The method of experimental utopia, to truly correspond to its project, should lead to a new usage of life, to a new revolutionary praxis. The contestation of existing society in its entirety is the only criterion of an authentic liberation on the terrain of the city, this also goes for all other aspects of human activity. Otherwise 'improvement' and 'progress' will always end up oiling the system to perfect the conditioning which we must overturn in urbanism and everywhere else.
>
> (*Situationist International* 6 1986: 7; see also Hess 1988: 216–17)

Lefebvre could see the origins of the situation in Existentialism and in the Surrealist antics of his youth. Shocking incidents, invasions and takeovers of public events were a smash-and-grab tactic for getting public attention (Latour and Combes 1991: 87). But here Lefebvre did not provide a systematic critique: in one of the paradoxical manoeuvres of French intellectuals, he can be seen muddying the waters in *Langage et société* by arguing that modernity itself was one giant situation (1966d). Yet he agreed with Baudrillard and Debord, lamenting the commodification of everyday life through transforming the banal into a spectacle that could be enjoyed simply for amusement or its superficial attractions – much as in many advertisements, where the absolutely banal is glamorised and made to appear dramatic.

> The *cybernanthrope* searches for a style. It finds it, it has found it because he has made it. It is the Prising style, the Inn style, the super-market style. Our friend sees the total Spectacle there, the superspectacle, crowning a spectacular epoque which presents itself in spectacle and sells through spectacle.
>
> (1971d: 199–200)

About Dada, Marcus says: 'the blind oath, the severed gesture, the buried curse, the dance it took an entire civilisation to forget and ten seconds to remember. The pieces Lefebvre would promise to finish smashing had been discovered. The momentum was there, the task was to increase it' (1989: 221–2). Inspired by Tzara, Lefebvre argued that it was necessary to go beyond Dada, to 'finish smashing the pieces' that Dada had left, to make a lasting change not in an artists' cabaret but in the broader sphere of everyday life. The Situationists resolved to do just that, making a project out of the idea that 'the empty repetitions of modern life, of work and spectacle, could be ... [hijacked] into the creation of Situations, into abstract forms that could be infused with unlimited content [such as invoking archaic symbols]' (*ibid.*: 238). Lefebvre summed up the passion of this project when he said, after he had left the PCF:

> I have never taken seriously anything but three realities: love, philosophy, Party. Three deceptions? To a point. I only wish for my detractors such moving and ardent deceptions.
>
> (1958: 343)

May 1968

In 1965, Lefebvre finally moved back to Paris to take up a post as Professor of Sociology at Nanterre. This new university in suburban Paris was to be the crucible of the student revolts 'à l'Americain' at the end of that decade. Lefebvre scorned the University, which

> was conceived in terms of the concepts of the . . . productivity of neo-capitalist society, but falls short of the implications of such a conception. The buildings and the environment reflect the real nature of the intended project. It is an enterprise designed to produce mediocre intellectuals and 'junior executives' for the management of this society, and transmit a body of specialised knowledge determined . . . by the social division of labour. . . . Situated in the midst of a civilisation which . . . is based on the City, it might be described as a place of damnation. . . .
>
> These functional buildings that are utterly devoid of character . . . were designed for the functions of education: vast amphitheatres, small 'functional' rooms, drab halls, an administrative wing. . . . [Here] manifest poverty sharply contrasts with the utopian and mythical richness of officially proposed culture and officially dispensed knowledge. . . . This contributes substantially to the disintegration of culture, formal knowledge and institutions.
>
> (Lefebvre 1968h, quoted from the English translation 1969d: 104–6)

Nanterre is, in effect, at the end of the long axis of the Champs Elysées, where the government and corporate office developments of La Défence mark the end of the vista. However, Lefebvre attributed a radicalising influence to the location of the campus, which attracted middle-class students in a working-class commuting area of Paris. While the campus was a long way out, it stood presciently on the old marching route of armies straight down that axis, under the Arc de Triomphe and down the Champs Elysées into the heart of Paris.

Insulted by the lack of facilities and the injustices of the educational system, inspired by the thesis of the 'festive revolution' promulgated by Lefebvre and his then-assistant Jean Baudrillard,[14] and provoked by the contradictions between privilege and the despair surrounding the campus, and between an ideology of equality and pedagogical practices that discriminated sharply between students and faculty, students held a protest meeting at the beginning of May 1968. Misunderstandings and an unwillingness to take the student protest seriously exaggerated the protest, which soon became an occupation that quickly spread to other campuses, including the prestigious Sorbonne in the city centre. It was an atmosphere in which Edgar Morin, the Dean, argued with angry students in a packed lecture theatre. For Morin, it was a return to the politics of the mob: he fancied himself shouted down by Fascists. But for the students, it was experienced as the unwillingness of figures in power to face their own hypocrisy, and a triumph over authorities who had lost all legitimacy.

For the *Situationnistes*, it was a dream come true. After widely publicised and notorious attempts to foster revolt earlier in Strasbourg, they found themselves invited onto the students' occupation committees. Situationist slogans and Lefebvre's aphorisms decorated the streets. The idea was simple, as Lefebvre's most 'Situ' saying put it, 'Under the pavers, a beach'; which is to say, just beneath the surface of the alienating, rationalised city lay a ludic, festive community. As the students pulled up the granite cobbles to hurl at the police, they exposed the layer of sand on which they were laid and levelled.

Lefebvre's summary of the events of the month, which saw workers affiliated with Communist trade unions break ranks with the wary PCF to march into Paris in support of student demonstrators, and during which the French President, Charles de Gaulle, left Paris fearing a *coup d'état*, and ended with order restored within weeks, is one of the most widely translated accounts of the May revolt (1968h; see 1969i). Lefebvre became the most widely translated French writer of the 1960s.

The effect of 1968 was to put Lefebvre and the *Situationnistes* into the political history books. But the importance of 1968 was, first, to establish the political importance of media, communications, and mass phenomena that cut across classes (thereby displacing the centrality of orthodox, Marxist analysis even before it became popular within the English-speaking world). The students did make demands that were not reducible to wages, working hours or democratic representation; they demanded a revolution in everyday life (see also Plant 1992: 96). Second, May 1968 was seen as a demonstration of the ineffectiveness of a 'festive revolution' for achieving political change: it was the nemesis of Lefebvre's political proposals. In response, there was a shift away from Lefebvre's anti-structuralistic emphasis on the early 'humanistic Marx', on alienation and personal liberation, towards the PCF-endorsed 'scientific

---

14 Baudrillard's 1972 text *For a Critique of the Political Economy of the Sign* (1981) can be read as a Situationist-inspired commentary on Lefebvre's position of the time, which maintained a form of Marxist essentialism concerning the identity of classes.

Marxism' of Louis Althusser. This returned the focus to the structures of the state, to an essentialised reading of history as a succession of 'modes of production' and a theory of social interaction that prioritised the politico-economic above all other elements of sociality (Althusser and Balibar 1972; Hindess and Hirst 1977). Lefebvre's later critiques of Structuralism (see Chapter 8) must be read as a rearguard action as he attempted to maintain his intellectual pre-eminence against more structuralistic analysts who had come to the fore during and after the events of 1968 – Michel Foucault (1986a), Manuel Castells (1977; 1994), and Althusser himself.

In *Le Manifeste différentialiste* (1971a), Lefebvre argued for a form of extreme pluralism. This *Differentialist Manifesto* demands an end to political *indifference* through forms of popular democracy, grassroots involvement and self-organisation (*autogestion*). The political is reconceived as the personal, echoing the great Situationist slogan that perhaps sums up the *zeitgeist* of the 1960s and its 'baby-boom generation': 'the personal is the political'. But this could easily collapse into something that could be lampooned as an impossible utopia, or an irrelevant exploration of unpragmatic politics.

> Can one conceive a revolution in the name of difference? . . . It takes up and returns to the light the Marxist project of a maximum revolution (total), a project abandoned at the side of the road. It demonstrates that without this idea of total revolution (the 'impossible–possible') there is no project, no action, conquest, reform. To obtain the least, one must think and will the most.
>
> (1971a: 159)

The beautifully dialectical notion of an 'impossible–possible' – in other words, a utopia that makes us think critically about the status quo – appeared irrelevant to many in the Cold War political world of the 1970s: one reader has scribbled 'the differentialist asparagus of Lefebvre' on the thirteenth page of the signed copy in my local library. The difference, however, between the potential and the already existing was the heart of 'differentialism' counterposing heterogeneity to homogenisation. As Lefebvre puts it: '*Differentialism* [is] an arrow to expose an issue, between the thesis of a closed world [the status quo] and that of a beatified world [utopia].' (1971a: 9). One must struggle for the right to be different, to exceed the narrow categories constructed in modernity and their neat alignment with commodities, images and commodified lifestyles. In this method for linking an exploration of possible futures with the analysis of existing worlds, Lefebvre is clearly applying his dialectical 'projective–retrojective' method, adopted in the 1950s by Sartre (see Chapter 9).

8

FATHER OF THE DIALECTIC AND CRITIC OF STRUCTURALISM

Lefebvre is perhaps best-known as the 'father of the dialectic' in France and was for many years also best-known outside France for his works on the dialectic. Focusing on dialectical materialism as a general method developed by Marx but applied by him to only a limited number of fields, Lefebvre proposed dialectical materialism as a universal method. While Althusser and 'scientific Marxists' saw economics and materialism as the legacy of Marx, Lefebvre saw dialectical materialism as the rigorous core of Marx's insight. The dialectic itself thus became the cornerstone of Lefebvre's philosophical critique of the formal logic of traditional philosophies. As noted briefly in Chapters 2 and 3, the basic difference may be summed up by saying that while formal logic, exemplified by simple mathematics, focused on the singular identity and differences between elements, dialectical logic focused on relationships between elements and the process by which new states of affairs arise out of deep contradictions in the status quo.

The dialectic is the centripetal core of Lefebvre's many different interests. This chapter focuses first on Lefebvre's approach to dialectical materialism and then on his argument that this furnishes a logic and methodology that is a universally useful approach. I have already argued that Lefebvre was a methodologist and populariser who wrote many of his works to either make dialectical materialism better understood or to show how a Marxist interpretation could be applied to the work of historical French thinkers. He aimed to make dialectical materialism easily accessible to students and the general public. His most translated and best-known work is *Matérialisme Dialectique* (1939b),[1] translated in 1968 as *Dialectical Materialism* (1968j). Although it is one of the most venerable of short and accessible student texts on Marxism in university libraries, it has been generally ignored, even at the same time as academics teaching in this area usually claim to know the book well. In France, the initial fate of *Matérialisme Dialectique* was cruel. Only a month after its publication,

---

1   Two fragments appeared in *La Nouvelle Revue Française* (1934), linking this work to Lefebvre's collaborations with Guterman. See 1935a, 1935b.

Soviet theoretical orthodoxy was adopted by the Parti Communiste Français (PCF), leading to the destruction of whatever could be seized from the first printing. The declaration of war in September 1939 and the rapid occupation of France ensured that no reviews and little discussion was possible of this underground classic.

It is the original – the first – textbook on the subject. Although it was widely translated, the reason for the eventual disappearance of *Dialectical Materialism* from the English-language Marxist scene was its lack of fit with Althusser-influenced interpretations of Marx. This divided his work into a 'young Marx' who focused on humanistic questions of alienation and ideology before the publication of the more mature, older works of 'scientific Marxism', such as *Das Kapital*. The later Marx focused on economic issues after having made what Althusser argued was a conceptual 'breakthrough' by understanding consciousness and ideology to be dependent on economic status, that is, class position. This young/old Marx continued to be the conventional division of anthologies of Marx's works (see Marx 1975). Lefebvre himself traced such divisions to the simplification of Marxism into a party doctrine, beginning with the rediscovery of the works of the young Marx in the 1920s and rearguard actions begun in the Soviet Union in the 1930s to rid official Marxism of their influence.

> At precisely the moment when hitherto disregarded concepts were being rediscovered (alienation, praxis, the total man and social totality etc.), and when those who had read the young Marx were clearing the way for the rediscovery of Hegel, the dogmatists were moving in the opposite direction. They became more contemptuous than ever of Hegel and Hegelianism, they rejected Marx's early writings as being tainted with idealism and as having preceded the formulation of dialectical materialism, they drew a line between Marx and his predecessors and another between the so-called philosophical and so-called scientific works in the Marxian corpus.
>
> (Lefebvre 1968j: 14)

Lefebvre understood Marx's career quite differently. Alienation is central throughout Marx's work, which is divided into the period of the development of historical materialism, during which Marx rejected Hegel. His highest achievement is to unify idealism and materialism in the *German Ideology*, written with Engels (cf. Lefebvre and Guterman 1939b [1968]: 60–80). Marx's 'mature' period is demarcated by the recognition of the importance of Hegel's dialectical method, which bore fruit in *Das Kapital* and *Critique of Political Economy*.[2] The reintegration of dialectical method with Marx's materialist critique of Hegel and Feuerbach provided a set of tools for the analysis of the

2 Lefebvre dates this to 1858. See 1939b [2nd edn, 1968]: 82.

underlying socioeconomic causes of alienation. Lefebvre thus follows the Marx of *The German Ideology*, emphasising the continuous, dialectical movement of knowledge and practical experience. Neither of these two could be privileged over the other. Lefebvre thus rejects the idea that Marx was a 'pure' materialist because of the importance Marx attached to alienation – a concept that was both concrete and abstract. As outlined in Chapter 4, the 'alienation' of workers in the sense of the expropriation, or 'taking away', of the products they created and the profits from them is a case of empirical separation, whereas the progressive alienation of people from their human qualities is an abstraction. Lefebvre's Marx is always first and foremost dialectical, and hence he stresses the first term: *dialectical* materialism. The two elements of this term needed to be integrated in the totality of an unalienated 'total person' who is both the subject and object of becoming – a formulation that anticipates and causes Lefebvre's work to be compared to Marcuse's critique of individualism (1964), which so influenced American students' social critiques in the mid-1960s. The 'total person' was a concept that Lefebvre developed from Marx's comments in *Economic and Philosophical Manuscripts*: 'Man appropriates his integral essence in an integral way, as a total man' (Marx 1975: 351; see Chapter 4).

For Lefebvre, the development of a society of 'total human beings' is not the result of an inevitable historical progression, nor of economic structures, but requires continuous effort to demystify social relations (1939b [1968]: 164). There are therefore no guarantees. This places an enormous pressure on existential choices and the need for responsible exercise of agency. Lefebvre shifts Marxism away from materialist determinism and places creative ability back into the consciousness – and will – of people. At the same time, knowledge and understanding and the opportunities for transformation are limited by material, historical conditions (Burkhard 1986: 264). However,

> Lefebvre's open totality lacked a motivating agent, a will to create and transform. Without the introduction of a source of human self-creative effort, Lefebvre's Marxism would sooner or later be forced to rely on either an idealist Absolute or a materialist determinism.
>
> (Burkhard 1986: 265)

Hegel's dialectic

Lefebvre took up the topic of the dialectic with Norbert Guterman in their *Cahiers de Lenine sur la dialectique de Hegel*, with a 130-page 'Introduction' to Lenin's 'Notebooks' on the topic. These were largely disregarded in Europe but were available to Guterman and Lefebvre from their Russian publication in 1929/30. Their 'Introduction' helped to make Hegel more central to debates within Marxism in France, although official Marxist doctrine avoided these 'Philosophical Notebooks' because of their focus on issues such as subjectivity, idealism and self-movement (for a full discussion see Anderson 1992). They

111

were incompatible with the party doctrine, which had come to focus on materialism and Marxisms anchored in economic determinism.

Dialectical logic, in its modern form, begins with Hegel as a response to paradoxes that could not be dealt with within the terms of Aristotelian 'formal logic'. Formal logic studies purely analytical transformations, abstracted from any specific content. In this sense, formal logic is concerned with *form* and rules of operation rather than the contents of logic. Thus 'A is A,' and 'If A is B but B is C', then 'A is also C'. Formal logic is in no way concerned with the material contents of this argument. Lefebvre cites Hegel's *History of Philosophy*, where the curious, apparent movement of thought independent of any material is identified. In terms of the example above, 'A' seems to move from identity with itself over to identity with 'C', even though this has nothing to do with the objects being thought about (1968j: 21).[3] Formal logic is dependent on having some sort of content 'As Hegel points out, a completely simple, void identity cannot even be formulated'. Furthermore, the argument 'A is A' implies that 'A is not "not-A"', obscuring from view the logical process by which negation operates (1968j: 22). Even if sufficient to its own specialised concerns, it leaves us with philosophical problems concerning how logic itself and its form is related to the content, to what is being thought.

> Logical theories of the real, as Hegel remarks ironically, have always been much too soft-hearted towards things; they have busied themselves rooting out contradictions from the real only to carry them over into the mind and there leave them unresolved. The objective world thus comes to be made up ultimately of isolated and immobile facts, of essences, substances or parts, which are external one to another.
>
> (1968j: 22–3)

They are thought of as external to one another, just as 'A' is posited as logically external to 'B'. This hardly does justice to the material and even encourages one to turn within, to the life of the mind, for the interest of movement. This situation can be summed up as a *logic of identities* of 'A = A' and 'B = B', which neglects negation ('not-A', 'not-B'), excludes transformation ('A becomes B') and is blind to its content, even though it is dependent on it. In everyday arguments, nothing is indisputably true, nothing is absolutely absurd or false. 'Each thesis is false in what it asserts absolutely, but true in what it asserts relatively (its content); and it is true in what it denies relatively (its well-founded criticism of the other thesis) and false in what it denies absolutely (its dogmatism)' (1968j: 27; see Hegel 1969, Book III). By comparing different theses or propositions,

---

3   Lefebvre provides no specific citations to editions or pages of most of the philosophical sources that he cites or paraphrases. References to sections and chapters have been included to supplement the source references to Lefebvre's own work.

one spontaneously seeks a better and higher unity.

Dialectic, or maieutic, the art of clarifying ideas through the exchange of questions and answers, becomes a method once this movement is recognised and uprooted from sophistry, or argument for the sake of it, which only brings falsity into collision with ungrounded 'truth'. Beginning with Kant, a synthesis of form and content had been sought. In Hegel's *Science of Logic* (1969), dialectic becomes a technique of 'analysing the multiple aspects and relations of words and things, without destroying their essence; a science which releases whatever is true in all the contradictory ideas between which common understanding oscillates' (1968j: 28). Thought moves amongst contradictions:

> The negative is equally a positive; whatever is contradicted is not reduced to a zero, to an abstract nothingness, but essentially to the negation of its particular content; in other words such a negation is not a complete negation but the negation of the determinate thing which is being dissolved, and therefore a determinate negation. The result, being a *determinate negation* has a content; it is a *new concept*, having been enriched by its negation . . . it contains the other but is also more than the other, it is their unity.
>
> (Hegel 1969, Book I; cited in Lefebvre 1968j: 30, italics added)

This *synthesis* is thus a 'third term', Hegel's discovery of which defines *dialectical logic*.[4] This third term unites and transcends the contradictories and preserves what was determinate in them. What vanishes in this movement is the formal element of contradiction that thrusts each term beyond itself, uprooting it from its limited identity with itself and inserting it into the movement of synthesis, or *aufheben*:

> Whatever is transcended does not thereby become nothing. Nothingness is im*mediate*, whereas a term that has been transcended has been *mediated*; it is a non-being, but only inasmuch as it is a *result* arising from a being; it still has within it therefore the determination from which it arose. This word (*aufheben*) has two meanings; it means to 'keep' or 'preserve' as well as to 'put a stop to'.
>
> (Hegel 1969, Book I; cited in 1968j: 35)

'Synthesis' thus contains a treacherous notion of *aufheben*. The position of synthesis could also be an outside term that transcends, or an 'other' that freezes and holds – possibly stabilising – a dialectical contradiction. It is in this sense that culture is a third, synthetic term (not a simple 'superstructural'

---

4 For a contemporary application of the idea of the third term, and a development of Lefebvre's work on social space, see Soja 1996.

element within a dialectical relationship with a Marxist economic 'base') in relation to the contradictions of capitalism. Hegel argued that every movement is a case of transcending, thereby anchoring a notion of surmounting progress into reason and recoding history as necessity. It does not abolish formal logic, only transcends it by showing that there is more than the logic of the instant and of simple facts. It does not abolish identity but gives it a content, an identification. Lefebvre sums this up, drawing on Hegel's *Encyclopedia of the Philosophical Sciences*: §143:

> The Hegelian dialectic seeks to restore life and movement to the sum of the realities that have been apprehended, to assertions and notions. It involves them in an immense epic of mind. All the contradictions of the world . . . all beings therefore and all assertions, together with their relations, interdependencies and interactions, are grasped in the total movement of their content, each one in its own place at its own 'moment'. The network of [isolated] facts, forces and concepts becomes Reason.
>
> (1968j: 36)

Dialectical materialism: Marx's and Engels' critique of Hegel

Hegel's philosophy, Lefebvre commented drily, 'is still not the world of Men, in all its dramatic reality' (1968j: 58). Marx's critique stems from the triumphant quality of mind over matter and the ongoing world of human action. Whereas Hegel had proposed a system in which all conflicts were ultimately reconciled philosophically, Marx sought a more worldly, a practical, utopia. 'Hegel's ambition coincides with that of philosophy, with the most secret desire of the lie of the mind, seen as expansion and dominion: to exclude nothing, to leave nothing outside itself, to abandon and transcend every one-sided position' (1968j: 46). Having asserted the primacy of content, the truth of form ends up being defined in terms of its logical coherence with itself: systematisation takes over.

> Just as much a doctrine and a logical method, Hegelianism represents a type of spiritual life that is still valid. Not to aim at acquiescing too hastily to ourselves or to the world; not to hide from ourselves the contradictions in the world, in man and in each individual, but on the contrary, to accentuate them, however much we may suffer, because it is fruitful to be torn asunder and because, once the contradictions have become unbearable, the need to transcend them becomes stronger than any resistance on the part of the elements that are passing away;

such is the principle of a spiritual lie both sorrowful and joyous, wholly rational and unconfused. . . .

. . . modern culture forces man to live 'in two worlds which contradict one another. On the one hand we see man living in the ordinary, temporary actuality of this world, weighed down by want and wretchedness, in thrall to matter; on the other hand he can raise himself up to Ideas, to a kingdom of thought and of freedom; inasmuch as he is Will he gives himself laws' (*Aesthetics*). But even as he does so 'he strips the world of its living actuality and resolves it into abstractions.' Thus flesh and spirit, everyday reality and thought . . . actual servitude and the theoretical power of the intelligence, the wretchedness of concrete existence and the splendid but fictive sovereignty of the Idea, all are in conflict. . . . Hegelianism . . . cannot efface or justify what causes us actual suffering.

(1968j: 47–8, 59)

Is it conceivable that the limited mind of an individual should be able to grasp the entire content of human experience? For Hegel, 'In relation to the Idea, the luxuriance of Nature, its ambivalence, its vitality, its fantasy and its incessant generation of new and aberrant types, are merely a form of impotence' (Lefebvre 1968j: 49). Having asserted the primacy of content over the form of thought, in *Encyclopedia of the Philosophical Sciences* §14, Hegel later argued that 'logical thoughts are not moments exclusive in relation to those thoughts, because they are *the absolute foundation of all things*' (cited in 1968j: 52). 'Thought is thus the secret source of content', which ends up enclosed in a circular system.

Although Hegel gave action a role in his philosophy, as one aspect of the absolute idea, he saw it as an imitation of the mind, a 'putting into action' of thought, not as an autonomous realm. He thus rejected Kant's earlier idea of separating 'practical reason' from other forms of thought and judgement. For Hegel, action becomes 'thought of action'. If action 'proclaims itself' as autonomous, as part of nature, then Hegel has left out a significant element and set of problems arising from the relationship between rational thought and action. Between 1843 and 1859, Marx and Engels dedicated themselves to developing the content of Hegel's system as a way out of the fatalistic consequences of Hegel's approach.

Like Marx and Engels, Lefebvre found the positive aspect of Hegel's dialectic in his *Phenomenology* (1949), where he was not content simply to record the content of thought but attempted to develop a method that comprehended its ongoing process of production, autopoésis and change. Seizing life only in terms of logical concepts and celebrating the 'realisation of mind' in social institutions such as the state – which then act repressively against people – is rejected as a form of alienation. 'This is why the whole history of alienation . . . is nothing more than the history of the production of abstract thought, of speculative, logical thought' (Marx 1975; cited in 1968j: 62–3).

Marx and Engels had built upon the work of Feuerbach, who exposed a fatal flaw in Hegel's system: if mind becomes nature and matter, then matter becomes mind, dissolving the basis of Hegel's dialectic. Feuerbach argued that philosophy was systematised religion, and he proposed setting individuals and their relationships with each other in the fore of any post-Hegelian philosophy. Marx's and Engels' addition was to reconceptualise individuals as concrete social beings in definite historical–geographic relationships. Adopting this materialism, Lefebvre argued, Marx and Engels were first and foremost seeking to deepen humanism and their critique of alienation. *Dialectical Materialism* seeks to give thought back its force by linking it directly to practice, and moving Hegel's dialect into concrete social analysis and finally applying it to economic relations before moving on to nature (cf. Engels, *Dialectics of Nature* (1954); Marx and Engels, *Correspondence 1873–4* (1934)). Lefebvre argues that we in turn must apply the method of dialectical materialism to the problems of our epoch.

> truth is to be found in totality . . . philosophy cannot be the supreme . . . total activity. The true is the concrete; philosophical abstracts have hardly any actual effect. There is no immobile absolute. . . . Speculation must be transcended.
>
> (1968j: 72–3)

Nietzsche and dialectical materialism

In their well-researched introduction and analysis of Lefebvre's texts on the urban, Kofman and Lebas comment that 'the most striking and neglected aspect' of Lefebvre's work 'is the debt to Nietzsche. . . . The emphasis on the body, sexuality, violence and the tragic, and the production of differential space and plural times, have direct resonances in Nietzschean thought' (1996: 5). While *Matérialisme Dialectique* was clearly a continuation and restatement of Lefebvre's earlier themes from *Philosophies* through *Avant Poste* (see Chapter 2), it should also be read in conjunction with his other 1939 text, *Nietzsche*, which was intended to fill another absence (Burkhard 1986: 265). As with Hegel (see Chapter 3), Lefebvre rehabilitated Nietzsche from Fascist thinkers, and broke with the vilification of Nietzsche by Communist intellec-

---

5   For example, Drieu la Rochelle *Socialisme fasciste: Marx contre Nietzsche* (1934). Lefebvre agreed that elements of Nietzsche's work could be manipulated into Fascism, including heroism, history as myth, and the combination of pessimism and tragedy and the link with Wagner. Yet Lefebvre argued that the concept of 'overcoming' (*überwinden*) usually associated with the Fascist adoption of the idea of the Overman (*übermensch*) should be 'equated with the Marxist concept of dis-alienated human existence, the 'total man'. Like the 'total man,' the *übermensch* represents the re-fusion of consciousness and being (Burkhard 1986: 267).

tuals, including Lukács.[5] Despite the importance of Nietzsche to Parisian intellectuals such as the Surrealists and the post-Durkheimian critical thinkers around Bataille, there was no accessible translation or introduction in French. In particular, he associated himself with Nietzsche's project of continuous social critique and the examination of social values. In the late 1930s, Lefebvre attempted a historic synthesis of Hegel, Marx and Nietzsche into an open and developing totality. His first attempts in the 1930s concluded in favour of Marx; however, he returned to this project later in his career to produce a more daring synthesis (1975a). In effect, a 'Nietzschean' Marx would 'wager' on one's understanding and agency to effect progressive social change (Burkhard 1986: 267–8).

In later works, Lefebvre re-examined the compatibility of a Hegelian *aufhebung* (see Chapter 6) with Nietzschean *überwinden* (or 'overcoming', see Chapter 2) and reassessed the possibilities of a synthesis. Dialectical logic emphasises the changeable quality of things as they encounter opposition, or *antitheses*, and are re-synthesised with those contradictory forces to become entirely new objects, or *theses: ab→c*. In this model, *difference* is the central feature and is the creative force by which objects come into being. Finally admitting his debt to Nietzsche in the mid-1970s, Lefebvre tried to bring this dialectical logic together with Nietzsche's circular model of 'overcoming' (*überwinden*) and the 'eternal return' in which objects continually metamorphosed but returned on age-old historical lines (which Nietzsche extracted based on his reading of classical Greek history): the original elements (*a* and *b*, above) never dissolved into a synthesis (*c*) but broke out again.

Thus in *La Fin de l'histoire* (1970d) he does not attempt a synthesis but describes them as complementary parts of his own project of the critique of modernity: a history of the development of consciousness, based on Hegel; a critical analysis of the state and the economic organisation of society drawn from Marx, and the ongoing critique of values and creative agency proposed by Nietzsche. This was announced over many years. For example, writing in 1959 on 'Irony, Maieutic and History', he quips:

> For Hegel time is a restless force, but in the final analysis it never destroys anything substantial. In truth – that is to say, in absolute truth, in being or spirit – everything is preserved and everything accumulates. If it is true as Hegel maintains, that things and men step worst foot forward, this is but a small facet of men and things. No room for irony, and no real negativity. The negative merely attacks appearances and superficial modalities in the appearance (or 'emergence') of details.
>
> (1995 [1962i]: 19)

Ironically, shall we say, a dialectic in which nothing truly changes is hardly Marx's dialectic, sharing much more with a process of *überwinden*. Lefebvre develops Nietzsche's notion of a Dionysian element of spontaneous social ferment – almost a form of vitalism,[6] but one anchored in the material – and the sublimated expression of the will to power that manifests itself in an ongoing re-valorisation and revaluation of life. This becomes Lefebvre's *fête révolution-naire* partly borrowed from, and partly developed with, the Situationists (1965f). He attempted to apply this framework to French society in his *Vie quotidienne dans le monde moderne*, translated as *Everyday Life in the Modern World* (1968i [1971]). A risky, experimental, revolutionary festival in which the values were rediscovered and recreated would be the only solution to alienation:

> Lefebvre compares the Paris Commune to, 'Tragedy and Drama [which] are bloody festivals, at the hearts of which the defeat, the sacri-fice and the death of the *héros surhumain* who defied destiny are accomplished.' The brief existence of the Commune represented both absolute tragedy and Promethean drama in festival form, played without the slightest frivolity, accompanied by a unique fundamental will to change the world, even at the price of voluntary self-sacrifice. The Commune's attempt to overcome alienation, to inaugurate history as lived and dominated by men [*sic*], forced open a new horizon of possibilities for the future, 'announced and prepared' the victory of the Soviet revolution as well as those more successful festivals Lefebvre believed still possible . . . and necessary.
>
> (Lefebvre 1965f: 22, 24; translated in Burkhard 1986: 270)

Any such move towards the importance of experience and the recognition of any form of vitalism would appear to draw on Bergson's work. However, Lefebvre does not make clear his position on such a rapprochement with the father figure of twentieth-century French philosophy, against whom Lefebvre had earlier rebelled. Another more explicit example of the development of the work of Bergson, Marx and Nietzsche into a unified whole can be found in the work of Deleuze and Guattari, later in the 1970s. The major distinction between their work and Lefebvre's, of course, is their refusal of a possible 'end of philos-ophy' and their location of the primary anchoring structures of society in the social imaginary, in other words in ideology. Thus revolution may only change the face of politics, a totalitarian monarch like the tsar giving way to a totalitarian dictator such as Lenin. Lefebvre argued much earlier that revolution must pene-trate to the roots of mystification to change consciousness and everyday life. 'The return of meaning comes from the fact that adventure,' or revolution for that matter 'signifies "that one invents it"' (interview with Lefebvre, February 1988; cited in Hess 1988: 58). His is a call to adventure and action; Deleuze and Guattari make a call to rethinking problems in new terms.

---

6   This aspect of Lefebvre's work has been developed by Michel Maffesoli (*L'Ombre de Dionysos* [1979] 1995), who in other respects broke violently with him.

Spatialising the dialectic

> The dialectic is back on the agenda. But it is no longer Marx's dialectic,
> just as Marx's was no longer Hegel's.
>
> (Lefebvre 1976e: 14)

Lefebvre makes an additional contribution: he shifts the ground of dialectical materialism from time to space. After his best-known work on space, he draws back from a periodicising historical narrative of the dialectical development of modes of space and their relationship with capital and visuality, substituting an analysis of the spatial extension of capital in the present.

> The dialectic today no longer clings to historicity and historical time, or to a temporal mechanism such as 'thesis–antithesis–synthesis'. . . . This, then, is what is new and paradoxical: the dialectic is no longer attached to temporality. Therefore, refutations of . . . Hegelian historicity cannot function as critiques of the dialectic. To recognize space, to recognize what 'takes place' there and what is used what it is used for, is to resume the dialectic.
>
> (1976e: 17)

Soja takes up this suggestion, proposing what he calls 'third space' as a translation of, on the one hand, Lefebvre's three-part dialectics of the social production of space (see Chapter 10). Gregory also notes this shift:

> Time, said Feuerbach, is the privileged category of the dialectic, because it excludes and subordinates where space tolerates and coordinates. Our tendency is to think of space as an abstract, with physical contexts, as the container for our lives rather than the structures we helped create. The difficulty is also one of vocabulary, while words like 'Historical' and 'Political' convey a dynamic of intentionality, vitality and human motivation, 'Spatial', on the other hand, connotes stasis, neutrality and passivity. But the analysis of social space, far from being reactionary or technocratic, is rather a symptom of strategic thought . . . that poses space as the terrain of political practice. An awareness of social space . . . always entails an encounter with history of – or better, a choice of histories.
>
> (Ross 1988; no page cited in Gregory 1994: 348)

However, the claim being argued here is that a spatialised dialectic foregrounds a new form of 'affirmation–negation–negation of the negation' found in the old forms of dialectical materialism. We are aware, of course, that neither Hegel nor Marx used the terms 'thesis, antithesis, synthesis' (it is, rather, from

Fichte) and that 'affirmation–negation–negation of the negation' is Marx's and Engels' formula. The third term of 'negation of the negation' is that alternative route which displaces or reconfigures – divides – the dualism of affirmation–negation. This is the philosophical implication of Lefebvre's proposition that dialectics could be extended into 'trialectics', in which a position is opened up for otherness within dialectical materialism. As we shall see, Lefebvre himself does not appear to fully grasp or exploit the importance of this shift: his description of a 'dialectique de triplicité' as merely a 'three-way dialectic' consisting of a thesis with not one, but two, anti-theses is confusing.

To use the example of Lefebvre's description of social space, it suggests that practice, thought and imagined space are elements synthesised together in a social spatialisation. But his third term is in fact treated more as a 'negation of the negation' than an equal player with the first two, and he uses language that harks back to his older work on the 'total person'. Perceived, conceived and lived out are used to describe practice, thought and imagined, respectively. The three make much more sense if they are rethought as a dialectical contradiction of: everyday perception/practice versus spatial theory/concepts relativised by a transcendent, entirely other, moment: creative, fully lived space. If we still insist on counting terms or positions, any notion of a totalising synthesis lies in a *fourth*, transcendent term, what Lefebvre calls *'l'espace'*, itself – best understood as 'the spatialization' (see Figure 8.2 and Chapter 10).

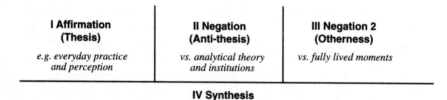

Figure 8.1 Common interpretation of Lefebvre's triple dialectic

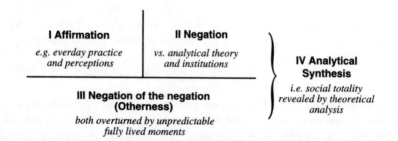

Figure 8.2 The implication of Lefebvre's dialectic of triplicity

Structure and experience

Lefebvre remained faithful to Marx's vision of history and to existential notions of subjectivity, always attempting to reconcile humanism with dialectical materialism (Kurzweil 1980: 57). He resisted the temptation to produce an anti-humanistic study of social structures. This humanism was the root of his objections to Structuralism. To him, Structuralism proposed an analysis of classification without assigning any importance to the content, or to the objects being classified. Citing Bataille (1987 [1957]), he dismissed Lévi-Strauss, who 'contrives to deal with the family and with social relationships without once mentioning sex or eroticism' (1991d: 296n [1974a). While studies of politico-economic structures produced apparently elegant portraits of society, the 'nitty-gritty' complexities of everyday social interaction were left out. Structuralist diagnoses of societal conditions and their prescriptions foundered on their ignorance or simplified concepts of actors' intentions and aspirations. It made Lefebvre one of the earliest and one of the most vehement critics of Structuralism as later formulated by Althusser and Lévi-Strauss. French Structuralism traced the links between social categories to sketch out social and economic systems or structures. Drawing on a linguistic model in which any given sign, such as a word or a symbol, was linked to its corresponding referent, systems such as those of kinship were analysed as metaphors and analogies of social structures of power. For example, gods and totems were analysed as signs of particular families or clans; mythical dramas and the battles of those gods were interpreted as allegories of struggles between social groups. The relationships of intermarriage, of obligation and duty between families and clans, compared favourably with the relationships between characters in myths and totems.

Generalising from particular cases and cultures, archetypal structures were sought. Finding their manifestation and reflections in rituals provided the guiding objective to the interpretation of cultures and of social action. Structuralism appeared to be a science of structures, in which the structure of cultural myths paralleled the lines of social power, patrimony and economic necessity. Moving from linguistics to anthropology to become 'structural Marxism', Structuralism dominated theoretical debates from the early 1970s until the 1980s. Yet

> When structuralists announced that kinship systems, languages, and epistemologies were structures without subjects, they did not look for the alienation of the subject, his loss of control through direct or indirect class conflict, but simply proclaimed the given-ness of their finding. . . . To move from these facts to the theoretical demonstration of the *necessity* of the subject's absence, as structuralists did, was an ideological mystification *par excellence*, even if this result was not intended by them.
>
> (Poster 1975: 254)

For Lefebvre, placing abstract social structures in such a privileged position and then deriving explanations of social phenomena from them was problematic. They quickly became fixed, reified and unquestioned. Those structures were placed beyond the reach of members of societies who played with, inverted and transformed those structures through everyday life.

> Structuralism was nothing more than the infusion of technocratic thought into the intellectual field. The Structuralist crisis of 'man' and 'humanism' was above all a practical and historical crisis brought on by a capitalist society where unchecked bureaucratic growth meant that institutions – medicine, teaching, research – no longer put humans first. In a society where objects were more important than people, where cars determine the way people live, why wouldn't the status of 'man' be undermined? But instead of analyzing . . . that society, Structuralism served as an underlying ideology *justifying* the devaluation of humans under capitalist modernization. Rather than theorizing the liquidation of the historical, Structuralism enacted and legitimated that liquidation. After all, Structuralism's concern was the ordering of objects, not the criticism of their function.
>
> (Ross 1996: 177)

The denial of historical change, and of people as the agents of those changes, was the same criticism that Lefebvre levelled so effectively at Sartre's *Being and Nothingness* in the 1940s (see Chapter 7). Forgetting about the role of the human subject made Structuralism's elaborate social and linguistic 'structures' and the systems that acted to socialise and structure people's lives seem lifeless. In effect, the denial of the human subject legitimised a new form of alienation. Thus 'the "anti-humanism" of Foucault, Lévi-Strauss and Althusser reflected the new situation, in which the working class no longer saw its historical mission and the bourgeois ego was no longer . . . autonomous and self-conscious,' but 'colonised' by advertising and organised around consumption, which had invaded both public and private life, transforming relationships and leisure activities equally (Poster 1975: 154). These thinkers were 'technocrats', an intellectual bureaucracy that ordered the world in cold classifications.

Against structural linguistics

Structuralism was an expression of its time, of the bureaucratised society of mass consumption, and of the extension of alienation ever deeper into the previously unregulated areas of everyday life. Rather than a structural linguistics of systems of meaning, the significance of language was its importance as a tool of administration and dominance – most importantly through mystification. To argue against Structuralism, Lefebvre shifted Marx's concept of commodity fetishism into linguistic terms. Thus, advertising invested commodities that referred not to use or price but to an alienated system of fantasy that was floated free of necessity and political content. Images of sexual virility, popularity and modernity or progress itself formed a parallel system of social status that distracted consumers, in effect pacifying them and making them easier to govern. Without integrating elements drawn from a common culture or from everyday necessity ('the practico-sensible' – 1966d: 345), 'The social world fragmented into a plethora of semiotic subsystems, like the world of high fashion . . . with no . . . unification. . . . The outcome was paradoxical: "loneliness in the midst of over-crowding, lack of communication in a proliferation of signs and information"' (1968i/1971h: 185; cited in Poster 1975: 252). 'Terrorism, today,' he wrote 'is the persuasion by the rhetoric and the menaces of propaganda' (1967b: 51).

By contrast, language was an *oeuvre* of the collective – a work of *poësis* through which people appropriated meaning and expressed themselves:

> The *oeuvre* is appropriation. It fashions from time and space, from the sensible, the material, a fragment of 'nature'. One would not know how to reduce it to a 're-appropriation' of a lost essence, such as Feuerbach imagines. The [speech] act that 'models' (actively) something cannot be understood by memory or souvenir, even promised an ontological dignity by philosophers.
>
> (1967b: 160)

Language stands against this authentic act as a system or 'institution'. In *Le Langage et la société*, Lefebvre argues that the two cannot be disengaged (1966d: 335) and then refines this notion by adopting Emile Benveniste's (1966) integrative theory of discourse: it is not possible to do what the Structuralists wanted; to separate out two 'levels of analysis' (the poësis of the act versus the structural system, agency versus structure) without tending to forget and mystify the fact that language is an equally human invention (1967b: 122): 'As for the institution, it is something human, a social abstraction detached from nature and by consequence, from the body, need and desire. The institution is *praxis* and not *poësis* in our vocabulary' (1967b: 160).

Central to the notion of *poësis* is the 'event' of human expressiveness, which emerges as the standard for determining whether or not communication is authentic or not. It is easy to confuse this concept of authenticity grounded in the body's movement with an essentialist notion of philosophical authenticity. Furthermore, this position can degenerate in the direction of arguing that spoken words are more authentic than written communication – if only because they are a more immediate, linguistic performance by an embodied person. The interest of Lefebvre's position is the centrality of the body, which, by acting 'appropriates' the resources of cultural codes and its material environment. Both can be studied, mapped, but that action is fundamentally unpredictable: the active body and the 'situation' it anchors and defines (see Chapter 4) is the wild card in the theorist's deck. But what of radio and recorded speech?

Lefebvre repeated his position again and again across numerous publications: at his best, he identifies the importance of the embodied, human actor (showing himself a precursor of the 1990s theorists of the body, both in feminism and in queer theory (cf. Haraway 1991; Butler 1993; Grosz 1994; see Chapter 8). At his worst – especially in uncareful translations (1971h) – his argument becomes blurred and oversimplified into a black–white contrast between authentic speech and language (structure). Lefebvre is often presented as arguing this oversimplified position, but we must always keep in mind that all of his arguments are dialectical. Lefebvre's antinomies are never frozen contrasts and are always linked moments in a process in which human creativity is central and is moving forward towards new syntheses, new positions. This problem happens at one point in Poster's otherwise excellent work. He ends up contrasting Derrida with Lefebvre.

Derrida's contribution was to show the impossibility of finding original, authentic meanings or referents without including something extra-philosophical, the act or gesture that combined language and intention into utterance. In effect, words referred to other words and were too easily detached from their referents. Nowhere was there an originary referent: even the most simple terms, which apparently referred to simple objects in 'the real world', were defined only by other words, which in turn were also defined by words, leading anyone rigorously searching for an end-point back and forth through the pages of dictionaries: they would discover that language was a self-referential system.

Lefebvre would agree! But he would deplore the alienated state of language, scoffing at those who concluded that signs ended up referring to nothing because he focused on the importance *in use* not as an abstract system (see his astounded comments on Guattari, 1967b: 130). 'The knowledge of institutions implies the radical critique of institutions' (1967b: 128). As he says of Foucault's vision of a totalising system of governance through classification in *The Order of Things* (specifically 1966: 395):

> The 'lived' reference to objects and to the world of objects to situations should fall such that only a system of signs without substance or determination other than their transparence exists. This transparency is not surprising: we have evacuated their contents. To present this as a victory of the intelligible – a mortal victory, the victory of Death – it is this attitude which can be surprising.

> (1967b: 131)

Yet he remains very close to Foucault in spirit, and he anticipates Deleuze's much later study of Leibniz, when he comments:

> the power to maintain the relations of dependence and exploitation, does not keep to a defined 'front' . . . like a frontier on the map. . . .
> Power is everywhere; it is omnipresent, assigned to Being. It is

124

everyday *in space*. It is in everyday discourse and commonplace notions, as well as in police batons and armored cars. . . . It is in the diffuse preponderance of the 'visual', as well as institutions. . . . Power has extended its domain right into the interior of each individual, to the roots of consciousness, to the 'utopias' hidden in the folds of subjectivity.

(1976: 86–7; cf. Foucault 1975: 10–12; Deleuze 1993)

Lefebvre takes the next step of asking whether or not it is possible to reclaim control over language, which was a human creation in the first place. Both speech and language were products of human action, essential to each other, and only realised by human actors. I repeat: it is not a question of speech versus language but, as he says, of *poësis* versus alienated *praxis*. Lefebvre was correct about the mystificatory potential of language and that words chosen to describe events or commodities could shape our understanding of them, making it difficult to notice or remember their actual use or value. Jean-François Lyotard, of the *Socialisme ou Barbarie* group, later followed this path, stressing the unpredictability of speech acts guided not so much by rational calculation as by longing and libido in what he called 'language games' (1985). On the one hand, cultural systems of meaning functioned as systems that structured everyday life and coloured people's view of the world, shaping their beliefs and opinions. On the other hand, these systems only functioned through the efforts of human agents, who created, actualised, imposed, believed or purchased the systems. Such structures were not closed systems but were full of holes and ruptures where they were inverted, where norms were manipulated and played with. Just in 'seeing what they could get away with', people developed and transformed social systems bit by bit, day by day. Those inversions, however, were something that Lefebvre sought to mobilise in a great 'festive moment' that would have a revolutionary impact.

There is a further problem with the emphasis on social and semiotic 'structures' when they are linked with norms to become what Lefebvre called '*L'idéologie structuraliste*' (1975d). The focus on systemic rules easily degenerates into an insistence on their rightness, their normativity – as Foucault, whom Lefebvre thought had ended up being a blind participant in furthering, showed only too well. This 'passage to the point of view of the norm, of the rule and of the system,' (Foucault 1966: 372) was a movement 'from a philosophy of liberty (which Sartre took up after Marx . . .) to a philosophy of constraints' (Lefebvre 1967b: 126). As has often been noted since, Foucault's 1960s work on the 'archaeology' of codes and classification left no room for political resistance – there were no 'margins' outside of the system.

Lefebvre mistrusted Foucault's privileging of knowledge, or the discursive, and the visible (notably in his Panopticon model of power, which drew on Lefebvre's and Debord's concept of the spectacle) over the *lived* (*le vécu*). It is the lived, Lefebvre's third dialectical term, which troubles the settled compromise of everyday life and dominating force that occurs in the administrative equation that Foucault refers to as governance. Lefebvre once commented that after Marx, and at the end of many a philosophical analysis, we discover that Hegel awaits – he has been there before us. Perhaps, after Foucault, we will find Lefebvre waiting for us at the margins, that borderline of transformation, to leap into the lived? He said, of Foucault among others, in 1974: 'The strategy of centring knowledge on discourse avoids the particularly scabrous topic of the relationship between knowledge and power . . . amounts to an overestimation of texts, written matter, and writing systems, along with the readable and the visible, to the point of assigning to these a monopoly on intelligibility,' and he wonders what connection exists between the bodies of academic analysis and 'a practical and fleshy body conceived of as a totality complete with spatial quali- ties (symmetries, asymmetries) and energetic properties (discharges, economies, waste) . . . the moment the body is envisioned as a practice–totality, a decentring and recentring of knowledge occurs' (1991d: 61–2).

Lefebvre's focus was on capturing the content of everyday life, in all its vitality. Years after his 1939 textbook, he proposed a method that would capture social experience in its multidimensionality as it moved towards an open future while continually reinvoking an established past. Social life moved forward both as a project and as the consequence of past, even forgotten, efforts. 'The progressive–regressive [or 'projective–retrojective' – see Chapter 9] method, he thought, was suitable to dialectical reason only because its object, social-historical experience, was formed through projects. Human projects carried within them the same backward and forward movement of temporality that Lefebvre ascribed to objective, social phenomena' (Poster 1975: 268). Ironically, an encounter with his old rival Sartre, in the form of an article from each translated in a Polish journal in 1957, gave rise to a rapprochement. They both agreed on the crisis of Existentialism and Marxism. Sartre republished this in his *Critique of Dialectical Reason* (1961). The problem of mediations led Sartre to advocate Lefebvre's 'projective–retrogres- sive' method of socio-historical analysis. 'Accepting Lefebvre's schema, Sartre added an existentialist touch by grounding the method in his concept of the project' (Poster 1975: 268). This method will be discussed in more detail in the next chapter.

9

EXISTENTIAL MARXISM: SARTRE

Henri Lefebvre's youthful essays anticipate Jean Paul Sartre's fully worked out philosophy of Existentialism, but they can only barely be called Existentialist, despite Lefebvre's claims. However, the flip-side of the coin is that the mature Sartre's notions of practice, of the situation and his 'projective–retrojective' method are all not just indebted to Lefebvre: they are *Lefebvrean*. If one turns this metaphorical coin over again, one discovers a similar indebtedness to Sartre on the part of Lefebvre, who reconciled with Sartre and gradually rejoined the Existentialist bandwagon in the 1950s (and was excluded from the Parti Communiste Français (PCF) partly for this tendency). The works of both appeared from the 1940s to the 1960s interwoven like twisted strands of wool as they built successively on the other's position. Both vied to align Existentialism and Marxism in a form of 'metaphilosophy' (1965e) that would itself supersede bookish philosophy, which remained simply discursive and conceptual. Metaphilosophy would take the form of a *praxis* within daily life.

The young Lefebvre's argument that life be lived as an *oeuvre*, an unalienated 'work', anticipates the Existentialist interest in the relation between consciousness and action (1924f). This vein of Parisian academic thought reappears in Foucault's later work on the ethical 'care of the self', in which character and biography emerge as a creative personal 'work', much like a work of art (Foucault 1986b). In the journal *Philosophies*, Lefebvre had argued that life be conceived of as an adventure in which the importance of not just self-discovery but also self-production was paramount. This self-production was intended to be 'authentic' – Lefebvre would spend a lifetime trying to sketch out the conditions in which such an authentic and personalised humanism would be possible in practice, moving in the course of this quest to become one of the strongest voices protesting against the alienation felt by people in twentieth-century industrial societies. This stress on action was an outlook that the *Philosophes* suppressed in order to unite their voices with others in the socialist struggle in France. This left Sartre to refine the *Philosophes'* outlook into a coherent existential philosophy. In the process, *oeuvres* became 'projects', and the focus was moved to the level of individual agents rather than the young Lefebvre's focus on the *impact* of ideology on individuals' outlooks (mystification) in *La Conscience mystifiée* (1936a).

With the publication of *Being and Nothingness* immediately after the war (Sartre 1958 [1943]), Lefebvre was outraged. He led the charge on behalf of the PCF, which was watching the cohesiveness of its position break up in the postwar reinstitutionalisation of the French state and corporate interests. He penned meticulous critiques, walking a tightrope in order not to simply denounce his own belief in the importance of overcoming alienation, but privately he seethed. Lefebvre was sidelined: Sartre had stolen his thunder and glory. He remarked bitterly in a recently discovered letter:

> You know why Sartre keeps me from sleeping? Because all his philosophy represents the development of my 'manifesto' which appeared 20 years ago in *Philosophies*. And I saw perfectly what it might develop into at the time. I turned out hundreds of pages. And I abandoned that with the success and the glory, and money and women for a hard and mediocre life, for militant thought dealing with real problems.
>
> (letter to Guterman, 31 July 1945; translated and cited in Trebitsch 1992: 81)

The 'manifesto' was 'Sept manifestes dadaïstes' (1924g) and its sequel, 'Positions d'attaque et défense du nouveau mysticisme' (1925a). Both were published in *Philosophies* as proto-Existentialist sketches that document a set of ideas in currency among the interwar generation of the 1920s and 1930s, who sought to break with the establishment philosophy, which had become associated with France's poor performance during the First World War. After the Second World War, with Existentialism the rage, the paradox was that Lefebvre's *L'Existentialisme* (1946) was one of the earliest critiques launched on behalf of the PCF. Sticking to a rigorous dialectical method, he criticised the social roots of Existentialism and its esoteric and individualistic character. These marked it as an attempt to palliate the consequences of the individualism bred by modern capitalist social organisation. Lefebvre set out to unveil the social roots of Existentialism in what he called the contradictions and neuroses of 'the bourgeois intellectual's world with its privatised consciousness' (1946: 21). The problem was that Lefebvre was also trying to reclaim Existentialism and radicalise it by providing dialectical materialism as a logic for all existential philosophies. His books on the topic of dialectical logic had remained unpublished throughout the war (*Logique formelle, logique dialectique* not being printed until 1947, and Volume 2, as *A la Lumière Dialectique*, in 1948). This attempt to, on the one hand, radicalise – to improve – Existentialism, and on the other hand, act for the PCF, which simply wanted Existentialism destroyed, only got Lefebvre into trouble with all sides.

This was not just a philosophical debate; it was part of the PCF's struggle for the hearts and minds of a new postwar generation. A story is told of the PCF bringing in underwear, which was in short supply after the war, stamped with its slogan – '*Renaissance Française*'. 'New underdrawers are vital to a civilized reconstruction of Europe,' quipped Janet Flanner, correspondent for the *New Yorker* (1946: np; cited in Campbell 1994: 8). Mark Poster (1975: 117) notes that 'no tactics were too low' to be used in this struggle' to dissuade the progressive elements of French society from turning away from Communism to Existentialism (even though Sartre was attempting to merge their positions). In one autographed copy, Lefebvre inscribed a quotation from the interior of *L'Existentialisme*:

> Under the pretext of describing the research of the self and going along the path of liberty, existentialism contents itself with recounting turpitudes, degouts, clichés and deceptions that meet in the course of their individual adventure, the unhappinesses, the prey of their own nothingness.[1]

Lefebvre's working-class chauvinism and his disdain for the middling position of the bourgeoisie is difficult to separate from PCF dogma. However, his misgivings about the intellectuals' 'disdain for the practical' and the Americanised 'privatised consciousness' of French urban classes, which aspired to a higher material standard of living even at the cost of destroying communities and personal ties, run throughout his work. Kristin Ross (1996: 108) notes that 'privatization, or losing oneself in the repetitions and routine of "keeping house," meant an increasing density in individual use of commodities and a notable impoverishment of interpersonal relations. For both Lefebvre and Castoriadis it constituted above all a flight from history'.

> [What] Castoriadis, Morin and Lefebvre all called 'privatization' – is a movement echoed on the level of everyday life by the withdrawal of the new middle classes to their newly comfortable domestic interiors, to the electric kitchen, to the enclosure of private automobiles, to the interior of a new vision of conjugality and an ideology of happiness built around the new unit of middle-class consumption, the couple, and to depoliticization as a response to the increase in bureaucratic control of daily life.
>
> (Ross 1996: 11)

Existentialism in its initial forms responded to this isolation without questioning its political, economic or cultural origins. Complaining that he was locked up with the lifestyle of 'keeping house' (desperately writing in order to

---

1 *Envoi* to J.T. Desanti, inscribed in *L'Existentialisme* (1946) signed by Lefebvre. Collection of Morrisette Library, University of Ottawa, Canada.

provide for his growing number of children and wife), Lefebvre jealously labelled Sartre's café-Existentialism a 'neurosis of interiority' (1946: 20). As argued in Chapter 4, Existentialism was an attempt to palliate the consequences of the individualism and 'false authenticity' required for and bred by modern capitalist states. But it led only to romantic protest: Lefebvre called it passive, emotional and magical – a childish fascination with the base and with appearances, a 'metaphysics of shit' (1946: 82). In contrast, he praised the virile quality of rationality, which possessed 'objective knowledge and effective power' (*ibid*: 81).[2]

Nonetheless, Lefebvre was deeply ambivalent, for he agreed with Sartre's critique of the excesses of scientistic reason and positivism but he feared Sartre's applause for the non-rational. Deeply marked by the war, and recalling his own, lonely articles against Fascism from 1933 to 1939 and his 1937 warning against the lure of politics transformed into the rhetoric of magic and nationalism in *Le Nationalisme contre les nations* (1937a/1988), Lefebvre feared the setting aside of critical judgement. Echoing his 1938 account of five years of Nazism in Germany, *Hitler au pouvoir* (*Hitler to Power* 1938c/1988), he thundered:

> Sartre wants to position himself within a bastard compromise between the philosophy of inhumanism and the new affirmation of the human. . . . To those who propose to liquidate on all levels the sequels of Hitlerism, it appears inadmissible to live on a bastard compromise.
>
> (1946: 224–5)[3]

Mark Poster, in one of the most systematic studies of existential Marxism in France, argues that both men shared an intellectual project that originated with Hegel: 'the restoration of subjectivity and *praxis* to their proper places' in critical life:

> Lefebvre was in a quandary because he was one of the few Marxists who could articulate a concept of reason that was not merely another positivism. . . . The crude point of divergence between the two doctrines was only touched on by Lefebvre: Marxism viewed man primarily but not exclusively as collectively related to nature, hence the emphasis on the economy; existentialism, in the first instance, probed man's relation to himself, his subjectivity. These positions were philo-

---

2   Lefebvre was a consistent traditionalist, chauvinistically adopting positive masculine metaphors and negative feminine ones. While he moderates this slightly through the 1980s, his stance towards feminism remained negative, in line with that of most French intellectuals, who reacted to the highly intellectual and psychoanalytic turn taken by French feminist theory, and the difficulty of critically deconstructing or de-gendering their language's linguistic reliance on a binary gendering of all objects and terms.

3   Compare the translation by Poster (1975: 118).

sophically complementary, but this fact would become clear only when each doctrine moved toward a focus on man's relations to others.

(1975: 119)

The dilemma was that Lefebvre's stress on alienation as the central 'ill' of his society led naturally to a demand that Marxism produce a theory of consciousness (1946: 233–52). However, the official dogma of the PCF allowed only for purely rational, economic models of action structured by external forces such as the need to produce the means to continue living. There was no desire, no place for pleasure or jealousy. How might any group of people come to revolutionary consciousness – to the decision to act to change the world? In contrast to this dilemma-ridden dead end, Sartre argued for the total and intrinsic freedom of the individual. Lefebvre noted the disappearance of any role for society or for the Other in the life of Sartre's individual. Proposing individual action as the panacea for all problems and the solution to anxieties stripped out attention to the importance of coordinated social movements with others, or the importance of contributing to long-term historical struggles. By asserting the independence of the individual will, Sartre appeared to be following Heidegger's turn to metaphysics in search of a resolution of alienation. Lefebvre, as noted in Chapters 2 and 3, preferred a turn to action – *praxis*. Lefebvre responded with phrases that are strangely reminiscent of the criticisms made of his own hybrid sources:

> The work of M. Sartre, direct disciple of Heidegger, presents a chaos, a formless magma of literature and philosophy. There, confusionism bears its fruits, and those most suspect. Add to this 'existential' confusionism the expression of a confused existence and an equally confused epoque of transition, [and] everything is open, all is permitted.
>
> (1946: 221)

Although they later resolved their differences, *L'Existentialisme* is one of the most striking failures to recognise a kindred spirit following a parallel course. Sartre's response was a theory of history that preserved his radical concept of total freedom. *Critique of Dialectical Reason* (1960) was Sartre's first existential Marxism. It arrived after Lefebvre and a number of other key intellectuals had been excluded or had dissociated themselves from the Communist Party while remaining critics of modern capitalism. The first part of *Critique* was based on a companion piece to Lefebvre's review of trends in Marxism written in 1957, the year that he was excluded from the PCF (see 1957d). Existentialism could rejuvenate Marxism because it offered an alternative to Stalinism. By exploring the limits of dialectical reason and arguing that it was the sole method that made history comprehensible, Sartre refined the position of Lefebvre and other radicals who had left the PCF.

Along with other French intellectuals such as Lefebvre and Morin, Sartre opened Marxism to the social sciences and to psychoanalysis. Only by paying attention to the detailed forms of alienation, their psychological structures and the social structures by which they were reproduced could the influence of economic structures (such as class, work, technology and capital) be mapped onto action and events. A multitude of different levels of experience functioned as mediators, warping the simple model of base and superstructure that orthodox Marxists continued (and some still continue) to uphold. To understand these, Sartre adapted Lefebvre's 'projective–retrojective' (sometimes translated as 'progressive' and 'regressive', see 1949c; 1953a; 1991d: 65) method of social analysis by tying it to an Existentialist concept: the project (see Hess 1988: 182–7):

> Human projects carried within them the same backward and forward movement of temporality that Lefebvre ascribed to objective, social phenomena.... If existentialism had omitted the relation of the project to the historical totality, Marxism needed the concept of the project to reveal the subjective level of experience.
>
> (Poster 975: 268–9)

Lefebvre's original method is a significant contribution to the toolkit of critical theory. The projective–retrojective method was, according to Lefebvre, implicit in Marx – notably *The German Ideology* – but it is Lefebvre who gives it the clarity and explicit status of a research method. It consists of three steps:

1 *Descriptive observation* informed by experience and general theory;
2 *analytico-retrojective* analysis comparing back historically to the known origins of other cases;
3 *historico-progressive* study of the genesis of structures, reconstructing the *projection* of trends to provide an explanatory framework for the present.

In their introduction to a translation of *Droit à la ville*, entitled *Writing on Cities*, Kofman and Lebas describe this method as it is deployed in *Production of Space* (1974b; 1991d). The retrojective moment (sometimes incorrectly referred to as the 'regressive moment')

> combines genealogical (returning to the emergence of a concept and exploring its concrete affiliations, detours and associations) and historico-genetic procedures (abstract and total, likened to the general history of society and philosophy). Progression refers to the opposite move, that of beginning with the present and evaluating what is possible and impossible in the future. He always emphasised this was a

method taken directly from Marx, reading Marx as the thinker of the possible, and not a realist.

(Kofman and Lebas 1996: 9; Lefebvre 1980b)

In *The Production of Space*, he describes this method as taking as its starting point the realities of the present: 'the forward leap of productive forces, and the new technical and scientific capacity to transform natural space so radically that it threatens nature itself.... The production of space, having attained the conceptual and linguistic level, acts retroactively upon the past, disclosing aspects and moments of it hitherto uncomprehended. The past appears in a different light, and hence the process whereby the past becomes the present also takes on another aspect' (1991: 65). Debord, however, best grasped the principle: the 'empty repetitions of modern life, of work and spectacle, could be 'detourned' – hijacked – into the creation of situations, into abstract forms that could be infused with unlimited content' – that is, with a utopian, projective inspiration to action (Marcus 1989: 238). *Détournement*, or hijacking, could be accomplished by shock, by irony, by direct confrontation and occupation, or simply by taking advantage of situations.

Sartre appears closer to everyday experience of bureaucratisation and consumption, and more rigorous philosophically, than Lefebvre, while avoiding the moralism of Marcuse and other Marxists, who saw the consumer and the citizen as dupes and which led to 'the nihilism of *One Dimensional Man*' (Lefebvre 1967b: 35; see Marcuse 1964). Those who wished to distinguish themselves from the seriality and sameness of consumer society found themselves locked in the privatised world of either consumption – 'in which individuals interiorised the command to become like other people simply in order to be like everyone' (Poster 1975: 298) – or the inheritors of class violence.

> The man of distinction, from which Lefebvre derived his discussion of the bourgeois, sought to distinguish himself from others and over against others, by his own merit. His self-definition was effected by splitting himself off from reciprocity [with others].
>
> (Poster 1975: 298)

In his turn, Lefebvre built on Sartre's work. Mark Poster and a number of French writers have argued that Lefebvre borrowed heavily from Sartre, yet a careful reading of his unpublished notes and manuscripts from the 1940s (see 1940; 1939b) and of his early works shows that he did not so much borrow as refine themes that had been present in his work over a long period. Some see much of Lefebvre's discussions of the contrast that he draws between dialectical and analytical reason, these were present in *Logique formelle, logique dialectique* (1947d). In his own critical analysis, Sartre drew on Lefebvre's philosophical argument, which contrasted formal Cartesian logic, or 'bourgeois reason', with dialectical methods with their transformations of thesis and antithesis into synthesis – an argument that had originated with Lefebvre in the late 1920s. Lefebvre's work in the early 1960s also turned to social and historical studies rather than philosophical theory, making Lefebvre appear to have 'exemplified a social and historical usage of Sartre's existentialism' (Poster 1975: 260), whereas the reality was much more dialectical.

Poster argues that 'Lefebvre drew from the *Critique* the dramatisation of the concept of totality into totalisations and totalising activities of the subject; from *Being and Nothingness*, the concepts of engagement, the situation, revolution as a "choice of oneself," the appropriation of "possibility"' through a "project," inauthenticity as a critical concept, and a concept of "creative freedom"' (Poster 1975: 258). This is both true and not true: the notions of engagement and the project are clearly Sartrean, but 'situation' is drawn from Surrealism and its postwar literary successor, *Lettrisme* (if indebted to anyone for this, it was to his students in Strasbourg, who included Guy Debord) and 'creative freedom' is redolent of Lefebvre's earliest works in *Philosophies* and his first serious book: *La Conscience mystifiée* (1936a).

Both Sartre and Lefebvre worked on the concept of everyday life (see Chapter 5), locating it as the 'pivot point' where the individual was integrated into social structure. It was both the 'colonised sector' of the alienated 'serial individual' and the promise of unalienated social relations. It was his work on technology and bureaucracy (1971d; 1961d; 1967b; 1959i: 130–7) – written at a time when writing about technology was in vogue among both European (Heidegger) and North American intellectuals (Innis, McLuhan) – that drew on Sartre and the tradition of phenomenology, which examined the relations between subjects and objects directly. However, Lefebvre's originating position and line of thought were different: his interest was in the realisation of philosophy by the working class (whereas Sartre appealed directly to youth) as creative action over long historical timespans – in *oeuvres*, such as personal character (the development of a narrative biography as a form of self-identity), the city (as an ongoing expression of its citizenry) and the non-bourgeois community. Where Lefebvre stopped was in any attempt to understand the importance of gender roles and the oppressive quality of the patriarchal family or its relationship to the community as the basis of public forms of gender and sex discrimination. Similarly, while he participated in protests against France's rearguard colonial war in Algeria, he had no critical position on racism or cultural genocide, gaps that would undermine the influence of his later theories of the global (1973e) on debates on globalisation (see Chapter 8).

Arguments 1956–62

Sartre was also significant as the first critic of Stalinism and of the dogmatic approach of the PCF (1959i: 80–1) at a time when many intellectuals were to quit the party in disgust following the Russian enforcement of Stalinist orthodoxy and sovereignty in Hungary in 1956. Others were thrown out of the PCF for minor violations of the strict code of allegiance and pre-approval of publications. In the late 1950s and early 1960s, there was a 'momentary confluence between the major thinkers of *Socialisme où Barbarie*,' such as Jean-François Lyotard, and theorists, many expelled from the PCF, such as Edgar Morin, Roland Barthes, Kostas Axelos, Henri Lefebvre, Pierre Naville and Pierre Fougeyrollas, who founded an independent journal of debates, *Arguments* (Poster 1975: 210).[4] Contributors included Alain Touraine, Pierre Naville, Colette Audry and Françoise Chatelet, Claude Lefort and Cornelius Castoriadis, and Michel Foucault.

For Lefebvre, the significance of *Arguments* was to develop links between the Left and the social sciences: 'Was Marx a philosopher or a sociologist?' was debated in *Sociology of Marx* (1966c/1968k). Lefebvre continued to argue that Marx was not merely a sociologist but also a philosopher *and* activist of dialectical materialism. While the PCF continued to ridicule him for years, Lefebvre pushed for a systematic re-examination of the conditions of possibility for rebuilding a credible Communist agenda. He directly asked about the realistic possibilities of revolution in 'The Revolution is not what it was' (1970a) and even that holy grail of Marxist thought – 'Is the working class revolutionary?' (1971b). He critiqued the abstraction of information theory (1958j), cybernetics (1971e), semiotics (1966d) and planning theory (1971f). Lefebvre also rediscovered his interests in Existentialism, popular democracy, self-management and Surrealism. These interests were fundamental to the *Arguments* agenda, bringing issues of the link between theory and practice, between the subject and object and between the cultural and economic to the forefront. Relations between action, thought of an action and knowledge in general raise the issue of the relation between the embodied subject and the structured world of politics: other writers such as Foucault (1986a), and Castoriadis (1984) were to take these issues much further.

This shift towards a cultural Marxism occurred much earlier in France than in other European countries, such as the UK. One can venture to speculate that in ridding itself of Lefebvre and championing Althusser's more economically oriented, so-called 'scientific' Marxism, the PCF succeeded not in controlling the French intelligentsia but in shaping the tenor of ideas that were exported from France in the early 1970s: Althusserian Marxism took hold in the UK in particular. Among Anglo-American academics, the debates of the 1950s and the positions explored in *Arguments* were repeated, twenty years later.

Métaphilosophie: desire and alienation

Philosophy had pretences to universalism but could not comprehend the tedium and banality of everyday life. It was unintelligible without a firmly developed, and social, theory of alienation under the conditions of modern capitalism. To realise a 'universal' philosophy, thought had to linked to lived experience and creative intervention in the everyday environment. Lefebvre sought a *Métaphilosophie* (1965e; 1967b; 1971a) that would link thought to action and respond to the complexity of everyday life by broadening Marx's concepts of alienation (see Chapter 4), production (see Chapter 8) and *praxis* (see Chapter 4). In this project, which was shared not only by the *Arguments* group but also by others such as the *Socialisme où Barbarie* group, not to mention other philosophers who were forging links with psychologists (for example Foucault) and exploring alternative thinkers such as Nietzsche and Heraclitus, rather than Hegel and Marx. Deleuze and Guattari (1976) and Lyotard (1974) in many ways surpassed Lefebvre by also questioning the presuppositions inherent in materialism and the dialectic. However, what remained central was dialectical materialism as a method, which Lefebvre now argued Marx had only had time to apply to the economic sphere, but which needed to be applied consistently, and to all fields of life. This argument is explicitly made in *Production of Space* (1974b/1991d).

The thrust of this revision of basic concepts was to renew the link between alienation itself and *praxis*, which would include not only activities oriented to the realisation of political theory but also the realisation of self, similar to Sartre's call for a concentration on projects. Lefebvre called this *poësis*, 'the experience and creation of human nature: the realisation of the self, including the creation of the city, the idea of "absolute love," psychoanalysis, the decision to change one's life – in short, the creation of new "situations"' (Poster 1975: 242). Yet *poësis* itself could not be sustained beyond specific 'moments': continual dis-alienation was an impossible, utopian condition (see Chapter 4). It existed in a dialectic with 'mimesis', the routinisation of the minutiae of a person's everyday life and 'residues' (contrast Pareto's notion of 'residua') of the historical process of structuring and stabilising interaction into institution-alised fields of everyday life – 'each activity that differentiates itself tends to constitute itself into a system, a "world"' (1965e: 17–18), becoming what Bourdieu was later to call a 'field'. These domains of social activity advanced beyond sociologists' crude division of 'spheres' of life – economic, religion (spirit), the arts (culture) (see Weber 1979). These three concepts were inter-linked in a three-part dialectic (see Chapters 5 and 7) under the rubric of everyday life. *Métaphilosophie* could thus be regarded as an integral part of his four-volume series on the *Critique of Everyday Life*, written between 1946 and 1981.

Poësis represents a broadened concept of Marxian production that aims at the realisation of desire and the will. The aim of work is thus understood not to be 'free time', as presented by the leisure industries, but non-work, spontaneity and even idleness (1972b: 168). The absence of work is understood as a need for unlimited indulgence (1965e: 109). Creating a 'slacker' philosophy before its time, Lefebvre sought a non-moralising conception of production that creates the external and internal nature of the 'total person'. Lefebvre's philos-ophy of needs and desires is built around the question of how people 'produce themselves'. A critique of needs is essential to seeing the interlocking construction of capitalism. Here he takes a position very closely related to the work of the Frankfurt School, most notably Marcuse (1964), arguing, for example, that capitalism continually constructs new forms of relative lack and desire, which provide a 'motor' for consumption. However, echoing earlier work by Bataille (1970; 1992), 'needs' are an inadequate concept, even though 'in order to . . . create, man [*sic*] needs the feeling of deficiency' (1965e: 79; see Sartre 1958). Need is for a specific purpose and in the present. In *The Anti-Oedipus*, Deleuze and Guattari (1976) decisively criticise this concept of desire as deficiency or lack. Any self-production must aim not at satisfying needs but at the realisation of desire. Lefebvre acknowledged that completely unalienated 'true-to-themselves' 'total persons' must be as one with their desires. The totality of his books and articles in the final instance concern 'only love', he once said. Like Lefebvre, Deleuze and Guattari question the alienating quality of the conventional separation of production and consumption:

> production immediately means consumption and realisation; realisation and consumption directly dictate production, though within itself. Therefore everything is production: productions of productions of actions and excitement, productions of realisation, of distributions and allocations, productions of consumption.
>
> (1976: 9, author's translation)

Taken together, these processes make up a social 'desiring-production' or the 'desiring-machine' churning out empirical products on the one hand, and fantasies, dreams and desire on the other hand. Understood together, Deleuze and Guattari create a concept of social production that transcends the Marxian suppositions about the relative autonomy of social spheres and the appropriateness of separating the economic from, for example, the spiritual.

While Deleuze's and Guattari's approach is often understood in relation to psychoanalysis, alongside Jean-François Lyotard (1974; see alsoHocquenghem 1974: 65), they propose a unified 'libidinal economy' of this desiring-production. Kleinspehn outlines the consequences that this has for the development of Lefebvre's notions of *poësis* and *oeuvre*, for it proposes an emancipatory theory of self-production within everyday life (1975: 108–14). Their critique avoids any reliance on economic notions of production. Not only is Lefebvre's notion of production still too narrow, but Kleinspehn argues that he understands needs and desires as *a priori*, pre-existing, rather than arising organically from the everyday life of people. With the Situationists, he despaired of the alienation of desires themselves, as a result of the slavish consumption promoted by what Debord had called 'the society of the spectacle'.

Only when the wish is understood in Deleuze and Guattari's sense and freed from its supposed sole bond with deficiency, the theory of the unfurling of satisfied desires and needs makes sense. If this is set aside, Lefebvre's claim, where the everyday must have been created as an *oeuvre* and the presently unknown and also unthinkable needs developed there, would be meaningless. The everyday, which Lefebvre wishes to understand as an *oeuvre* again becomes the product of factors external to it. If Lefebvre understands needs and wishes solely as precoined, already existing, requirements, he falls back again on an economic determination which he actually criticizes.

(Kleinspehn 1975: 111–12)

The liberation of desires in a festive uprising is a theme that thus unites Lefebvre with Deleuze and Guattari, with Lyotard and the writers of *Socialisme où Barbarie*.[5] However, each writer has a different 'take' on the status and effect of desiring. For Lefebvre, desire itself appears simply hedonistic or a regressive manifestation of a mystified consciousness. He sides with the Situationists that the social imaginary is colonised by a sophisticated, image-based and virtual regime of consumer capitalism, and that the route to liberation lies through the integrated, lived bodily experience of the 'total person'. By contrast, Deleuze and Guattari privilege the tendency of personal desire to clash with the rational ethos, deferred gratification, and toleration of divisions of 'work' from pleasure and self-fulfilment that are required for modern capitalism to function. The demand that needs and wishes be granted here and now was one of the most important demands of the workers and students of the May 1968 protests in France. This aspect of social protest challenges any purely reformist changes (1966c: 71; 1968k; Kleinspehn 1975: 113; Lyotard 1974: 160ff).

These theories were formulated within the context of a triumphant consumer capitalism that appeared to have obliterated connections to community, tradition and ethnicity. Subsequent events have placed capitalist modernity – even in its moment of maximum globalisation – in a dramatic check by the return of ethnic nationalism, regional linguistic separatism and religious fundamentalism. Only Lefebvre's work, hinged on his pioneering critique of the mobilisation of sentiments of solidarity and authenticity by state nationalism, takes into account the ability of reactionary social movements to exploit the same structure of desiring-production and to offer a pseudo-liberation based on the manipulation of a mystified consciousness of collective identity (see Chapter 4; 1937a; 1938c). On the one hand, there is much to be pessimistic about. Even desire is colonised and we are directed, pell-mell, by the 'bureaucratic

---

5 This section draws on Thomas Kleinspehn's 'Excursis on the relation of political and libidinal economy' (1975), in which he briefly compares Lefebvre with the French theorists of libidinal economy during the post-1968 period.

society of controlled consumption' in which the pressure to consume is to all intents and purposes a form of terror whose violence

> is always latent, pressure is exerted from all sides on its members, who can only avoid it and shift its weight by a super-human effort; each member is a terrorist because he [*sic*] wants to be in power (if only briefly); thus there is no need for a dictator; each member betrays and chastises himself; terror cannot be located, for it comes from everywhere and from every specific thing; the 'system' (in so far as it can be called a 'system') has a hold on every member separately and submits every member of the whole, that is, to a strategy, a hidden end, objects unknown . . . that no one questions.
>
> (1984c: 147)

However, this system also stimulates 'authentic' desires that are related directly to the desiring body and the 'non-instrumentalized spaces of urban life' (Gardiner 1995: 101) and the domain of the everyday. Desire 'refuses to be signified' (Lefebvre 1984c: 172). As soon as it is, it is colonized, yet there are countless momentary breaks in the monotony of the everyday that might one day come together in a revolutionary festival.

Nationalisme contre les Nations was published in 1937, the year of the destruction of Guernica by the Nazis and Franco's Fascist supporters in Spain. It shared little of the optimism of the Left's united 'Front populaire' and broke with the PCF's nationalistic celebration of the heritage of the French Revolution. Lefebvre's analysis of the *sentiment national* criticised the fetishism of the idea of 'nation' and the appropriation of a people's past by the state. In effect, this 1937 book could be read as the historical ground for late twentieth-century critiques such as Homi Bhabha's *Nation and Narration* (1989; Lefebvre 1988g [1937a]: 110). Turning the Marxist critique of the state on the practices of Stalinism and the Communist parties of the 1930s, Lefebvre was one of the first to understand 'the nation' as a theoretical concept and to question its appropriateness to a Marxist vision of the future. He pitted his broader understanding of the importance of the concept of the nation as distinct from 'the people' against historians' attempts to locate the exact beginning point in time of nations (1989a: 581–6; Trebitsch 1988: 10–12).

Before, during and after the drama of May 1968, Lefebvre pushed these ideas towards an encounter with the terms and conditions of an existing society, first with fieldwork on the declining peasantry of his beloved Occitaine, and later with the centrality of the urban experience. Kristin Ross commented on the rising colonisation of everyday life, which pushed out self-realisation, and excluded spontaneity, art and humanity in the name of 'good government' and with the compensation of new domestic appliances:

With the waning of its empire, France turned to a form of interior colonialism; rational administrative techniques developed in the colonies were brought home and put to use side by side with new technological innovations such as advertising in reordering metropolitan, domestic society, the 'everyday life' of its citizens. Marxist theory had made considerable progress in refining theories of imperialism in the domain of international relations. Lefebvre now pushed that theory to apply the insights garnered from an international analysis to new objects: to the domain of inter-regional relations within France, for example, or the space of domesticity and practices of consumption. But it was above all the unevenness of the built environment of the city, its surroundings, and its social geography that came to crystallize, for Lefebvre, the contradictions of postwar life.

(1996: 7–8)

10

THE PRODUCTION OF SPACE

Lefebvre may have thought that 'everyday life' was his most important contribution to Marxist social theory. He may have insisted on the fundamental importance of dialectical materialism. However, his most influential contribution, across intellectual disciplines, has been his investigation of the social construction and conventions of space. Lefebvre understood the spatial as an issue cutting across disciplines, an ideal example to illustrate his demand for an end to the technocratic specialisation of academia and the organisation of government. He progressively extended his concept of 'everyday life' into first the rural life of the peasantry, then into suburbia and ultimately to discuss the geography of social relations in general terms. Lefebvre makes space both more material and more amenable to public debate and direct action by comparing cultural landscapes (such as Tuscany) as well as discussing the inequality and despair of class landscapes (like many upper-class enclaves and gendered consumption areas: 'gay' areas from the large, San Francisco's Castro district, to the small, Ottawa's Centretown 'Pink Triangle'), in relation to the ghettos of the poor and the plots of tenant farmers. Lefebvre's works on the city and on space – published under titles such as *Urban Revolution* (1970a) and *Right to the City* (1967d; 1968b; 1996) form a manifesto for independent social movements and community action. Although he may never have expected it, his *magnum opus* has become *The Production of Space* (1974a). As Kristin Ross argues, Lefebvre spearheaded the twentieth-century re-emergence

> of a new image of society *as* a city – and thus the beginning of a whole new thematics of inside and outside, of inclusion in, and exclusion from, a positively-valued modernity. Cities possess a centre and *banlieues*, and citizens, those on the interior, deciding who among the insiders should be expelled and whether or not to open their doors to those on the outside.
>
> (1996: 150)

At a second spatial level, an extended analysis of the state, *De L'État*, covered four volumes in which Lefebvre attempted to synthesise the political economy of Poulantzas with his own intuition of the waning relevance of states in the face of the emergence of truly global phenomena, such as the oil embargo of 1973 (1976a; 1976b; 1977; 1978b). The cartel of oil-producing states, most of which were in the Middle East, demonstrated the importance of distant events and the power of foreign actors over the oil supply of the energy-addicted economies of Europe and North America. Other global phenomena were increasingly evident: international tourism, trans-border data flows and global telecommunications and broadcasting. On the one hand, *De L'État* was criticised for taking up Poulantzas' ideas, and on the other hand, it was not read by those for whom it was most intended, the non-Marxist Left such as the self-management (*autogestion*) and anarchist movements in Spain and the United Kingdom, and the environmental movement in West Germany. Lefebvre 'reassembles existing concepts submitting them to a negative and radical critique' (Kofman and Lebas 1996: 8). He is, in this sense, an exemplary *reader* of theory as well as a radical producer of non-systematic theories but key insights and methodologies. In so far as this is true his work remains open-ended: a toolkit for progressive action now.

Urban and global spaces of capital

From the early 1960s, Lefebvre was in increasing demand as a commentator on the changing social realities of the new suburbs and satellite cities of the major European capitals (see Chapter 8). Research funding in France placed a premium on urban sociology, which drew heavily on the methods that Lefebvre had developed in the Institute of Sociology at Strasbourg. In the early 1970s, he directed the Institut de Sociologie Urbaine (Paris). His research on suburban development continued his early studies of the flight of rural peasants into the postwar 'new towns'. He put urban development and administration on the radical agenda. The city was an *oeuvre*, much like a work of art, and this was only barely covered over by the commodification of its spaces along property lines into 'lots'. The alienated life-spaces of detached suburban houses only barely masked the possibilities for community involvement and dis-alienation.

The city itself, the way that investment in roads, buildings, subways and other elements of urban infrastructure benefited some but not others, was brought into mainstream political debate. His great studies of rural–urban problems (1970b) and the 'urban revolution' (1970a), *The Right to the City* (1996 [1968b]), on *Marxist thought and the city* (1972b), and the book considered by many to be his masterpiece, *The Production of Space* (1991d [1974b]), all date from the early 1970s (see Chapter 8). In France, Germany and many other European countries, it was Lefebvre who put environmental concerns – only a small part of what he calls *l'espace* – on the agenda of the Left. Bridging the split between the 'red' Communists and the 'green movements', he attacked the patterns of excessive consumption that led to the squandering of resources, pollution and the one-sided development of whole regions of the world as eco-tourist preserves in which the environment itself was consumed.

While officially he retired, he remained at the heart of the vibrant intellectual scene in Paris throughout the 1980s – even if he was still considered an outsider. His outspoken critique of Structuralism through the 1960s had earned him a position in the vanguard of the post-structuralist reassessment of language, ideology and communications, and this was applied in turn to develop an urban political agenda based on the right of access and possession of the city as a common good and an ongoing, collective production.

He spent much of the late 1970s and early 1980s travelling, lecturing in different countries, and writing about the development of a global space of capitalism. His work on the state and on space (1991d; 1976a; 1977; 1978b) anticipates much of that on globalisation and research on the relationship between the local and global (cf. Castells 1989). In particular, he spent the better part of a year in the United States and influenced Californian Marxist geographers and literary theorists, who would popularise the idea of 'postmodernism', such as Fredric Jameson (1984) and Edward Soja (1989b; 1996), and other geographers who bitterly criticised it, such as David Harvey (1989). The common influence on these two poles was a consensus on the importance of the spatial character of a capitalism that increasingly relied on long-distance linkages and attenuated social relations ('distanciation'), bringing places closer together in one sense at the same time as compressing the time allotted for almost every task – a shift that Harvey tries to sum up in the phrase 'space–time compression'.

In 1986, Lefebvre was one of the founders of the journal *M – Mensuels, marxismes, mouvements* along with a group of ex-students and colleagues who formed what was sometimes called the 'Groupe de Navarrenx', which met at the family home in Navarrenx that Lefebvre had inherited from his maternal grandmother and aunt. The plurals of the title indicate the unorthodox, yet identifiably Marxist, stance of the magazine, to which Lefebvre contributed short editorial comments and outlines of his key arguments on worker self-management, citizenship and civil disobedience. However, his old ill-health had returned and he retreated from active involvement.

Lefebvre's ideas made the leap from French into English partly as a result of his own lectures, partly as a result of the many translations of *Dialectical Materialism* (1968j [1939b]). The most translated French author of the early 1960s, and the 'Father of the Dialectic' to one, even two, generations was bound to have some impact. But another route was via even more radical activists. He had relayed the 'space' of Dada and Surrealism on to the Situationists, the student radicals of the late 1960s, and the German Green movement of the 1970s. These groups in turn spread his ideas, hooking up with social movements in many countries. The ideas of Debord and the Situationists directly inspired the punk anarchists of the 1980s in the UK – including Class War. Lefebvre, cloaked as Situationism, not only was a populariser, but a theorist who put ideas in order and into forms that could be easily translated into popular action before he put them into words.

Illness prevented much activity at the end of the 1980s, and any further publications in 1989 and 1990. What was Lefebvre's reaction to the fall of the Berlin Wall? Wicke (1991) has argued that this is a perfect example of a spontaneous 'festive revolution', which evolved out of riots after rock concerts marking fifty years of the East German state were cancelled in Leipzig. We can only speculate that silence kept him friends in East Germany's intellectual elite and the political establishment to whom he had been a sometime adviser. However, this silence is thunderous and dark. *Revolution is not what it used to be*, as the title of one book, written with Catherine Régulier, put it (1978a).

The popular revolutionary who had little to say about popular revolutions? The Marxist who inspired postmodernism? In the end, Lefebvre remains an enigmatic hybrid. His position was ambiguous and remains poorly understood. He was a difficult intellectual ally. His sources and inspirations – including the Situationists, students, and the series of women who were his typist-muses – were unacknowledged, and, to the extent that they are glossed over in his autobiography, were disavowed. He crossed party discipline to take up a more radical position than institutional politics allowed, but at key moments in European history – the Hungarian Uprising in 1956, and the fall of the Berlin Wall in 1989 – he was silent. While he endeavoured to bring philosophy to an end by turning it towards practice, he was enmeshed in philosophical publications at crucial moments. Only his students, in the course of May 1968, managed the synthesis of theory and practice that he sought.

At the scale of the globe, Lefebvre was one of the first to argue the necessity of a 'planetary' scale of analysis. Rather than comparing and contrasting, for example, religions, Lefebvre was interested in the interlinkages and mutual awareness of religious thought at a global scale. He devoted much time to travel – particularly in Latin America and the United States – to spread this argument. In *The Production of Space* (1974b), he proposed a grounding for this analysis that tied all scales of place, region, nation and globe into a broadened concept of social production. Paradoxically, it is both a significant failure and an intellectual triumph as it succeeds in interrelating most aspects of spatiality while not succeeding in clarifying key points about his three-part dialectics of space (see Chapter 10) or breaking with a tradition of gendered analyses that locate public patriarchy as the defining mode of social space while leaving the maternal and feminine tied to the interior, on the one hand, and nature, on the other (Blum and Nast 1996). In *The Production of Space*, the spatiality of society and political action is examined. Not only are places produced through naming, but they are interrelated with each other in a series of 'historical modes of production of space'. Furthermore, they are interrelated with political and economic processes in that the activities associated with each place form its identity and exclude other activities (see Chapter 8). Everyday routines, the conventions of debate and interaction, all take place at one or another spatial scale and in space, making their spatial characteristics a crucial issue for utopian thought and for any attempt to change society. Such banal arrangements ground the inequalities of local cultures, from the repeated routines of everyday life to the cultural monuments and icons of the state. What was required was not a piecemeal analysis (for example, separating geography from politics or sociology, as the academic disciplines had done), but a comprehensive study of this 'spatial dialectic' of identities, activity and images associated with any given place. This work made Lefebvre a crucial theorist of critical strands of postmodernism and studies of globalisation.

There are two phases to Lefebvre's research on the spatial. The first deals with what he called 'the urban'. The second deals with social space and what he called the 'planetary' or global. Defining the essence of 'urbanity' as the simultaneity of many discrete social interactions brought together in a 'centrality', Lefebvre analysed the impact of changing social relations and economic factors under capitalism upon the quality of access and participation in the urban milieu. His important definition of the city was never properly absorbed, especially by British theorists. 'What is the urban?' he asked. The urban is not a certain population, a geographical size or a collection of buildings. Nor is it a node, a trans-shipment point or a centre of production. It is all of these together, and thus any definition must search for the essential quality of all these aspects. The urban *is* social centrality, where the many elements and aspects of capitalism intersect in space, despite often merely being part of the place for a short time, as is the case with goods or people in transit. 'City-ness' is the simultaneous gathering and dispersing of goods, information and people. It goes without saying that some cities achieve this more fully than others – and hence our own perceptions of their greater or lesser importance as cities *per se*.

The earlier works focused almost exclusively on this aspect of 'urbanity' and are critiqued for their vagueness and anti-Structuralism bias by Manuel Castells (1977). His book, *The Urban Question*, was almost exclusively an Althusserian Structuralist *response* to Lefebvre's pre-1972 work (e.g. Martins 1982: 166; Gottdiener 1985), but it was through this response that English-language readers first became aware of Lefebvre's spatial turn.[1] After the first set of works explicitly concerned with urban struggles and the experience of May 1968, *Production of Space* forms the keystone of the all-important 'second moment' of Lefebvre's analysis of the urban. This may be seen as beginning with his 1972 contribution to the colloquium 'The Institutions of the Post-Industrial Society', sponsored by the Museum of Modern Art in New York. The location is important: Lefebvre noted that he was always inspired by New York from his first visit at the end of the 1930s (1980a: 234; 1972d).

---

1 Castells' objections, the difficulties that Castells acknowledges with his alternative formulation, and the problem of its inapplicability to Lefebvre's later work is assessed in the author's 1986 thesis (Carleton University, Ottawa).

As reconceptualised in *Production of Space* and restated later in *De l'État* (vol. 4, 1978b) Lefebvre almost single-handedly moved the analysis of 'space' from the old synchronic order of discourses 'on' space (typically, that of 'social space' as found in sociological texts on 'territoriality' (Hall 1966) and social ecology to the analysis of the process by which meta-level discourses 'of' space are socially produced. Rather than discussing a particular theory of social space, he examined the struggles over the meaning of space and considered how relations across territories were given cultural meaning. In the process, Lefebvre attempted to establish the presence of a 'lived' spatialisation within the hegemonic 'logico-epistemological' theories of space promulgated by philosophy, geography and urban planning and the everyday attitude that ignored the spatial altogether. Thus a large portion of *Production of Space* is devoted to developing a radical phenomenology of space as a humanistic basis from which to launch a critique of the denial of individual and community's 'rights to space' under the abstract spatialisation embodied in capitalism and technocratic knowledge structures of the state. This phenomenological base, and the sociological critique that developed from it, has made this later work especially puzzling for mainstream urban studies scholars raised in the tradition of political economy or ecology.

The work on the city and on other scales of space is the reason Lefebvre's work has remained important in the English-speaking world – not his once prominent role as the Father of the Dialectic, or the lost history of his contributions to passing the idea of a personal revolution, of everyday life from the Dadaist of the 1920s to the student countercultures of the 1960s and the 1980s punks and anarchists, including the British group Class War (1988). 'Rediscovered' by academics such as Edward Soja and Mark Gottdiener, and cultural theorists such as Fredric Jameson, Lefebvre spent part of 1983 in California accompanied by the architect Serge Renaudie, who acted as translator and assistant. During this trip, an enduring connection to contemporary social critics of all stripes was made – including postmodern theorists – and the final relay was closed in the extensive circuitry of intellectual transfers that Lefebvre effected.

Why is this work important? Lefebvre goes beyond previous philosophical debates on the nature of space, and beyond human geography, planning and architecture, which considered people and things merely 'in' space, to present a coherent theory of the development of different systems of spatiality in different historical periods. These 'spatialisations' are not just physical arrangements of things but also spatial patterns of social action and routine as well as historical conceptions of space and the world (such as a fear of falling off the edge of a flat world). They add up to an socio-spatial imaginary and outlook, which manifests itself in our every intuition.

This system of space operates at all scales. At the most personal, we think of ourselves in spatialised terms, imagining ourselves as an ego contained within an objectified body. People extend themselves – mentally and physically – out into space much as a spider extends its limbs in the form of a web. We become as much a part of these extensions as they are of us. Arrangements of objects, work teams, landscapes and architecture are the concrete instances of this spatialisation. Equally, ideas about regions, media images of cities and perceptions of 'good neighbourhoods' are other aspects of this space, which is necessarily produced by each society as it makes its mark on the Earth.

What is the use of such an 'unpacking' of the production of the spatial? Lefebvre uses the changing type of historical spatialisation to explain why capitalistic accumulation did not occur earlier, even in those ancient economies that were commodity- and money-based, that were committed to reason and science, and that were based in cities. One well-known explanation is that slavery stunted the development of wage labour. Not convincing! No: it was a secular space, itself commodified as lots and private property, quantified by surveyors and stripped of the old local gods and spirits of place, that was necessary. Space is a medium – and the changing way in which *we* understand, practice and live in terms of our space provides clues to how *our* capitalist world of nation-states is giving way to an unanticipated geopolitics – a new sense of our relation to our bodies, world and planets as a changing space of distance and difference.

Lefebvre's interest eventually expanded to the scale of what he called 'the planetary' (in the sense of globalisation) but is much more down to earth. He dated his interest in urban life from 1956. His work is directly tied to the twentieth-century experience of urbanity with its attendant anonymity, crowds, choices and alienation. Louis Aragon's Surrealist *Les Paysans de Paris* (1953) pushed to the extreme the naturalist literary genre originated by Balzac, Sue and Flaubert, which was fascinated by the nineteenth-century growth, the artificial patterns and vitality of the city (see Shields 1995). Early in the twentieth century, taking up the public spaces of the new parks, exhibition grounds and shopping arcades, Aragon paints a surreal picture of a city practically hyperventilating on encounters, gatherings and the pleasures of the eye and crowds. Lefebvre was also affected by the movement to the city, and subsequent changes in the countryside, which took place after the Second World War. From his early youth, when he was sent to Paris to study, his life moved in what he called a 'dialectic' of the city and the country. His academic training was anchored in rural sociology, but he was attracted by the possibilities of a more urban focus. During his research on the rural, he examined the late 1950s creation of new towns, in particular Mourenx and Lacq in the southwest. Lefebvre witnessed a massive extension of the urban into the rural and a strong flow out of small towns and the countryside into new suburbs, or *banlieues*. The result was a dissolution of the density and clarity of the old core cities.

The urban

Lefebvre adopted the argument of Marx and Engels that it was necessary to break down the dialectic of the city and the countryside. They said 'The greatest material and intellectual division of labour is the separation of the city

147

and the countryside' (Marx and Engels 1965: 81ff). It is often forgotten that their early arguments ran in the reverse direction to many contemporary Marxist models: in *German Ideology*, they argued that industrial development of factory work was necessary to keep the huge new urban population from rebelling against their overwhelming poverty. This was the key contribution of Marxist thought on the city, argued Lefebvre in *Pensée Marxiste et la ville* (1972b: 48). Nonetheless, for historical reasons, Marx does not insist sufficiently on this identity between industrialisation and urbanisation (1973c; 1973d). In our time, the recognition that the 'urban' is the meaning and truth of industrialisation is politically essential. The crisis of the urban cannot be resolved by 'urbanistic' means. The problem is socio-ideological, not rational-technical (1972b).

The city was the seat of intellectual development and administration – by necessity given the growing, restless population, given the wealth generated by urban trade, and given the plagues and contagions, which demanded the development, administration and enforcement of forms of quarantine and regulation. All these gave city-based governments an advantage over those based in the rural hinterlands. From the cities, financial, ideological and governmental control spread out to regiment the countryside. Marx and Engels had argued against the terms in which social change was understood in the nineteenth century. Sociology was born in the attempts to understand this development. Theorists such as Ferdinand Tönnies and literary figures from Thomas Hardy to Eugene Sue, and later, Gustave Flaubert, chronicled the expansion of nineteenth-century metropolises as poor rural families were forced off the land into unemployment or wage labour and urban slums. The rural was romanticised as a place of tradition and well-being. The countryside became a metaphor of peace contrasted with the Dickensian factories and pollution of the nineteenth-century city (Williams 1973). However, a return to the countryside was no solution to the inequalities of capitalism then. Nor was the 1960s suburbanites' quest for quasi-rural lots and houses a solution for alienation in the twentieth century. And continued development of more and more far-flung suburbs geared to ethnically and class-specific types of family only exacerbated the segregation of minority groups and 'ethnic others' into slums and ghettos.[2]

With the urbanisation of society and the explosion of the urban, the city as a place of encounter becomes the city as centralisation of wealth, decisions and

---

2 For example, two heterosexual parents, two–three children and a level of wealth sufficient to maintain two cars is assumed in the design of North American suburban houses, the layout of tract development and the poor provision of public transport. This model of housing and family interlocks with career patterns, which support this middle-class lifestyle, and is policed by inflexible planning regulations and the difficulty of obtaining mortgages for alternative forms of housing – whether energy-efficient, cooperative, or housing for smaller or larger families. Despite attempts to change this, such suburbs remain hostile environments for anyone who does not fit this model, as any young person can attest.

information but not people. In the fourth volume of *De l'État*, he argues that people are segregated and this situation is maintained by the state apparatus (1978b). Thus urban conflicts are immediately state–people conflicts. The birth of the urban settlement ushers in one of the most basic divisions of labour, permitting intellectual work to take place apart from the manual labour of subsistence. Marx and Engels compare it to the sexual division of labour. Lefebvre argues that the city brings into being the first bourgeois and proletarians: the first merchant-capitalists and workers. But it is also the urban condition that makes the material interdependence of people on each other most apparent. Hence, it is *both* the site of the development of capitalism and the condition that might inspire a wholehearted recognition of people's common interests. The city is both 'obstacle to the new society . . . and its prototype' (Lefebvre 1972b: 60; Marx and Engels 1965: 83ff). Lefebvre worried about not only the marginal and excluded, but also the passivity of better-off inhabitants, who would accept the narrow social norms and lack of opportunities in the new suburbs.

Lefebvre's battery of works on urbanism include the books, *Du rural à l'urbain* (1970b), *Révolution urbaine* (1970a) and *La Pensée Marxiste et la ville* (1972b). In English, *Production of Space* (1974a) represents his key work on spatiality, while *Writings on Cities* (1996) provides a selection from Lefebvre's urban essays, which remain largely untranslated, including his first book on the topic, *Le Droit à la ville* (1968b). However, the entire series of *Critique of Everyday Life* (1947a; 1961j; 1981a) and its follow-up *Elements de Rhythmanalyse* (1992a; see 1996) are intrinsically tied to everyday life in an urban context. Moreover, Lefebvre goes beyond conventional understandings of the city. He extrapolates from his doctoral studies of rural land rents to conceive of a system of spatial divisions – a *system* of lots and property of which the city is only one element. This 'second nature' is laid over the natural topography: a *socially produced* system of capitalist space.

> Each network or sequence of links – and thus each space – serves exchange and use in specific ways. Each is *produced* – and serves a purpose; and each wears out or is consumed, sometimes unproductively, sometimes productively. There is a space of speech whose prerequisites, as we have seen, are the lips, the ears, the ability to articulate, masses of air, sounds, and so on. This is a space, however, for which such material preconditions are not an adequate definition: a space of actions and of interactions, of calling and of calling back and forth, of expressiveness and power, and already at this level – of latent violence and revolt; the space, then, of a discourse that does not coincide with any discourse on or in space. The space of speech envelops the space of bodies and develops by means of traces, of writings, of prescriptions and inscriptions.
>
> (1991d: 403)

Space in the dialectic

As argued in earlier chapters, Lefebvre takes a further step by experimentally 'spatialising' the dialectic itself. Within what the English-speaking world refers to as 'Marxism', Lefebvre, Benjamin and Lenin have been the lone commentators on the spatial characteristics and expansion of capitalism. It is thus not surprising that translations into English of *Production of Space*, which began to appear in the late 1970s and early 1980s, mark what Dereck Gregory refers to as a decisive break in English-language geography, the *geo-graphos* of David Harvey and Edward Soja, amongst other prominent writers who began to discover, through Lefebvre, the specifically French appreciation of the qualitative character of *l'espace capitaliste*. Gregory reviewed this development, commenting on the works of key representatives of the 'geographical imagination':

> Soja calls this a 'provocative inversion,' a reversal of the original mapping of historical materialism into geography, which set in motion a spatialisation of critical theory whose intellectual momentum pushed far beyond Harvey's historic-geographical materialism. . . . Not only was a spatial analytics incorporated within historical materialism as a central moment in its critique of capitalism, but many of these newer formulations were now directed toward a postclassical, Western Marxism that turned on more than the critique of political economy.
>
> (Soja 1989b: 39–41, 56–75, cited in Gregory 1994: 96)

This process involves two aspects, one that geographers have seized upon (e.g. Soja 1996: 44–6) and one that goes beyond the question of space to the positioning of otherness within dialectical logic itself (see Chapter 8). For the first, Lefebvre notes that all struggles and the sedimented achievements of the history of civilisation all take place in space: It has 'always been the reservoir of resources, and the medium in which strategies are applied, but it has now become something more than the theatre, the disinterested stage or setting of action.' Spatial extension, scale and character are the common elements, measure and loci of all 'materials and resources, finished products, be they businesses or "culture" . . . it brings them all together' (1991d: 410). Exploitative or utopian, social relations must also be spatial to count as more than dreams. Space is thus Lefebvre's ultimate repository of the authentic, providing an ontological groundwork to reassert the primacy of the 'real' over the imaginary. Even the simulated world of hyper-capitalistic advertising images relies on fetishised commodities materialised, emplaced, and shown to function in the tactile and weighted world of three dimensions. These objects may be respatialised to include imagined literary and cinematic spatialities to convey and connote social aspirations. Mere rocks may be re-scripted with manipulated desires, but even then they can be dissected and analysed as a blend of different moments, modes and forms of spatialisation.

The effect is to reunite over-specialised areas of knowledge by substituting or giving an overriding emphasis to the spatiality of action, objects, laws, semiotic codes, economic processes and cultural practices rather than analysing them in terms of the priorities prescribed by the specialised domains of knowledge, which tend to attach themselves to different phenomena and processes. This would mean, for example, analysing the action of a protest march in terms of:

- Spatial manifestation (marching bodies, direction, mass of people);
- Objects (truncheons, individual bodies versus the crowd, 'lines' of police);
- Laws (restrictions on free assembly, rules governing highways, codes of behaviour);
- Semiotic codes (the inferred meanings and connotations of protest, of marchers);
- Economic processes (the dependence of merchants on orderly conduct and access via streets);
- Cultural practices (the unusual character of pedestrians blocking traffic or even walking).

This is not intended to be an exhaustive but merely an illustrative, analysis. A spatial approach might bring to light neglected opportunities for political advantage, or make the marchers aware of the manner in which the march itself could be regarded as a utopian form of collective unity and highlight the contrast between armed representatives of the state confronting the citizenry itself. Lefebvre asks in his typically dialectical style:

> What exactly is the mode of existence of social relationships? . . . The study of space offers an answer according to which the social relations of production have a social existence to the extent that they have a spatial existence; they project themselves into a space, becoming inscribed there, and in the process producing that space itself. Failing this, these relations would remain in the realm of 'pure' abstraction – that is to say, in the realm of representations and hence of ideology: the realm of verbalism, verbiage and empty words.
>
> (1991d: 129)

With that triad, we might also highlight the importance of Lefebvre's sketch of the potential to be found by introducing a spatial structure into the temporal logic of Hegel's dialectic. Soja tentatively envisions this as not 'an additive combination of its binary antecedents but rather . . . a disordering, deconstruction, and tentative reconstitution of their presumed totalisation producing an open alternative that is both similar and strikingly different' (Soja 1996: 61). What he derives from Lefebvre as 'Thirding decomposes the dialectic through an intrusive disruption that explicitly spatialises dialectical reasoning. . . . Thirding produces what might best be called a cumulative *trialectics* that is radically open to additional othernesses, to a continued expansion of spatial knowledge (Soja 1996: 61). Soja appropriates this as a specifically spatial shift in the sense of social and geographical space. Indeed, 'the dialectic thus emerges from time and actualises itself, operating now, in an unforeseen manner, in space. The contradictions of space, without abolishing the contradictions which arise from historical time, leave history behind and transport these old contradictions, in a worldwide simultaneity, onto a higher level' (Lefebvre 1991d: 129). However, the shift is more of a philosophical questioning of the temporalising character of the dialectic. In Hegel's view, 'affirmation' is undifferentiated in itself and thus a homogeneous entity, unknowable because lacking in any difference. Reading this through Heidegger, it is a purely spatial concept, similar in all respects to an undifferentiated field of which no single point or aspect stands out. 'Negation', however, introduces temporalisation – the negation of space, in the form of the *punctum*, the point or instant (the most elementary of temporal concepts). Negation of this negation must subsume both the spatial field and the point that is pure difference in itself. For Hegel, this takes place by means of the spatialisation of the point itself, drawing it into the line, the trajectory, and initiating flow, movement and passage. In the Hegelian scheme, we could say that the third term is analogous to historical development: 'progress'.

Lefebvre's proposal is to respatialise the dialectic, holding the negation of the negation not as the point set in motion (line) but as a radical 'outside', a 'beyond' or otherness, constitutively distinct from the original binary of field and point, or affirmation and negation. In effect the shift is from 'affirmation–negation–negation of the negation' to 'affirmation–negation–otherness'. This is, however, not fully pursued by Lefebvre himself, who remains closer to the classical Hegelian model. Nor is it fully clarified in Soja's work, which draws on some (could they be called post-colonial?) theorists of alterity such as Homi Bhabha and bell hooks. However, he does not fully return to the dialectic itself to work out the logical structure of this new triadic form, a form that can only be called postmodern and that would find its roots to lie not only in Hegel, Marx and Lefebvre but also in the work of Emmanuel Levinas' 'alterity', Edward Said's 'Orientalism' and Gloria Anzaldua's 'bordercrossing', and in the work of others who have sought to piece together the logic of stories told 'alongside' official histories (Bakhtin).

As argued in Chapter 8, spatialising the *aufhebung* or sublimation of contradictions or tensions into a synthetic triad of both–and is a major change. Here, 'both–and' could be restated more precisely as 'both' (both affirmation and negation) – 'and' (the third, other). This is spatialised in the sense that notions of the dialectic are often over-simplified into a temporal supersession. Here, Lefebvre reintegrates within the structure of the dialectic Nietzsche's concept of an irreducible tension, *überwinden*, which is not simply superseded but returns. The result is a postmodernised, cubic *dialectic* in which terms are mutually dependent and relativise each other. Lefebvre presents the possibility of fixing the dialectic as a counterposed assemblage of three terms that are mutually supporting and mutually parasitic for their status within the dialectic. Only the synopsis, delivered out of the dialectical analysis – and not a part of the dialectic proper – gives the possibility of an overarching synchronic synthesis.

Soja also attributes the idea of the third term to Lefebvre's late work, discovering a 'thirding' of long-standing dialectical interests in the everyday (*perçu*) and the technocratic (*conçu*) by the 'lived' (*vécu*). However, the concept of the *vécu* goes back to his presentation of *l'homme total* – the fully realised, fully living person in the 1930s.

Translating *L'Espace*

The spatial is the tie that binds together the urban and the rural as two expressions of the same social system of capital. Lefebvre, pondering the ever more industrialised landscapes of his childhood Occitaine (*Les Temps de méprises* (1975c), ch. 9), argued that the production of an appropriate system of spatial attitudes, habits and territorial divisions has been essential to the survival of capitalism. This industrialisation of the countryside was not anticipated by Marx and early theorists of capitalism. Lefebvre argued that it is necessary to redirect historical materialism towards a 'spatial problematic' (Soja 1985: 108). In practice, Lefebvre presents a series of 'approximations' that first centre around the problematic of everyday life and are enlarged in later books to encompass the spatialisation of social relations in general. In relation to capitalism, this might be summarised as a set of theses. First, social space is the location of the reproduction of relations of production and of 'society' in all its complexity. Second, the internal contradictions of capitalism have been managed through the development of a mediating system of spatiality and of modes of occupying geographic space. In volume 4 of *De l'État* (1978b), this is developed as a third argument, that the production of this capitalist spatialisation is accomplished through the activities of the state, which oversees what he calls the 'statist mode of production'.

> Spatiality is not only a product but also a producer and reproducer of the relations of production and domination, an instrument of both allocative and authoritative power. Class struggle, as well as other social struggles are thus increasingly contained and defined in their spatiality and trapped in its 'grid'. Social struggle must then become a consciously and politically spatial struggle to regain control over the social production of this 'space'.
>
> (Soja 1985: 110; quotation marks added)

'Space', or more properly 'l'éspace', is used *metaphorically* and *allegorically* by Lefebvre. Unfortunately, Lefebvre's phrase 'the production of space' (used differently by Harvey (1989) and Soja (1985); see also my discussion in Shields

1991, ch. 1) conveys a multitude of spurious ideas. As noted below, Lefebvre attempts to broaden the definition of 'production' but leaves his argument hostage to misinterpretation and reduction back to established, Marxist concepts of production. A second misunderstanding arises that the core of Lefebvre's thesis is a reduction of social space to its social production. However, he constantly works against a simplistic causal analysis by asserting the importance of a dialectic in which space and the geographical is integrated into the understanding of the social just as time and history are.

'Space' has been understood in vastly different ways dating back to medieval scholasticism. The lesson of this history is that 'space' is far too loaded a term to be bandied about or to assume that it can be used in a purely technical manner. An examination of the very different concepts and semantic fields around the various words for 'space' in even closely related Western languages reveals that 'space' entails not only a concept of physical dispositions (distance, area, etc.) but also has social uses (e.g. the notion of 'social spaces' such as a place or space for a specific activity (a 'leisure site', a forum or a stadium) or 'front and back spaces' (Goffman 1969). There are still further abstract usages, for example, 'cyberspace', 'head space' or 'discursive space'. All these 'levels' of meanings interact to make a culturally specific set of connotations when the word is used.

Lefebvre's *'l'espace'* is a term that always makes one want to complete it: 'the space' of everyday life; of geometric concepts; of the city. Each is completely different. In referring to this third aspect as *'spaces* of representation' Lefebvre creates an apparent tautology: one aspect of 'space' is these 'spaces . . . '. It is like saying that space is made up of space. If this is taken as a logical statement, then Lefebvre's logic is jumbled from the start, but because he operates with a metaphorical notion of *l'espace*, or 'the space', it is quite possible that his overall *l'espace* is on a completely different plane to *'les espaces de représentation'*. This is much more easily understood as the reflexive quality of a spatialisation that weighs on subsequent social action, dreams for, and perceptions of, the world as a space of distance and difference. Lefebvre tries to tell us that the system of space is not just spatial practice, in the sense of its social construction, but equally the representations of it and discourses about it, and it is also equally its reflexive effects, promoting here, limiting there.

One problem, then, is a problem of translation: our 'space' is not the French *l'espace*; nor is it the German *raum*. None of these corresponds to what Kant and Leibniz called *'spatium'* (a spatial field or area); nor do they signify what Descartes referred to as *'extensio'* (extension, pure space). The semantic fields of these words do not neatly coincide. Just as the Inuit have many different words to convey the (very important, in their history) nuances of what we naively lump together as 'snow', so, if 'space is important', we are in desperate need of a vocabulary to conceptualise the varied production and consumption of varied spaces, places and landscapes. Because Lefebvre is referring to not only the empirical disposition of things in the landscape as 'space' (the physical aspect) but also attitudes and habitual practices, his metaphoric *l'espace* might be better understood as the *spatialisation* of social order. In this movement to space, abstract structures such as 'culture' become concrete practices and arrangements in space. Social action involves not just a rhythm but also geometry and spacing. Spatialisation also captures the processual nature of *l'espace* that Lefebvre insists is a matter of ongoing activities. That is, it is not just an achieved order in the built environment, or an ideology, but also an order that is itself always undergoing change from within through the actions and innovations of social agents. In short, all 'space' is social space, and a systemic approach is necessary that avoids a partial, discipline-based analysis (for example, planning, geography) and keeps the intersections on space with an overarching regime or spatialisation in sight: 'It is no longer a matter of the space of this or the space of that: rather it is space in its totality or global aspect that needs not only to be subjected to analysis scrutiny . . . but also to be *engendered*' (Lefebvre 1991d: 37).

Social spatialisation subsumes the tendency to over-simplify back to a society–space dialectic within a term that is both a verb, as in a group that engages in spatialising itself in the form of a territory, and a noun, as in an accomplished cultural achievement, 'a spatialisation'. It is both a thing and a process, both an achievement and an ongoing practice. 'Thus production process and product present themselves as two inseparable aspects, not as two separable ideas' (1991d: 37). Thus we can follow the spirit in which Lefebvre responds to the multiplicity of approaches to, and appropriations of, space recounted above by arguing that what is needed is a unitary dialectical framework that integrates 'under one roof' all the other possible but limited perspectives: what he goes on to call '*l'espace*' and in translation has been called 'social spatialisation'.

> It is a question of discovering or developing a unity of theory between fields which are given as being separate. . . . Which fields? . . . First, the *physical*, nature, the cosmos, – then the *mental* (which is comprised of logic and formal abstraction) – finally the *social*. In other words, this search concerns *logico-epistemological* space – the space of social practices – that in which sensible phenomena are situated in, not excluding the imaginary, projects and projections, symbols, utopias.
>
> (1974a: 19)

Lefebvre finds two precedents for this holistic analysis. First, the work of Surrealists such as André Breton, who attempted to unify through narrative the physical sense of lived space with the symbolic meanings of space. The second precedent is the operation of modern technocracies, which attempt to unify the lived space of the everyday environment with the conceptual–mathematical space of science. Through urban and regional planning practice (1974a: 26–9), and through super-rationalisation and homogenisation, the emotional investment of places with meaning is wiped away.

This is a difficult project, and Lefebvre often fails to maintain his focus on this new 'combinatory'. He must maintain the Marxist categories of production and historical materialism if his analysis is to have a political impact, yet his proposal suggests a new outlook in which these terms are superseded. This leads to much tortuous writing and a tendency (ably exposed in Gregory 1994) to reduce the contemporary social spatialisation to a capitalist 'strategy which has created the new totality, whose elements appear to be joined (joined in authority and by qualification) and disjoined (disjoined in that same fragmented space and by that same authority, which uses its power in order to unite by separating and to separate by uniting)' (Lefebvre 1976e: 27–8). Fundamental to Lefebvre's hesitation is his difficulty in *spatialising power* in the manner proposed by Foucault, for example, where power is embedded as force (*puissance*) in a dense network of bio-powers. For Lefebvre, power is 'political' rather than ethical; it is sovereign and conceived from above.

Lefebvre criticised the separation of space and time, materiality and meaning in analyses. A typical example was the mass-produced suburban dwelling, the *pavillon*. As director of the Institut de Sociologie Urbaine de Paris,[3] he led a research team that produced an extended study of suburbia. This broke with the tradition of focusing on housing in terms of needs to produce one of the first social science analyses of home as a symbolic system, a foretaste of the development of material culture and studies of the domestic (Lefebvre 1966a). Without memory or concern for allowing inhabitants to 'dwell' in its fullest sense, householding was reduced to its economic skeleton. Parodying Heidegger's nostalgia for the country dwellings of the Black Forest, Lefebvre sought to retain the importance of memory without lapsing into a reified nostalgia for a mythified past, which is thus false in the Lefebvrean schema. At the same time, however, the *pavillon* offers the utopian promise of the stable family unit – a unit that Lefebvre could not recognise as patriarchal, as having weaknesses, or being itself mythified. Kofman and Lebas (1996: 16) identify one key quotation in which Lefebvre identifies the links between the spatial and the temporal. Speaking of the city, he said:

> Space is nothing but the inscription of time in the world, spaces are the realisations, inscriptions in the simultaneity of the external world of a series of times, the rhythms or the city, the rhythms of the urban population . . . the city will only be rethought and reconstructed on its

3 Soja claims Lefebvre for 'geography' against 'sociologism'. Lefebvre would scorn such a disciplinary appropriation of his work. Suffice to note that Lefebvre maintained his affiliation with that vanguard discipline for far longer than his sociology professorship in Strasbourg (1961–65), and he never published in a geography journal in his life – a discipline that was not engaged in social critique, even including the more progressive journals such as *Espaces et sociétés* and *Hérodote*.

current ruins when we have properly understood that the city is the deployment of time . . . of those who are its inhabitants.

(1967e: 10)

Spatialisation takes on all the weight, historicity and promise of time. If Benjamin finds history prophetic, space – retrojectively–projectively (cf. Chapter 9) – includes both sedimented historical 'truths' and flashes of utopian potential, which destabilises any present regime. Kofman and Lebas also sketch the link that Lefebvre attempted to draw between what he argued was a semiotic multiplication of images and the transformation of everyday life and the city. Much of *La Production de l'espace* is taken up with issues of the non-discursive versus discursive aspects of space. 'Do the spaces formed by practice–social activity . . . have meaning?' What sort of semiotic analysis should be applied? 'Can the space occupied by a social group . . . be treated as a message?' How could we 'read' it? 'Ought we to look upon architectural or urbanistic works as a type of mass medium?' And, 'May a social space viably be conceived of as a language or discourse?' (1991d: 131). These are the preoccupations of the time and cannot be dismissed as some have.

Beginning in *Langage et société* (1966d), he argued that in this multiplication, signifiers became detached from concrete references. This multiplication was one component of an escape of signs and symbols from control by social and political institutions. On the one hand, this permitted the extension of the imagination, but on the other hand, resulted in a growing 'mystification' of language and of everyday life. The new, modern states extended their mythologies of national uniqueness and claims of antiquity and respectability – wrapping themselves in representations and myths that preceded reality. This required that the state be organised around promoting and supporting these myths. Language became more diverse but also fragmented into the jargons of increasingly specialised fields (Kofman and Lebas 1996: 20). This line of argument is expanded and developed by his then research assistant, Jean Baudrillard (1981).

Beyond human geography

Against the tendency of theorising space in terms of its own codes and logic, what is necessary, argues Lefebvre, is an approach that seeks to understand the *dialectical* interaction between spatial arrangements and social organisation itself. Lefebvre thinks of space in terms of its social production as a particular 'kind' of space and system of places and landscapes, spaces and regions. This is a spatial–territorial ordering with a historically and culturally specific morphology that reflects a consistent order. Gottdiener (1985) goes as far as referring to a spatial 'design'. Much of Lefebvre's work is taken up with establishing the role of this spatialisation in contemporary capitalism. Struggling to fit the concept into Marxist terms, he first tries humorously suggesting that spatialisation is a superstructural element that has, however, the status of a material element of the base. This only reveals the shortcomings of such a non-dialectical dualism. Space is both produced and productive: it is something that evolves historically rather than being created separately from a society. One of Lefebvre's biggest problems is to overthrow the conventional, formalistic (Martins 1982: 173), attitudes whereby space appears to us as non-dialectical, *a priori*, rather than as only one reflexive moment in a dialectic (Lefebvre 1974a: 337–41) between social action and the spatial and geographical aspects of society, the economic mode of production and the cultural imaginary.

Lefebvre's project is to displace views that understand this social space as a product of overall social relations. Social action always takes place in space, and political debates presume a set of spatial arrangements to argue over. Thus geographers have objected that such a dialectic is essentially meaningless, except in purely theoretical terms. It adds nothing to the possibilities of practice, nor does it aid analysis. Society *is* spatial as one characteristic of its essential being; the terms are inseparable. Lefebvre's theory does away with the distinction between cultural or social geography and sociology, yet he muddies the argument by insisting that space is an *oeuvre* that can be understood by broadening the concept of production (1991d: 113–15; see also Chapter 9; see Kleinspehn 1975), drawing back from fully immersing the social terms within their spatial context and embodiment. In order to maintain the analytical separability of elements, Lefebvre refuses to spatialise his analysis fully. By contrast, a historian would insist on the historicity of every element, object and facet of a historical investigation. On the one hand, Lefebvre does not live up to his ambitions, but on the other hand, the advantage is that he maintains the use of politically charged terms, which give his work force. He also maintains the turbulence of the dialectical relations of space, notably around the *oeuvre*, not allowing us to relax into the seductive 'view from above' inherent in master terms such as spatialisation for one minute.

Gregory notes that while he accentuates the 'instrumentality' of social space, Lefebvre presents social space as concealing the strategies that underwrite modern capitalism, and 'more subversively, that a theory of the production of space that makes those strategies visible, that renders the contours *en clair*, is capable of underwriting a politics of resistance that must be (and indeed, can only be) a "politics of space"' (Lefebvre 1976e: 17; 1973c)

Rather than accepting the logic of spatial orderings as given in the bourgeois divisions of the social science disciplines, or in the official ideology of professional planning, Lefebvre argues that a rigorous approach would seek the material grounding of all these partial, ideological theorisings about space in the real conditions of the social existence of men and women (1974a: 19). One possible extension of this research would be to pursue the question of a gendered experience of space, as Julia Kristeva (1981) does in the case of time or as Elizabeth Grosz attempts for space (1994; 1995).[4]

---

4   Grosz also considered the issue in *Space, Time and Perversion* (1995). A large number of sources

Product–*oeuvre*–concrete abstraction

It is essential to acknowledge that much of Lefebvre's discussion is framed within an explanation of the production of space. How can spatialisation be both a product and a productive medium in which other products are created and in which exchanges take place? Bo Grönlund refers to this as Lefebvre's ontological transformation of space (1993). Pursuing the question of the 'inner truth' of social space, Lefebvre in effect attempts to construct the equivalent of Marx's analysis of the commodity form for spatial analysis.

The concept of production as it emerges from Hegel and from Marx and Engels is his inspiration and is enlarged (Lefebvre 1974a: 83ff) from its narrower, industrial, sense (production of products, commodities) to include the production of works in the built environment (*oeuvres*) and of spatialised meanings and other codings of the social environment. Lefebvre proposes that Marx's concept of commodity production represents a model by which the multiple dualisms of his analysis of space can best be accommodated and the philosophical dualisms of most, static, Marxist analysis overcome. An often quoted (and misquoted) passage from *Dialectical Materialism* explains:

> In any product, however trivial, the subjective and objective aspects . . . the activity and the thing, are intimately linked. These are isolated objects that have been separated from Nature. . . .
> And yet these products still remain objects of Nature. . . .
> Every product – every object – is therefore turned in one direction towards Nature and in another towards man. It is both concrete and abstract. It is concrete in having a given substance, and still concrete when it becomes part of our activity, by resisting or obeying it, however. It is abstract by virtue of its definite, measurable contours, and also because it can enter into a social existence, be an object amongst other similar objects and become the bearer of a whole series of new relations additional to its substantiality.
>
> (Lefebvre 1968j: 119 [1939b])

However, unlike other commodities or products, space has both a material reality and a formal property that enables it to constrain other commodities and their social relations. It continually recreates or reproduces the social relations of its production. 'Space has the property of being materialised by a specific social process to act back upon . . . that process. It is, therefore, simultaneously material object or product, the medium of social relations, and the reproducer of material

are available that consider the issues of gender, sexual identity, the body and space. Recent additions that are particularly useful include Blum and Nast 1996; Hayden 1981; Miller 1981; Valentine 1989; Deutsche 1991; Morris 1988; Wilson 1991; and Rose 1993. Shirley Ardener's book *Women and Space* (1984) provides a further empirical reference.

objects and social relations' (Gottdiener 1985: 129). In this manner, Lefebvre grounds the multi-faceted nature of the interrelation between society and its space in a dialectical framework, transforming Marx's original ontological categories by the addition of a spatial dimension. For Lefebvre's Marx, social space is simultaneously a means of production as land and part of the social forces of production as space. As real estate property, spatial relations can be considered part of the social relations of production (the economic base). In addition, space is an object of consumption, a political instrument, and an element of social struggle.

This short-circuits any base–superstructure dualism, making it difficult to think in terms other than a dialectical juxtaposition rather than a hierarchy. The multi-dimensional thesis is in direct contrast to the more customary reduction of space to part of the trinity: production, consumption and exchange (as in Castells 1977). To these three, common in politico-economic analyses of space, Lefebvre argues that together they form a fourth realm of social relations: spatialisation, or the production and deployment of wealth or surplus value in space. The spatial may be seen to be an arbitrating concept in cultural regimes of socio-economic hierarchies (implemented through physical spatial division), and an indicator of socio-economic consistency, compatibility or continuity of privilege, class and practice.

> According to Lefebvre, space can only be grasped dialectically because it is a concrete abstraction – one of Marx's categories, such as exchange value, which are simultaneously a material, externalised realisation of human labour and the condensation of social relations of production. The concrete abstraction is simultaneously a medium of social actions, because it structures them, and a product of those actions.
>
> (Gottdiener 1985: 128)

Three-part dialectics

How can one conceptualise in one unitary 'social theory of space' the various 'levels of space' (the physical, the mental and, most importantly, the cultural aspects of social spatialisation), which are specified and analysed one by one in the various professional discourses about 'space'? As argued in the earlier section 'Spatialising the dialectic' (see Chapter 8), Lefebvre proposes a *threefold* dialectic within spatialisation (*dialectique de triplicité* 1974a: 48ff), which consists of:

1   *Spatial practice* with all its contradictions in everyday life, space perceived (*perçu*) in the commonsensical mode – or better still, ignored one minute and over-fetishised the next.

2   *Representation of space* (which might equally be thought of as discourses *on* space); the discursive regimes of analysis, spatial and planning professions and expert knowledges that conceive of space (*l'espace conçu*).

3   *Spaces of representation* (which might best be thought of as the discourse *of* space), the third term or 'other' in Lefebvre's three-part dialectic. This is space *as it might be*, fully lived space (*l'espace vécu*), which bursts forth as what I have called 'moments' of presence (Chapter 5). It is derived from both historical sediments within the everyday environment and from utopian elements that shock one into a new conception of the spatialisation of social life.[5]

A brief example might show the interrelation of these elements in the case of one spatial object, the human body. Lefebvre notes that there is a tendency to 'cheerfully commandeer social space and physical space and reduce them to an epistemological (mental) space – the space of discourse and of the Cartesian *cogito*'. This 'abstract body' is easily manipulated by technocratic capitalism. Even so, 'the practical "I" ' of everyday perception (i.e. the *perçu*) 'is inseparably individual and social . . . one may wonder what connection exists between [this "I"] this abstract body, understood simply as a mediation between "subject" and "object", and a practical and fleshy body conceived of as a [monadic] totality complete with spatial qualities (symmetries, asymmetries) and energetic properties (discharges, economies, waste)'. However, when the body is conceived as a fully lived, practical and theorised body – 'the moment the body is envisioned as a practico-sensory totality,' something that is at present alien, other, to the manner in which the body is understood, at that moment a 'recentring of knowledge occurs' (1991d: 61–2).

Each aspect of this three-part dialectic is in a relationship with the other two. Altogether they make up 'space'. All these aspects can be latent, ideological or expressed in practice in a historical spatialisation, and may either reinforce or contradict each other in any given site or moment. Lefebvre does not provide clear definitions 'up front' and in fact refines these three aspects by comparing and contrasting them in subsequent sections of his book. This introduces a great deal of confusion, for one is never quite sure which of his forays into defining this three-part dialectic is the definitive one. Its roots lie in the religious mysticism of Joachim de Flore, and his preservation of the terminology of his earliest work, in which the experience is counterposed with law and spirit (see Chapter 3). The first of these three aspects, 'spatial practice', is easily confused with his notion of 'lived space', a dis-alienated moment of the embodied 'total person' at one with their context.

---

5   Nicholson-Smith translates this as 'representational spaces', but this makes it difficult to comprehend in relation to other aspects of Lefebvre's terminology.

Spatial practice

This is the production and reproduction of specific places and spatial 'ensembles' appropriate to the social formation. It would include building typology, urban morphology and the creation of zones and regions for specific purposes: a specific range of types of park for recreation; test sites for nuclear weapons; places for this and that; sites for death (graveyards) and remembrance (memorials, battlegrounds, museums, historic walks and tours). Through everyday practice, 'space' is dialectically produced as 'human space'. This production is not *ab nihilo* – as if space comes into being from a pre-existing, non-spatial practice that 'secretes' space. Rather a particular form of space, or spatialisation, is created out of the *matériel*, the bits and pieces of arrangements and territories that are our historical patrimony. It is our legacy to create our own spatiality, and the ability and freedom to do so is the prime index of quality of social life. This indicator is quite separate from and more reliable than stylistic measures, which are cultural and historico-geographically specific.

This aspect of 'space' helps to ensure social continuity in a relatively cohesive fashion and the reproduction of the social relations of production. For example, Lefebvre asks (1974a: 55) 'How could the Church survive without *churches*?' What is the relationship of space and ideology and social formations? Such cohesion through space implies, in connection with social practice and the relating of individuals to that space, a certain level of spatial 'competence' and a distinct type of 'spatial performance' by individuals.

So what is contemporary spatial practice? Using an iterative method,[6] Lefebvre attempts to sketch quickly the way in which spatialisation is just the gap between objects and therefore neutral, unimportant and not an object of struggle. This 'commonsense' understanding characterises both taken-for-granted everyday life (daily routines) and the logically rationalised urban (the milieu of routes and networks that we pass through on our way from home to work or play). We do not see that they are all linked together as part of an over-arching arrangement, or spatialisation, complains Lefebvre. This commonsensical vision of space is limited to 'perceived space' and in fact ignores practice just as it ignores the qualitative meanings, the images and myths of places and regions. All this needs to become fully integrated into a 'total space', what Lefebvre refers to many times as lived space.

Unfortunately, this early and crucial section of *Production of Space* is probably the most loosely written part of the book, and in trying to give it sense, it has further suffered in translation. Lefebvre tries to sketch the everyday importance of spatialisation, which is a complete and seamless set of practices and arrangements (for example, planned suburbs, or cities connected by agreed routes and flight paths) despite its divisions and inconsistencies (preserving

---

6　The relevant pages are part of a first chapter which summarises the book that follows so that it could be published in advance in a journal in order to promote the book.

nature in one place, paving over arable land in another). The reason he introduces his discussion of 'the perceived' is partly linked to his hypothesis that the
visual is the key to understanding the evolution of this aspect of spatialisation in
neo-capitalist Europe. Codes of axial perspective are built into cities, into
people's everyday actions in terms of judgements of distance (and are at the
same time a theory of space that will appear again in the second aspect – see
next section). The stress on perspectivalism leaves the impression that somehow
'spatial practice' is defined only visually by 'perception' (*l'espace perçu*) without
practice at all. This can make sense in English only if 'perception' is understood
as practical perception (cf. 1991d: 40) and 'common sense'. What remains
more important, however, is the notion of taken-for-granted and unreflective
practice.

> 'Modern' spatial practice might thus be defined – to take an extreme
> but significant case – by the daily life of a tenant in a government-
> subsidised high-rise housing project. Which should not be taken to
> mean that motorways or the politics of air transport can be left out of
> the picture.
>
> (1991d: 38)

For example, a shopping centre, such as the Eaton's Centre in Toronto,
represents a spatial ensemble that both encourages and requires (for commercial
viability) a specific type of 'crowd practice'. The aggregate, wandering,
consumer crowd of today is complemented by the celebratory and festive
galleria-type shopping mall. This type of spatial performance is quite different
from the much less commercialised public behaviour of the *boulevardier* or
flâneur who strolled the nineteenth-century shopping arcades of Paris. This
historical model legitimised the new Canadian and American shopping arcades
of the 1980s, such as Eaton's, the West Edmonton Mall and Mall of the
Americas, even while it was transformed into a new, hyper-commercialised
model (an architectural typology that was subsequently exported around the
world – see Shields 1989).

Representations of space

Représentations de l'espace are the logic and forms of knowledge, and the ideological content of codes, theories, and the conceptual depictions of space linked
to production relations. These are the abstracted theories and 'philosophies',
such as the 'science of planning' cited by Lefebvre, geography and cartography,
including geographical information systems (GIS). Taken alone, this 'level' of
the dialectic today involves the abstract presentation of lived experience in space
reduced to quantified movements along vectors between x–y coordinates. These
various discourses are linked to production relations and to the order that
these impose. Most crucially, these 'representations' are central to forms of

knowledge and claims of truth made in the social sciences, which (today) in turn ground the rational/professional power structure of the capitalist state. This is thus:

> conceptualised space [*l'espace conçu*], the space of scientists . . . techno-cratic subdividers and social engineers . . . all of whom identify what is lived and what is perceived with what is conceived. (Arcane speculation about Numbers, with its talk of the golden number, moduli and 'canons' . . .).
>
> (1991d: 38)

Spaces of representation

Espaces de la représentation are 'discourses *of* space' in the sense that this aspect of his triad forms the social imaginary, the presuppositions that often structure problem definitions and thus influence the sort of solutions that are thought of as being possible and achievable. This aspect is reflexive. It is thus at the heart of any fully 'lived' space (*l'espace vécu*). It is an essential terrain of struggle on the way to realising ourselves as 'total persons' (see Chapter 3). Integration of this would be essential to achieve out of the three-part dialectic a 'total space' of engagement and presence.

This sphere offers complex re-coded and even decoded versions of lived spatialisations, veiled criticism of dominant social orders and of the categories of social thought often expressed in aesthetic terms as symbolic resistance. Lefebvre cites Dada and the work of the Surrealists, particularly the paintings of René Magritte, as examples of art, literary comment and fantasy regarding other, possible spatialisations. Also included in this aspect are clandestine and underground spatial practices, which suggest and prompt alternative (revolu-tionary) restructurings of institutionalised discourses of space and new modes of spatial *praxis*, such as that of squatters, illegal aliens, and Third World slum dwellers, who fashion a spatial presence and practice outside the norms of the prevailing (enforced) social spatialisation. For example, in many countries, inequitable property ownership often privileges absentee landlords over landless peasants. Lefebvre calls this

> space as directly *lived* through its associated images and symbols, and hence the space of 'inhabitants' and 'users'. . . . This is the dominated . . . space which the imagination seeks to change and appro-priate. It overlays physical space, making symbolic use of its objects. Thus representational spaces may be said . . . to tend towards more or less coherent systems of non-verbal symbols and signs.
>
> (1991d: 39)

Signs? Nicholson-Smith's English translation (1991d) chooses the odd phrase 'representational spaces' rather than the literal translation, 'spaces of representation'. This translation of the text (and every translation is also an interpretation) brings out the importance of Lefebvre's thinking at this time about the semiotics of metaphor and metonymy and the entire mechanics of representation through a sign system. The text is strewn with the debris of near-forgotten theories of linguistics and semiotics. It would seem more obvious to tie the problem of 'lived space' to spatial practice rather than the social imaginary. However, referring to his Nietzschean ideal of the 'total person' (Chapter 4), he is interested here in the 'fully lived', pre-conscious and authentic shards of spatiality that animate people, providing meaning to the entire assemblage of lives and spatialisations.

Lefebvre dictated his books and avoided editing, leaving inconsistencies, which are also clues to a troubling problem that continued to haunt Lefebvre – the paradox of an almost impassable gulf between the sign and any authentic reality. This gulf left even the 'total person' either alienated from their nomo-thetic world or in a state of inarticulate and incoherent union and bliss, which could not be represented, and thus could hardly be expected to serve as a libid-inal, mobilising force for social change, as he and others had hoped might happen during the occupations of the spring of 1968. This paradox would drive Lefebvre back to reassess the work of Nietzsche after the completion of *Production de l'espace* (1974a; 1975a; 1991d).

Slums, *barrios* and *favellas* are seen by Lefebvre as localised 'reappropria-tions' of space that may furnish examples of such 'representational spaces' or 'spaces of representation' by which certain sites are removed or severed from the governing spatialisation and returned to the realm of 'communitas'. These are prophetic, temporary autonomous zones (Bey 1991). Lefebvre differentiates the popular 'appropriation' of space from the 'dominated' space of the nation-state, or of the capitalist city. The latter is the site of the hegemonic forces of capital, the former the site of possible emergent spatial revolutions. The local and punctual 'détournement' (re-adaptation, hijacking) of space, as in the tradi-tion of occupying key spatial sites or buildings as a means of protest, is similarly an example of the seizure and re-functioning of hegemonic space. It is this aspect of spatialisation that operates as an overcoding meta-concept that imbues other conceptual categories and symbolic systems with an often unrecognised 'spatial life'.

Lefebvre gives the example of the body: what is the spatial practice of the body? 'Considered overall, social practice presupposes the use of the body: the use of the hands, members and sensory organs, and the gestures of work as of activity unrelated to work. This is the realm of the *perceived* (the practical basis for the perception of the outside world)', which Lefebvre labels 'spatial prac-tice'. 'As for *representations of the body*, they derive from accumulated scientific knowledge, disseminated with an admixture of ideology'. A long tradition comes to mind – from the first medical axioms of Hippocrates through anatomic studies by Renaissance artists such as Michelangelo to theories of vaccine, antibodies and allergens in the environment. But the body considered a '*lived* experience', as itself a space of representations, returns us to metaphors to evoke the symbolic and mythic. 'The "heart" as *lived* is strangely different from the heart as *thought* and *perceived*'. Here we are in the realm of desire and mythification. Right-handedness as a norm, the attachment of moral values to different parts of the body – from wrists, ankles, to genitalia is one example of the colonisation of the *lived* and the use of the body as a space of representations against itself. The attachment of hygienic values to still other parts of the body – lips, anus, fingers – is yet another chastisement that reconfigures the dialectical linkage of practical perception–conception–lived image. When we shudder with disgust at transgressions of hygiene taboos we directly experience the overriding power of this interconnection as involuntary trembling seizes us and our 'skin crawls'. The 'lived' (*vécu*) is largely the domain of psychoanalysis and ethnography for Lefebvre, whose writing predates the emergence of cultural studies, where it is treated more fully as psycho-corporeal. Yet his project is to locate the revolutionary potential lying within the 'lived' as a deep motivation to utopian change.

Take the example of Canadian protests almost every summer in the first half of the 1990s against the injunction that women may not bare their breasts in public. On hot summer days, young women have challenged these laws and preconceptions by walking, topless (and bra-less) in towns, earning them notoriety in the national media. The shocked local burgers of these small towns, the titillated professional press and puzzled judges have been forced to examine the spectacle of burly cops covering up and arresting semi-naked women. How could Lefebvre's three-part dialectic contribute to an analysis? First, it highlights the practical logic at work: it is hot and the bra is a garment *designed* to constrain. Second, there are representations, legal codes, that decree the equality of citizens' bodies in Canada: If men are able to 'go topless', should women not also be allowed to? And is not their right to do so if they so choose guaranteed within the Canadian constitution? Judges deliberated, while town clerks drafted new by-laws or changed the wording of local statutes. Third, the bare-breasted woman invokes a range of cultural stereotypes – the fearless amazon, a sort of *National Geographic* primitiveness (Giblin 1977; Lutz and Collins 1993), maternity, ideologies of 'naturalness' propounded by those in favour of nudism, and a history of feminist activism associated with 'bra burning'. The breasts are – to stereotype mainstream Canadian culture – morally overcoded with desire. Do these women not contribute, then, to the erosion of civilisation? Are not these women exhibitionists? Or do they, at least innocently, subject themselves to the voyeuristic pleasures of others? Practical or not, stylish or not, the covering of one's chest for such reasons is a double burden imposed on the purported 'victims'/objects of this gaze. It is a sumptuary 'fix' to a cultural–psychological failure. Whether one agrees or not with the tactic, one is impressed with the daring civil disobedience involved here, and with the clarity with which problems of the body are highlighted. What is the source of this clarity? It lies in the recasting of the body as *lived*. The *lived* exhibition of the upper torso harnesses practical logic and legal representation together with utopian potential: an embodied dream of a time when bodies are not manipulated as pornographic images, and where voyeurs do not prey on other bodies for optico-sadistic pleasures.

All three aspects operate at all times. However, the varying balance and degrees of repression of one aspect or the domination of another marks out *historically specific*, as well as socially produced, spatialisations. Spatialisations find their grounding in a process of production through practice governed by the influence of historico-socially constructed spaces of representation. Spatialisations are then refined and rationalised in representation and discourses on space, which act upon production practices by specifying the appropriate movements of bodies (gestures, etiquette), materials (commodities), and relations (communications) in space. In this manner, the empirical and common-sense 'stuff' of space – the physical environment – is materially and historically constituted. Consequently, it is clear that Lefebvre's real object of study is the *process* of the production of space, and its configuration in any given historical period. He does not bother to engage in the philosophical debates on space itself. In such an approach (by linking space securely to production), it is possible to argue consistently for the *specificity* of spatialisations according to successive modes of production. Lefebvre's is a very periodicising stance: he makes – overstates – the production of the spatial the essence of each historical epoch. In different historical conjunctures, the three 'facets' of spatialisation will, in Lefebvre's view, dialectically combine in distinct structural systems and even as hierarchies. In a moment of rhetorical naivety, Lefebvre asks his readers:

> Did the [ancient] Orient know the difference between Representations of Space and Spaces of Representation? . . . the ideogram is both at once, containing, indissolubly, a presentation of the order of the world (of Space and of Time) and an implication of the concrete spaces and times (practical and social) in which symbolism is deployed, works of art composed, and buildings, temples and palaces built.
> (Lefebvre 1974a: 53; cf. the less direct translation: 1991d: 42)

Just as Lefebvre is clearly operating within a Eurocentric spatialisation of the world, in which the orient is the inverse, the mirror of a culture and zone called 'the West', so we too operate with our own evolving spatialisation. For him, 'the orient' is not just some myth or the title of a novel but a geographic region with such a level of self-evident internal coherence that further specifications (Japanese? Korean? Han Chinese?) are not necessary. Which spaces do we treat in a similar way today? 'The North'? 'The Pacific' (as in 'Pacific Rim')? The 'Third World'?

Lefebvre attempts to answer the question of how individual competence in spatial behaviour is achieved by pointing to the unacknowledged frameworks that make up his 'spaces of representation'. These interlink with formalised ideological 'discourses on space'. To reduce the complexity of social action to the status of a reflection of economic features, as in many politico-economic approaches, is to 'accept [that] spatial organisation is indistinguishable from the formation of its mental image' (Martins 1982: 164). This collapses discourses on space (Aspect 2) and the discourses of space (Aspect 3) into spatial practice (Aspect 1).

> Space is not merely economic, in which all the parts are interchangeable and have exchange value. Space is not merely a political instrument for homogenising all parts of society. On the contrary. . . . Space remains a model, a perpetual prototype of use value resisting the generalisations of exchange value in the capitalist economy under the authority of a homogenising state. Space is a use value, [similar to] . . . time to which is ultimately linked because time is our life, our fundamental use value.
>
> (Lefebvre 1978b: 291)

A spatialisation in its physical form as the historical landscape and built environment may be seen as one component of the *means* of production as the 'means of labour': its elements (roads, harbours, fenced fields) and the way it is arranged or spatialised enable work to be done. But it is also part of the *forces* of production. Thus:

> Space deserves membership in the set of productive forces. Ownership of space certainly confers a position in the economic structure. Even when a piece of space is contentless, its control may generate economic power, because it can be filled with something productive or because it may need to be traversed by producers.
>
> (Cohen 1978: 51)

Space is also part of the *social relations* of production, because the reproduction of the social formation must obviously be achieved in and through space–time as a *medium*. Based on the above three dimensions, space may be said to possess the same ontological status in the mode of production as capital or labour. Like a machine or any force of production, the social relations governing the activities associated with it are made to conform with the way in which it is used to acquire wealth. But, as has been over-abundantly argued in previous sections, space, now as spatial organisation, is not only a part but also a *product*. Lefebvre suggests that this makes the spatial organisation of a society different from any other social factor or commodity. This 'design' would include ingredients such as mass housing, transportation, parks and 'wilderness spaces', specific relations to perhaps wider spatial systems such as proximity to markets. Based on the nature of space as a product, Lefebvre speaks of the *consumption of space*, pointing to such phenomena as industrial relocation and eco-tourism, where spatio-environmental factors are important attractions. The spatial environment is converted into a commodity along with and besides being property. This is partially the result of contradictions between the natural environment and resource development – mining, logging, farming. Together with demographic growth, this has produced shortages of 'good' environments, leading to a condition where a true political economy of space is possible. The environment is commodified (air that is air-conditioned, water that must be purified, sun that must be filtered) and can be consumed (through purchase of the right technology, living in a favourable district of one's city, or tourism).

Because spatial organisation and design also constitute the physical form of a hierarchy of power, *spatial relations* are themselves important factors in the reproduction of existing social formations and in the process of governance: 'Space has become for the state a political instrument of primary importance. The state uses space in such a way that it ensures its control of places, its strict hierarchy, homogeneity of the whole and the segregation of parts. It is thus an administratively controlled and even policed space' (Lefebvre 1978b: 288; cited in Gottdiener 1985: 126). The hegemony of the capitalist class is renewed through spatial segregation and the effects of the 'normalising force' of state intervention in structuring spatial design (cf. Lefebvre 1978b). Not just ethnic but also class conflict is deployed in space, rendering it as spatial conflict. But spatial conflicts cut across class lines, because they are not produced by unequal relations of production alone.

Lefebvre spends much of *Le Droit à la ville* (1968b) establishing that a Marxist analysis of space that remains faithful to the dialectics of *Das Kapital* must insist on the dialectical relations between the development of the industrial 'base' of capitalism and the elaboration of urbanised society. Thus, for Lefebvre, the 'truth' of the capitalist city's morphology is industrialisation, and vice versa. This linkage occurs specifically in the form of an increasing tendency towards the transformation of space as landscape into property as exchange value. Twenty years before it became a common theme in sociology, Lefebvre was arguing that spatialisations have developed first from emphasising a natural space, through a historical space of territorial power and conquest, into today's arena of speculative capital (through private property, zoning, preferential taxation schemes and planning controls) operating across a fractured global space of localised ghettos. The wage labour system requires that land be held as private property and worked as a commodity, thus driving those who formed the peasantry in earlier modes, working the common lands, off the land and into the cities as potential wage labourers – an industrial proletariat. For capitalist social relations to dominate, this transformation of the holding of land and its economic and social position was essential.

The case of Rome demonstrates the historical change from the city-as-*oeuvre* of ancient Rome into a form of 'exchange value' (product) in its development during the twentieth century. The classical cities of antiquity were *oeuvres* in the sense of their use value as sites of ritual and as 'stages' for the monumental 'boasts' of 'despotic' rulers. The capitalist cities of the twentieth century convert what remains of the classical city-*oeuvres* into the newly commodified terrain of speculative real estate. In this transformation, the city ceases to be the central social form and becomes inserted into a far larger, capitalist, network, which is today a global system. The centrality of the older city (Rome) is replaced/displaced by new economic decision-making nodes. In this process of commodification of land, the monumental and festive aspects of the old cities also undergo fundamental changes. They are turned into museums of dead historical sites, as in the cases of Venice and Florence (Lefebvre 1976a: 89–96). Alternatively, they may be appropriated as consumer images of their former selves and reproduced in theme parks such as Disneyland.

This transformation inserts the classical city-oeuvre into a form that is not only analysable as the built component of a capitalist spatialisation but is also susceptible to an analysis of the city as a commodity without losing any of its specificity. Agents and the objects of production are combined 'in a specific structure of the distribution of relations, places, and functions.' In the case of industrialised capitalism, this 'specific structure' is the metropolis. The structuring function of the urban, which exerts controls over the daily life of the *agents* of production (i.e. individuals) and over the patterns of exchange of the *objects* of production (i.e. commodities) is the spatial and physical infastructure of capitalism. However, this infastructure, in its physicality, necessarily imposes the weight of 'sunk costs' on the organisation of the present and on future development patterns. 'Reproduction (of the relations of production, not just the means of production) is located not simply in society as a whole but in space as a whole. Space, occupied by new capitalism, sectioned, reduced to homogeneity, becomes the seat of power' (Lefebvre 1976a: 83).

A history of space

Spatialisation has a history. Having established the notion that social space is 'produced', Lefebvre historicises it, turning to a stereotypical, linear, Eurocentric modelling of historical progress. This is by far the least credible aspect and the largest element of the contents of *La Production de l'espace*. Lefebvre is controversial in first replacing Marx's history of modes of production with a history of spatialisation, and second, in cutting this up into periods, finding an essentialised spatialisation for each mode of production (see Figure 10.1):

absolute space	nature
sacred space	city-states, despots and divine kings, Egypt
historical space	political states, Greek city-states, Roman Empire, perspective
abstract space	capitalism, politico-economic space of property, lots

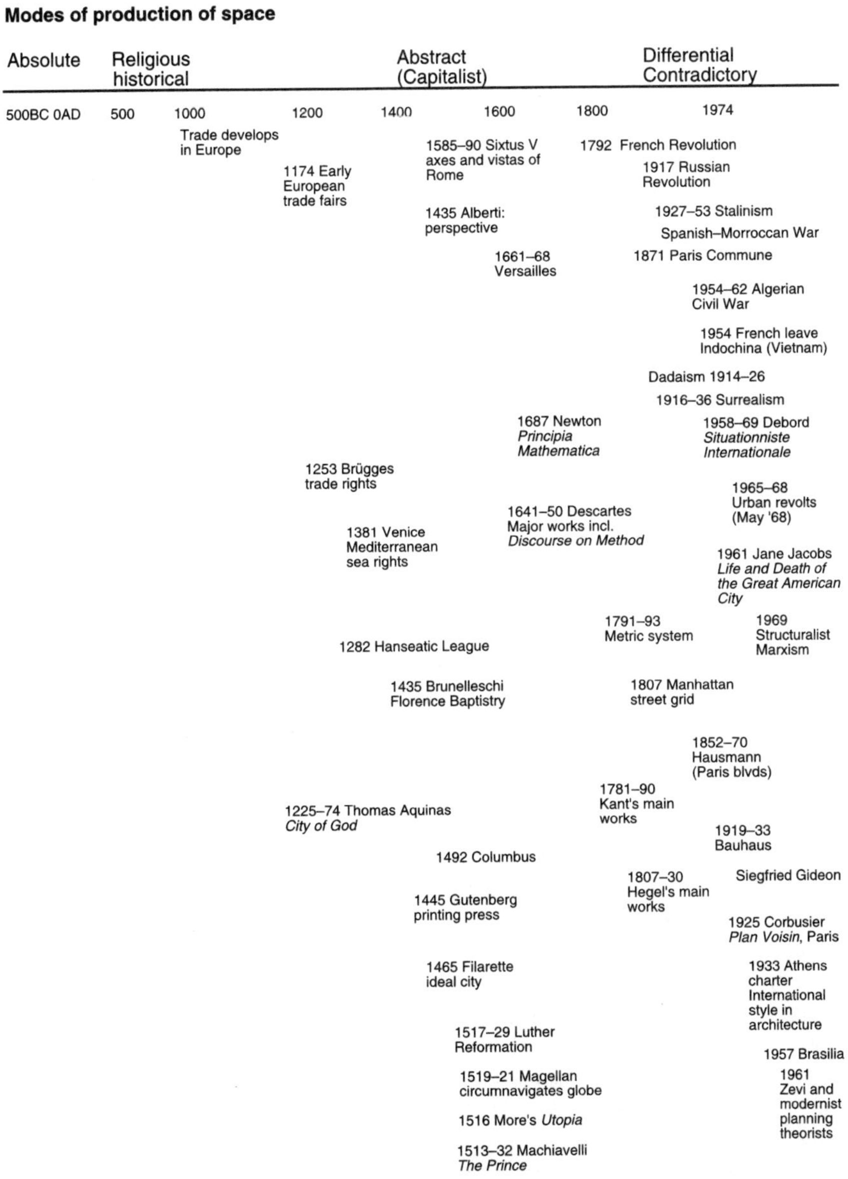

Modes of production of space

Absolute	Religious historical	Abstract (Capitalist)	Differential Contradictory
500BC 0AD 500 1000	1200 1400	1600	1800 1974

Trade develops in Europe

1174 Early European trade fairs

1585–90 Sixtus V axes and vistas of Rome

1792 French Revolution

1917 Russian Revolution

1435 Alberti: perspective

1927–53 Stalinism

Spanish–Morroccan War

1661–68 Versailles

1871 Paris Commune

1954–62 Algerian Civil War

1954 French leave Indochina (Vietnam)

Dadaism 1914–26

1916–36 Surrealism

1687 Newton *Principia Mathematica*

1958–69 Debord *Situationniste Internationale*

1253 Brügges trade rights

1641–50 Descartes Major works incl. *Discourse on Method*

1965–68 Urban revolts (May '68)

1381 Venice Mediterranean sea rights

1961 Jane Jacobs *Life and Death of the Great American City*

1791–93 Metric system

1969 Structuralist Marxism

1282 Hanseatic League

1807 Manhattan street grid

1435 Brunelleschi Florence Baptistry

1852–70 Hausmann (Paris blvds)

1781–90 Kant's main works

1225–74 Thomas Aquinas *City of God*

1919–33 Bauhaus

1492 Columbus

1807–30 Hegel's main works

Siegfried Gideon

1445 Gutenberg printing press

1925 Corbusier *Plan Voisin*, Paris

1465 Filarette ideal city

1933 Athens charter International style in architecture

1517–29 Luther Reformation

1957 Brasilia

1519–21 Magellan circumnavigates globe

1961 Zevi and modernist planning theorists

1516 More's *Utopia*

1513–32 Machiavelli *The Prince*

Figure 10.1 Timeline of Lefebvre's history of space in Europe (After Bo Grönlund, 1993, Nordplan, Stockholm)

| contradictory space | contemporary global capital versus localised meaning |
| differential space | future space revaluing difference and lived experience |

This second move turns his history into a series of epochs that are easier to remember, but it is anti-dialectical, suggests that time is the ultimate ordering system of space, and directs attention away from struggles in everyday life to grand themes in the economic and political structure of a time. In each period, the previous spatialisations persist, but this approach opens up a series of formalistic debates on whether or not the classification system is accurate – exactly the impasse that Lefebvre criticised in Structuralism. In effect, Lefebvre undoes the force of his spatial analysis by providing an exact set of 'modes of production of space' that can be substituted into orthodox Marxism's historical modes of production.

Although he is a great narrator, much of the 485 pages of *Production de l'espace* is thus a failure in Lefebvre's own terms. If the most modern type of space carries all the earlier types, sedimented and surcharged within itself, as Lefebvre will claim, his stress on *succession* despatialises and reasserts the centrality of history as an organising idea in European – and Lefebvrean – utopian thought. How did he lose sight of the dialectical relationship between different spatial modes? Thus in the contemporary world, all his forms or modes of spatialisation jostle each other, sometimes being juxtaposed in ridiculous proximity. Lefebvre's book is thus as contradictory as the contemporary space he analyses. After this work, he shifted away to much more philosophical topics rather than further develop his arguments in the form of detailed studies of spatial change.

Absolute space

Lefebvre's history begins with the *absolute space* of nature (Deleuze's and Guattari's 'great ungendered stasis'), which forms the archetypal 'space'. This still lurks into the present spatialisation in the form of Bachelardian nooks and corners, and in fragments of nature. Upon this 'first nature' of 'pure space' is constructed an overlying social space that emerges out of the measurements and paths of tribal practice: frontiers, liminal zones and temporary camps. The notion of 'wilderness' is itself a representation of space (1991d: 181 [1974a: 220]). Lefebvre embarks on a complex analysis of the body (human body, agent) as also therefore a 'social body'. Absolute space is intrinsically tied to the daily foraging of primitive hunting bands and the earliest farming villages. In such primitive communities, space was conceived of *analogically*, an analogy between the village form and the different functions of various areas and a 'holy body' being drawn. Space was thus visualised through an anthropomorphism that shaped the mental representation of space, the discourses on space. Thus physiological and mental 'frontiers' (the separation of the natural and the supernatural) are reproduced in the village and in its surrounding environment (Lefebvre 1974a: 223–4).

172

THE PRODUCTION OF SPACE

How does Lefebvre discern such periods? The method is *post hoc ergo propter hoc*, a projection of the present onto the past to form essentialised and reified historical periods. For whom? Where? The history is European, but Lefebvre merrily draws from global data. For example, he fills in a European past with images drawn from an East African present. He cuts and chops up space into history while criticising the fragmentation of our understanding of spatialisation produced in other studies. The armchair anthropology, in the tradition of Karl Marx, Herbert Spencer and Max Weber, draws little on detailed ethnological research or on peasant economics. An antediluvian spatialisation of 'absolute space' is constructed to provide a cultural universal: a datum from which all societies will be depicted as beginning their individual histories of spatialisation. In effect, such a datum is necessary to his narrative: it is the launch pad for the development that Lefebvre will sketch out, but it is of little interest in and of itself other than as a blank screen for the projection of Lefebvre's unoriginal notions of primitiveness. If there is an aspect of this history that works well, it is Lefebvre's attempt to present punctual exemplars – Periclean Athens, Rome at the time of the pontiffs, Paris in 1968, and so on. Missing however, are crucial examples that one might include, as a European, in a comprehensive history of spatialisation: the Moorish occupation of Spain, the rivalry with the Ottoman Empire and the construction of France, indeed of Europe itself, such that that regime can be constructed as one of what he refers to as '*transitory* sets of circumstances . . . (one thinks for example of Arab civilization in Andalusia)' (Lefebvre 1991d: 167). The abiding sense that Lefebvre gives is of the occupation of a unitary Europe by 'outsiders', who leave no trace of their presence. There is no mention of the sedimented inscription of the geometric sensitivity of Moorish architecture and administration of space. Finally, there is only silence within, no 'outside' to, this totalising history: 'spatiohistories cannot happen outside of capitalism – at least not any worth recording. Even when Lefebvre theories produced difference, it is always a consequence of the agency of capital' (Gibson-Graham 1993; cited in Blum and Nast 1996: 578).

Sacred space

Above the most archaic level of absolute space, the emergence of *sacred space* is marked by the construction of the first city states (strikingly, this coincides precisely with Deleuze's and Guattari's analysis of the '*Urstaat*' (1976: 217)). Sacred space is actually both sacred *and* political. It represents a political supersession of absolute (natural/primitive) space by the first truly 'social' spaces of the despots of the Asiatic mode. Deleuze and Guattari speak of a first 'territorialisation' of the environment: its designation as *territory* and the people and the land being symbolically joined in the body of the despot. The absolute space of the primitive village and semi-nomadic tribe is transformed into the space of the sacred city, whose forms are organised around the theme of identification and imitation (1991d: 236 [1974a: 274]). This spatialisation distances itself from the overbearing presence of nature in the earlier formation, setting up a man-versus-nature distinction subduing the forces of unknown nature through the first social technologies of organised religion. These political cities organise and dominate their surrounding rural region. Absolute space does not disappear but is merely subdued and displaced. It is significant that it disappears into the interior, into phenomenologically enclosed spaces – caves, nooks and crannies, alleyways, and the domestic. From this point onward comes the production of the spatialisations of the classical polis, which is relativised between the 'civilised' public space of the city-state and the 'barbarian' space beyond. The geocentrism of the classical polis is designated by Lefebvre as *cosmological* space. This rendered the Asian, Greek and Roman cities (concrete expressions of the spatialisation) as *imago mundi*, with particular elements (obelisks) marking their centre of the world and others (Pantheon) representing the forces and gods of the cosmos, which were never banished by secular society. Thus the environment and its forces are reconstructed as a reflection of the competing socio-political forces in the community. This public space is strongly marked as masculine, against the feminine of nature and the home.

> [Lefebvre was] emphatic about the implicit gendering of... [the] 'body' and more circumspect about the seemingly casual sexualisation of its 'promiscuities' and 'penetrations'.... Lefebvre identified from within the genealogy of modernity the immanent production of a supremely abstract, hyper-rationalised space that was fast becoming decorporealised through a tripartite constellation of geometric–visual–phallic power.
>
> (Gregory 1994: 157–8)

However, he does not break with the heterosexual gender assumptions built into his own analytical framework. Blum and Nast brilliantly expose Lefebvre's sexualised notion of space, drawing heavily on Lacan's psychoanalysis of the relationship between patriarchal sexual identities in which the masculine (phallic) is constructed in relation to the maternal and natural. Their seminal article on the topic argues that

> his schema begins with an originary and Edenic maternal space (the natural) to which he seems to want to return.... Second, his framework depends upon a heterosexuality that is fixated in a number of rigid, gendered distinctions... equating the paternal with activity, movement, agency, force, history, while the maternal is passive, immobile, subject of force and history.... Lefebvre's version of heterosexuality turns on an active–passive binary. If activity [labour] is that which materially inscribes the body in history, and only those inscriptions which are coded masculine are considered, feminine bodies necessarily become invisible... 'feminized' sociospatial practices and

struggles are completely ignored. . . . *structurally* female agency is fore-
closed, rendered unrecognizable and made theoretically impossible;
practically such exclusion winds up rejecting everyday forms of
nonmasculinist agency.

(1996: 577)

In a similar vein, Curry has questioned his intellectual style, which covertly
relies on the very spatial order he critiques to ensure that his book is published
and distributed, and that copyright is held. Furthermore his authorial voice
must be granted legitimacy by readers:

> In citing Hegel, Marx and Nietzsche, positively, Descartes and Spinoza
> critically, Lefebvre situates himself in that intellectual space and at the
> same time makes it clear that what he is offering is an analysis of space
> that legitimates the subject through his association with men who are
> of lasting importance. In legitimating the subject, he places himself in a
> space of authority . . . that *is* a hierarchy, which extends beyond the
> realm of 'pure ideas' yet is implicitly expressed in the presentation and
> organization of those ideas.
>
> (Curry 1996: 194)

Historical space

Primitive accumulation, the separation of production from survival and reproduction as labour, lays the groundwork for Lefebvre's third stage, *historical
space*. Lefebvre distinguishes between the spatialisation of the Greek city-states
and that of the empire of the city of Rome. Under the Romans, an increasing
primacy of patriarchy and empire over subterranean powers of desire takes
place. The Christian Middle Ages are seen by Lefebvre as the re-emergence of
these 'cryptic' or subterranean powers. The medieval use of symbolism (vertical
lines, icons) in religious architecture established a connection between the
terrestrial feudal order and its holy origin. In this symbolic space, a new lumi-
nosity and open or public space is noted by Lefebvre. Public spaces and urban
design lead to the increasing objectification of Renaissance perspective, and
finally the reification of capital itself (1972b).
  Renaissance human scale marks for Lefebvre the transition from a sacred to
a secular social order. Humanism as a unifying code allows the organisation of
harmonious built spaces (e.g. Siena). Lefebvre argues that the key form of the
Renaissance is the city, where the revival of Vitruvian architectural categories
goes hand in hand with the perspectival approach: dominance of the visual (*le
perçu*) and the primacy of the façade. Perspective corresponds to a built social
space with room left for citizens' action. In this *perspectival* space the dominant strategy of *abstract space* proper emerges: a three-fold primacy of
geometry (Galileo, Descartes), of the visual, and of the phallic (cf. Lacan; see

Blum and Nast 1996) as the approved mode of expression (through an 'empty' and neutralised space) of power and the state (Lefebvre 1976a: 328–35).

Lefebvre's story is also about vision and the ocularocentrism that emerges with perspective in the Renaissance and comes to dominate and be entrenched in capitalist spatialisations. Even when we recognise that Lefebvre counterposes the integrated, fully lived experience of the body, and that 'the body, at the very heart of space and of the discourse of power, is irreducible and subversive' (Lefebvre 1976e: 89), we generally see the possibilities for transcending and recasting 'the relations between bodies and spatialities within these new configurations' of capital and culture as lying in further visual strategies in which we discover ourselves in the new technologies of visualisation and their strategies, mapping ourselves out on the model of the capitalist domination of urban space: Olalquiaga effuses:

> Bodies are becoming like cities, their temporal coordinates transformed into spatial ones. In a poetic condensation, history has been replaced by geography, stories by maps, memories by scenarios. We no longer perceive ourselves as continuity but as location.... It is no longer possible to be rooting in history. Instead we are connected to the topography of computer screens and video monitors.
>
> (1992: 93; see also Gregory 1994)

Do these really 'give us the language and images that we require to reach others and see ourselves', as she goes on to argue? Gregory argues that Lefebvre urges us to recognise the *corporeality of vision* that, as a dialogical gaze, the line of sight, 'reaches out, *from one body to another*' (Gregory 1994: 416).

Lying alongside this history of vision is a history of the spatial expansion of capitalism. Thus the medieval city is sketched as a commercial city based on the emergence and extension of exchange, progressively incorporated and centralised in the marketplace and customs hall. Commodities and commerce, which are at first liberating operations, only later, in the market and in capitalism, develop their negative consequences. The development of industry and urbanisation, beginning in the fourteenth century, stimulates the growth of the new industrial cities. The proletarianisation of an increasing proportion of the population and the destruction of feudal social relations contribute to a social organisation based on the 'need to work'.

Abstract space

In the context of capitalism, *abstract space* emerges in artistic expression with Picasso (Lefebvre 1991d: 301–4 [1974a: 346–9]), as well as with the modern architects (Gropius, Mies van der Rohe, Le Corbusier, etc.): its distinctive feature is homogeneity and fragmentation at the same time. Lefebvre portrays Haussmann as being the precursor of this spatial practice in which the space of the city is broken, fragmented and segregated (by his street works and boulevards) in order to produce a new unity, order and homogeneity (of state power). Thus there is a unity of the whole despite division of the parts. This new spatialisation is dominated by a fundamentally visual logic, which transforms (1) solids into images and simulations, (2) 'dwelling' into 'habitat' (housing), and (3) finally reduces space to the object of 'planification' (planning and 'urbanism'). Under capitalism, space is pulverised by the social relations of private property; by 'the demand for interchangeable fragments, and the scientific and technical capacity to treat space on ever vaster levels' (Lefebvre 1978b: 289; cited in Gottdiener 1985: 126; see also Lefebvre 1991d: 355).

Modern landed property, by blocking the return to the land, also reproduces wage labourers: 'landed property leads back to wage labour. In one regard, it is nothing more than the extension of wage labour, from the cities to the countryside, i.e. wage labour distributed over the entire surface of the society' (Marx 1973: 277). Indeed, private property, as the form of the insistent cultural connection of one family, one house and one lot, grounds the patriarchal family and structures the practice of dwelling as a family, most recently as a nuclear family, into the *doxos* of capitalism (Ardener 1993). When the stability of our intimate lives is so thoroughly rooted in capitalist practice it was not surprising to Lefebvre that there was little willingness to support initiatives for change among the majority.

The *mythology* of the private 'lot', as he refers to it, stands opposed to not only the 'truth' of the lot itself as a unit of speculation but also to the essential reality of the urban, which is that of the collectivity. Private property forms one of the bedrock elements of the modern spatialisation across divisions of class, ethnicity, age and gender. Only a few religious communes and the remnants of aboriginal cultures begin to mount a challenge. As a spatial element and a clearly demarcated territory, it demonstrates the phenomenon of rendering space tangible and, in particular, visible. This rational and visual bias whereby space is reduced to a void or 'space of possibilities' between boundaries is a clear trend under the regime of abstract space, which Lefebvre analyses at length (1974a: 384ff). The character of the space is implicitly defined as the set of possibilities (enterprises, moods, etc.) allowable or most obviously achieveable within the lot. Limitations are set in turn by the influence of the boundaries or the character of the neighbouring spatial elements: for example, in an area with other single-family dwelling lots all around, any given empty lot tends to take on the definition of those by which it is surrounded.

In *Poverty of Philosophy*, Marx writes 'In each historical epoch, property has developed differently and under a set of entirely different social relations' (see Harvey 1982: 343). In advanced capitalism, if not land owners, all are potential land owners. As a doctrine and a 'representation of space', it allows the grounding of a whole rational, bureaucratic system of spatial definitions: look, you can see it right in your own home! Legal doctrine is mapped onto space, and social codes of propriety are prescribed through zoning laws. At the conceptual–symbolic level, the 'lot' not only grounds the whole realm of 'private property', but also by drawing individuals into the property structure of capital, every person has at least some capital, therefore a vested interest. By implying the homogenisation of space in terms of the dollar value of land, it reflexively conditions other aspects of socio-economic life. Every home owner's plot is a 'space of representation'. It condenses the essence of 'property', of a spatialisation whereby 'space' is abstract, homogeneous and exchangeable, and of social relations at all levels. All the contradictions of an abstract spatialisation can be found in the exemplar of private property, which furnishes a paradigmatic summation.

Contradictory space

Under capitalism, space becomes more and more fragmented. The contradictory process of centralisation/peripheralisation exemplified in planning practice since Haussmann leads to a progressive *urbanisation* (note that Lefebvre is substantially redrawing the semantic field of this term, as is his common practice) of society whereby all persons are drawn into a *gesselschaft*-type web of rationalised social relations of production and consumption. The increasing centralisation of power within the city (the 'headquarters function') occurs: that is, the 'centralisation of decision making power which extends its arms over all social space' (Martins 1982: 171). Simultaneously, a *ruralisation* of the privileged form of the 'urban', the city, takes place. In this counter-flow, the 'urban' is segregated into hierarchised and isolated social ghettos. Physically, the city morphology is redrawn in a series of suburban expansions.

> Social space became a *collection of ghettos*: those of the elite, of the bourgeoisie, of the intellectuals, of the immigrant workers, etc. These ghettos are not juxtaposed, they are hierarchical, spatially representing the economic and social hierarchy, dominant and subordinated sectors.
>
> (Lefebvre 1978b: 309–310)

This is a dispersal of people to urban peripheries and their segregation within a 'complex hierarchisation of residential and non-residential estates' (Martins 1982: 171, note that Lefebvre's *'ensembles urbaines'* is here translated in the British custom as 'estate').

> Cities are transformed into a collection of ghettos where individuals are at once 'socialised', integrated, submitted to artificial pressures and constraints . . . and separated, isolated, disintegrated. A contradiction which is translated into anguish, frustration and revolt.
>
> (Lefebvre 1972b: 168)

178

In the present situation of a dominant capitalism that aims to absorb all non-capitalist relations of production, the extension of capitalist relations beyond the places of work to every moment and site of daily life makes the city the preferential place for the realisation of surplus value through consumption. Lefebvre argues that the extension of capitalism could not be achieved within industrial premises alone or through the simple reproduction of the *potential* labour force through consumption; it requires the occupation and administration of the whole of social space. This involves:

1   the marginalisation of all non-capitalist spaces and activities (not necessarily their destruction but through imposed transformations, which create contradictions on the level of the articulation of that 'space' with the social totality);
2   the organisation of private and public consumption by means of advertising and state bureaucracy; and
3   the extension of capitalist relations to the non-productive, cultural sectors of leisure such as the arts, information and architecture by the instigation of conditions of lack and their submission to profit rule of supply–demand.

The state plays an important role, as Deleuze and Guattari (1972) hypothesised, in that the deterritorialisation of capital is countered by the reterritorialising impulse of social actors, production and commodity flows by the state.

> At the heart of *Kapital*, Marx points to the encounter of . . . the one side, the deterritorialised worker who has become free and naked, having to sell his labour capacity; and on the other, decoded money that has become capital and is capable of buying it. . . . For the free worker: the deterritorialisation of the soil through privatisation.
>
> (Levebvre 1976a: 222–4)

As Martins summarises:

> Together these processes created a new relation between space and social relations. Space was no longer the mere territorialisation of social relations nor an instrument for their organisation. Space as a whole became both a product and an instrument for the reproduction of the relations of production.
>
> (1982: 170)

In this process, production-side contradictions between capital and labour and consumption-side contradictions between use and exchange values are all encompassed within contradictions 'inherent to the reproduction of the relations of production transformed as "contradictions of space"' (Lefebvre 1972). This abstract spatialisation functions on sets of dichotomies, including the split of subject and object, and the development of dominant centres and dominated peripheries. Along with dichotomies, a whole series of contradictions tear this spatialisation asunder. In its advanced stage, then, abstract space becomes something qualitatively more polarised: *contradictory space*.

Fredric Jameson, a key mediator of Lefebvre's work on space into North America, once summed up the principal contradictions of this contemporary form of abstract space in the following fashion:

1   *Quantity versus quality*: The repression of quality, which re-emerges as 'leisure': 'from the space of consumption to the consumption of space in leisure and leisure space, or: from everyday life to the extraordinary by way of the festival . . . from work to non-work' (Lefebvre 1974a: 409; cf. 1991d: 353).
2   *Global versus local*: The contrast of a global spatial practice and system under multinational capitalism and the 'myth' of the parcel, lot and smallest commercial units of space, which is the lived reality for most. Abstract space is both of these at once without any possibility of synthesis.
3   *Use value versus exchange value*: As in Marx's formulation, the use value of land is transformed into the homogeneous exchange value of real estate. At the grand level of the spatialisation, *oeuvres* are transformed into products: mere opportunities for enterprise. Where this is not possible, they are transformed into images of themselves either through their literal reproduction (Disneyland reproduces fragments of various 'cities' and 'countries', providing living stereotypes) or through the operation of photography, which transfers the landscape to countless tourist postcards (see Baudrillard 1983).

These contradictions are discernible at all levels from the empirical of daily life all the way through to the political, aesthetic and theoretical (e.g. the way in which the production of the architect is already ideologically limited in advance by essentially visual, reductive procedures (Lefebvre 1991d: 361–2 [1974a: 416–419]) – in other words, the impoverishing influence on buildings by their initial conception in the form of the 'project' or sketched outline.

> Space . . . is treated in such a way as to render it homogeneous, its parts comparable, therefore exchangeable. . . . The subordination of space to money and capital implies a quantification which extends from the monetary evaluation to the commercialisation of each plot of the entire space. . . . Space now becomes one of the new 'scarcities', together with its resources, water, air, and even light.
>
> (Lefebvre 1970b: 261–2)

The paradox of abstract, contradictory space is that it produces ever fresh contradictions even while flattening or occulting them: city planning is universally recognised as a disaster, yet it has succeeded in effectively silencing those who suffer from it the most. Abstract space involves the repression of the lived and qualitative experience of space by abstract and dehumanised 'planned space' and homogenisation (1974a: 61). This is also therefore a repressive space. The operation of the 'space of representation' encompassing the ritual, the sensual and the sexual is repressed under the rule of the phallocentric and visual (*le perçu*). The sensual is reduced to the 'unconscious' and the sexual to what he terms the 'genital', an anti-erotic and mother–father–child family under the spell of fertility. Compared with the rest of the economy, this heterosexual production unit is marginalised in the domestic apartment 'cell' (1991d: 49 [1974a: 60–1]). Against the psychoanalytic reduction of the body to the symbolic and the reduction of identity into language, Lefebvre argues that we bodily and spatially exceed our own representations and images. Referring to Irigaray (1993), Grosz (1994) and Butler (1993), Blum and Nast add:

> [we] continually exceed the disciplining patriarchal codes of contemporary social orders. As many have written, there are significations and valorizations of female bodies that disobey, resist and overcome their dominant coding as 'lack', thereby undoing one of Lefebvre's underpinning and naturalised dualisms.
>
> (1996: 578)

They ask, how does this excess pervade all sexualities to the point that Lefebvre's categories become problematic themselves? Nonetheless, they find his work path-breaking because, even in the mid-1970s, he charts

> the changing ways in which constructions of the maternal and paternal have been paradigmatically extended across politics and 'space'. Second he exposes the bourgeois origins of Lacan's mirror-stage and the spatial privilege and violence subtending the pivotal role of the phallus in the conception of sexual identity and agency in patriarchal capitalism.
>
> (Blum and Nast 1996: 577)

He denounces Lacan's founding of social identity not in labour or action but in the acquisition of language and sexual prohibitions such as the incest taboo and the bar against sexual desire for the mother, such that 'her sex and her blood, are relegated to the realm of the cursed and the sacred – along with sexual pleasure [undifferentiated from the satisfaction of others' needs and desires for the infant], which is thus rendered both fascinating and inaccessible' (1991d: 35–6). Law comes to dominate over spirit; language dominates over the body (Blum and Nast 1996: 562).

In contradictory space, a series of other reductions turn history into theme

181

park nostalgia, created works (*oeuvres*) into ever more grandiosely advertised but disappointing commodities, originals into images, and people into workers. A spatialisation harmonises all these aspects together and blunts contradictions:

> Neither capitalism nor the state can maintain the chaotic, contradictory space they have produced. We witness at all levels, this explosion of space. At the level of the immediate and the lived, space is exploding on all sides, whether this be living space, personal space, scholastic space, prison space, army space, or hospital space. Everywhere, people are realising that spatial relations are also social relations. At the level of cities, we see not only the explosion of the historical city but also that of all the administrative frameworks in which they had wanted to enclose the urban phenomenon. At the level of regions, the peripheries are fighting for their autonomy or for a certain degree of independence. . . . Finally at the international level, not only the actions of the so-called supranational companies, but also those of the great world strategies, prepare for and render inevitable new explosions of space.
>
> (Lefebvre 1978b: 290)

It is precisely the interdependence of these spaces that is the essence of the current spatialisation. This idea becomes a key theme in Jameson's vision of a 'global spatialisation' (1984). Saunders (1981: 157) commented that the effect of the progressive extension of the capitalist production of space is to concentrate the decision-making centre while creating dependent colonies on the periphery: 'around the centres there are nothing but subjugated, exploited and dependent spaces: new colonial space' (Lefebvre 1976e: 85). While capitalism is consolidated and maintained through the production of differential spaces, and 'if space as a whole has become the place where reproduction of the relations of production is located, it has also become the terrain for a vast confrontation' (1967e: 85) between centres and peripheries, the displaced proletariat and the over-centred bourgeoisie. As Deleuze and Guattari add:

> The process of de-territorialisation here goes from the centre to the periphery, that is, from the developed countries to the underdeveloped countries, which do not constitute a separate world, but rather an essential component of the world-wide capitalist machine. It must be added, however, that the centre itself has its organised enclaves of underdevelopment, its reservations and its ghettos as interior peripheries.
>
> (1976: 231)

In summarising the critical response to Lefebvre, Soja notes that the difficulties encountered by materialist analysts, particularly orthodox Marxists, centre around the fact that Lefebvre appears to be substituting 'spatial/territorial conflict for class conflict as the motivating force behind radical social transformation' (1980: 208).

Lefebvre was recognised as having dealt brilliantly and insightfully with the organisation of space as a material product, with the relationship between the social and spatial structures of urbanism, and with the ideological content of socially created space. But surely Lefebvre had gone too far? He had raised the urban spatial 'problematic' to an intolerably central and autonomous position (Soja 1980: 207).

Beyond history to a differential space

Lefebvre's project of historical periods, the accuracy of his dating of changes and his ignorance of the conditions and spatialisation of most of the world detracts from his credibility and distracts from his overall message. However, his project returns to relevance when he takes aim at the future, proposing the possibility of generating a new spatialisation – a more equitable world – out of the contradictions of contemporary spaces and relations of globalisation.

The criteria for a positive development here will have to fulfil all Lefebvre's proposals covered in earlier chapters – escaping from a 'mystified' consciousness; decreasing alienation; acknowledging the importance of *oeuvres*, of the ethics of 'adventure' so as to promote the possibility of people realising and empowering themselves as 'total persons'. What would be an example of this? The reawakening of a 'politics of difference' (as opposed to the tendency of homogenisation), in which the rich creativity of the excluded can be developed into a concrete alternative to the present spatial system. Lefebvre detected this in his Latin American travels and stays in the slums and *favellas* of Brazil, which appeared to be moments in which alternative local spatialisations were brought into existence. Was he a naive romantic? The social question of the complicitous silence of the inhabitants of everyday spaces becomes the political question of how, rather than squandering their energies cruising along the predictable and neatly incised channels of the spatialisation like the surface of Mars, people can be directed to act along the fractures that deeply score the unstable 'surface' of the present spatialisation. How can this homogenising 'contradictory space' become a *differential space* that particularises and humanises?

Against conflict approaches, which begin with the assumption of the primacy of conflict in the relations between economic groups as the basis for the study of society, Lefebvre's formulation poses the disturbing question of people's cooperation, docility and complicitous self-implication in systems of inequality. Orthodox Marxism had little basis for a response to such issues, except for the weak theory of 'false consciousness'. In answer to these issues, the spatial problematic draws attention to the symbolic and distorted forms of resistance practised *through* the spatialisation itself: eruptions of instability through the carefully spread net of the Cartesian three-dimensional grid of rational and homogeneous modernity (for example, the riotous mini rebellions that quickly dissipate in public areas planned for riot control). *Space* itself becomes at once the medium of compliance and resistance. In *Urban Revolution*, he argues:

> Capitalism has not just integrated existing space, it has extended itself into completely new sectors. Leisure is becoming an industry of prime importance. We have conquered for leisure the sea, mountains and even deserts. The leisure industry and the construction industry have combined to extend the towns and urbanisation along coastlines and in mountain regions . . . this industry extends over all space not already occupied.
>
> (Lefebvre 1970a: 265)

Rational capitalism produces rationalised 'spaces of production' under the aegis of the nation-state, but the repression of desire that this involves leads the production of 'spaces of leisure' (free zones of escape, denial, resistance through folly and unproductiveness). The importance of desire and 'jouissance', or play, to capitalism makes Lefebvre suspicious of postmodern theories, such as those of Deleuze and Guattari (1976), who argue that desire is the ultimate driving force behind history, progress and social interaction – a 'libidinal economy' that is the foundation for any political economy. However, he does recognise the importance of the libidinal: these are also the 'counter-spaces' of festival, adventure and the potential space of the carnivalesque inversions of the social order (the unleashing of libidinal intensities) and thus revolt (liminality) against the normative order (1991d: 54ff [1974a: 66ff]). The eruptions of the libidinal in rioting, looting, over-consumption and extreme forms of adventure are the mark of a differential space exploding through the repressive system of a contradictory spatialisation.

Lefebvre's insights grew out of his experiences with the Surrealists and also with the Situationists, who much earlier had launched a project to map the potential of urban areas as sites that would support the unleashing of various forms of desire, liminality and emotion. One example of the *Situationnistes'* urban project is Abdelhafid Khatib's psycho-geographic report on Les Halles, the central market of Paris – now a garden and subterranean mall complex combining municipal services, libraries, shops and the largest metro/train station in Europe. The focus was to be exploration and *dérive* at night (the market was most active after 3am). These ideas – psycho-geography and *dérive* – were derived from the Copenhagen–Brussels–Amsterdam ('CoBrA') group of architects. *Dérive*, or drifting, was a matter of wandering about aimlessly to see where one would end up and what surprises one might discover, rather than purposefully traversing the city to a predetermined destination. The task was rendered impossible for Khatib because Algerians were subject to a curfew. After twice being arrested, he submitted an incomplete report and was excluded.

All sorts of tendencies to a counter-space are at work around us, with all

184

their ambiguities. Of these, the most striking are leisure sites, which represent the ultimate commodification of nature and of space, but which are also the moment of non-work, or jouissance, and festival, which negates the entire dominant spatialisation and social system. For Lefebvre, as for many of the French authors marked by the experience of May 1968, that 'celebration' and ludic 'eruption' of intensity and desire marks the type of rupture that could convert a dominated 'leisure spatialisation' into focused resistance and revolt through a sudden respatialisation. Hence the Situationist slogans invented in the mid-1960s tended to concern respatialisation: 'Think globally, act locally'.

A new vision of the city of the future – not as commemorating a nostalgic urban past or celebrating a technological utopia – is necessary in which the city is recognised as the site of exchange, *par excellence*, of festival and ludic centrality (the domain of the 'carnivalesque'); and as the ephemeral reflection of the social spatialisation: the constantly rebuilt and reappropriated. The city must be the spatial *form* of full exchange and of assembly.

At the level of the body, Lefebvre's analysis is even more trenchant. He provides a blueprint for the alignment of a radical otherness within a spatial dialectic of the body. His use of inherited notions of male–female heterosexual identity in which the female is a negation of masculine activity presents a parodic and non-dialectical affirmation (male) and negation (female). Blum and Nast argue that this 'negation sustaining contemporary forms of heterosexuality can be resisted'. How? They do not formulate this completely in dialectical terms but say: 'even granting that a negation-dependent form (A / not-A) of heterosexuality is dominant in Western cultural contexts, it is always exceeded. . . . lesbians, to varying degrees, have worked to wrest a positive sexuality from *double negation* (not-A / *not-A*) in the process forging possibilities for nonphallic economics of desire' (1996: 578). This excess, the positive element of the double negation, is the third element, that 'negation of the negation' of the spatialised, three-part dialectic that Lefebvre sketches out: it is the third term that relativises the all-inclusiveness of the simple dualism of affirmation and negation.

11

CONCLUSION

The ramparts of the town enclose no secure palace, no fortress. Even so, as everywhere, a few secrets. . . . These ramparts could stop no invader. Invaded themselves by weeks which have transformed them into walks, they are hardly frequented except by birds, children and lovers. In many places, laundry is hung out to dry. Its fortified city, one of the most ancient of France, in the confines of Bearn and the Basque country, is the refuge of Henri Lefebvre . . . retired from the world but listening to its heartbeat and rumours, attentive to its humours, its troubles and to its possibilities.

> Latour and Combes 1991: 15; see also Lefebvre 1991c)

The span of Lefebvre's work crisscrosses the terrain of twentieth-century intellectual concerns. His early works were prescient, foreshadowing changes to come in philosophy and its relation to the body, to politics, and to the progressive social sciences. His later works, published in the 1940s and 1950s, are 'crossroads in the reorganization of the intellectual field of the second half of the twentieth century.' In his most eloquent and creative period, in the 1960s and 1970s, he transfigures Marxism, nurtures a corporeal, material approach to everyday life and capitalism and projects the dialectic into areas we only now, at the end of the century, begin to grasp. His final, shorter pieces, published during the 1980s, are reminders, pointed aphorisms whose well-placed character hints at his ongoing engagement with utopian social projects.

This range and the lack of translations of the earlier works make it difficult to place Lefebvre's theoretical terms in their proper contexts. It is thus difficult to discern the contours of his conceptual apparatus. The defining axes of his unorthodox but unwavering Marxism have been argued to be, first, his university training in philosophy and Catholic theology; second, his formative experiences with Surrealism and Dada, which highlighted the importance of authentic, 'fully lived' experience; third, pioneering translation work with Norbert Guterman of the works of the young Marx on alienation and dialectical materialism; fourth, the post-First World War malaise and banality of everyday life; fifth, his exclusion from the Parti Communiste Français and his embrace of the more radical, populist position of the Situationists; sixth, the turn to the urban and the spatial as a strategic response to the stalemate of Communism and Capitalism in 1970s France. Using the three terms of Joachim de Flore's trinity: Lefebvre was interested in the commonsensical perceptions and routines of everyday, banal *life*. Always attracted to the popular and marginal, he nonetheless adhered to the rigorous framework of dialectical materialism, the defining method and *law* of his works. With this, he did not pursue legalistic definitions against the lived world of embodied practice; instead, he sought to extract or let out the moments of spirit – those points of rupture within the repetition of everyday life that could arrest time, link the local and microscopic with cosmic themes and throw this vision of totality back against the limited world view of capitalist duties and fetters.

We can define three key contributions that have radicalised the Marxist agenda over the course of the century: first, the stress on a thoroughgoing dialectical spirit against any and all dogmatism and party discipline mark Lefebvre as a patron saint of the independent Left. His focus on alienation as the motivating insight of Marx presents us, in the ruins of most movements toward a political utopia, with a reinvigorated sense of the costs and losses associated with the globalisation of technocratic 'progress'. Lefebvre contrasts the banality of the everyday with the potential for peak experiences embedded within it. This leaves us with a nascent humanism to assert against the technological reworking of the body and mind, and the standardisation of outlook, vision and dreams that goes along with it.

In a sense, one might describe this Marxism, again, as less political and more ethical: it is closer in spirit to grassroots disenchantment and to issue- and identity-oriented social movements. Its 'tools', so to speak, are tailored to the needs and resources of local, independent, actors and networks. This is true even where he failed to follow through on each and every insight.

A spatialisation of the dialectic moves geography into the centre of critical theory and yokes historicity and spatiality together. But more fundamentally, the spatialised, open dialectic that has been discovered in Lefebvre's work opens the possibility of reintegrating the disparate, progressive movements. By opening the position of the negation of the negation as the place of alterity itself, otherness is brought into the dialectical schema without being reduced to the logic of the 'other' as merely a straightforward 'negation' of self, of thesis – of affirmation. As such we can grasp *through* Lefebvre a legacy that lies beyond even his own accomplishments. We might attribute this to the dialectical style of his texts – to their excess – to the way in which they continue to ask pertinent questions that rise above even his answers. For example, as Blum and Nast comment:

> Because transcending masculinist capitalism is central to Lefebvre's project, it is crucial to take note of the blind spots and impasses that have led him to complicity with that which he otherwise repudiates.

Given the widespread influence of his work, we must be wary of inad-
vertently appropriating aspects of Lefebvre's study that might thwart
rather than stimulate liberatory initiative.

(1996: 577)

The spatialised, or *cubic*, *dialectic* is the most fundamental shift that is associated with Lefebvre's general turn to space. This included his interest in the
changing historical geography of capitalism and the globalisation of socio-
economic relations. It must not be forgotten, however, that this was also a turn
to rhythm and to space–time. Beyond *The Production of Space* stretched a
decade and a half of further publishing, including his posthumous book
Rhythmanalyse (Lefebvre and Régulier-Lefebvre 1992a).

While mapping out the intellectual terrain of Lefebvre's work, I have
attempted to avoid imposing administrative boundaries – Lefebvre's sociology
versus Lefebvre's geography versus his own puckish spirit and life story. I have
noted the highs and lows, however. It is out of respect that we respond to
Lefebvre's own critical spirit with an assessment of both successes and failures.

The claim made for Lefebvre's significance in the opening chapter was that
he was more than an eyewitness of events or a participant in a series of
European avant-garde political movements. He was a conducting wire of ideas
and accumulated experience from generation to generation of that avant-garde.
His ideas electrified not one generation but a century on the Left, and they
found their mark not just in France – or even in Europe – but also left a mark in
distant communities, *barrios*, struggles and debates, most notably in the
Americas. Even where he is not quoted directly, fading from memory, he introduces a coherence and radicality to utopian humanism that directs it not only
against alienating 'societies of bureaucratic consumption' but also against the
technocratic foot soldiers who administer oppressive apparatuses over the landless poor, the wage slave and the environmentally poisoned.

The challenge to this humanism most poignantly lies at the interface
between popular movements and the machinations of global capital and international systems of economic sovereignty. This interface is not only the visible
police cordon that confronts demonstrators protesting against the denial of
human rights by states invited to our own countries to receive lucrative trade
subsidies. It is also that fissure between a vision of the world that sees citizenship rights as fundamental to all liberties, including economic freedom. This
line is also the audible gulf between discourses, a gulf that must be crossed by
re-coding demands from popular into technical and legal jargon. It is true that
aspirations and campaigns are often blunted at this wall. However, the borderline does not thereby vanish. It represents both a barrier to aspirations and,
crucially, the limit condition of the otherwise unbridled development of technocratic capitalism. This border reappears in campaigns for a landmine treaty, in
campaigns against environmental exploitation, in the unnecessary slaughter of
species, and in the battles of Guatemalan and Mexican peasants in Chiapas

against the reinforcement of the owners of land and capital under the North American Free Trade Agreement. In all of these, what Lefebvre called 'the impossible–possible' confronts a complacent defence of the necessity of the status quo. Lefebvre's contribution is to strengthen our faith in our own intuitive and collective experiences and our knowledge of the good and the ethical.

BIBLIOGRAPHY OF HENRI
LEFEBVRE'S WORKS

Texts are entered chronologically under their original French titles, with the exception of recent editions in French or available English translations, which are listed separately by date of publication and cross-referenced to the French original. Information on translations into other languages and other comments are given in parentheses following the standard bibliographical information, and the occasional omission of page numbers and other publication information reflects the limitations of access to private editions or the lack of indexing for the interwar period. The considerable disagreements between previous bibliographical listings of Lefebvre's work have been settled by examining the original publications. Where necessary, notes have been added to point out binding problems or the unusual numbering of journal issues.

† Denotes works referenced in other sources but not found.

n.d. 'Schema sur l'irrationalisme français'. Typescript. Mid-1930s book proposal. Copy held in the Guterman Collection, Butler Library, Columbia Library. 8pp.

1924a. 'Fragments d'une philosophie de la conscience'. *Philosophies* 4, pp.241ff.

1924b. 'Lesvignes: Odor di femina'. *Philosophies* 2 (May), p.224.

1924c. 'Sur une note de M. Ramon Fernadez *Les intermittences du coeur*'. *Philosophies* 2 (May), pp.225–7.

1924d. 'Une tentative métaphysique. La thèse de M. Lavelle'. *Philosophies* 3 (September). pp.241ff.

1924e. 'Incidences (André Gide)'. *Philosophies* 3 (September). p.334.

1924f. 'Critique de la qualité et de l'être: Fragment d'une philosophie de la conscience' *Philosophies* 4 (November), pp.414–21.

1924g. '7 manifestes dada (Tristan Tzara)'. *Philosophies* 3–4 (November), 443ff.

1925a. 'Positions d'attaque et de défense du nouveau mysticisme'. *Philosophies* 5–6 (March), 471–506. (Part 2 of the 'Philosophy of Consciousness' project on being, consciousness and identity originally proposed as a thesis topic to Leon Brunschvicq.)

1925b. 'Déclaration des droits de l'esprit'. Paper presented to the Société des Amis de la Sorbonne; original ms. destroyed. (See *Annales de la Société des Amis de la Sorbonne* 1. See Lefebvre 1959i: I, 299; II, 387; see also 1989a.)

1926a. 'La pensée et l'esprit'. *L'Esprit* 1 (May), 21–69ff.

1926b. 'Le même et l'autre: Introduction', G. Politzer (trans.). Schelling 1926, *Recherches philosophiques sur l'essence de la liberté humaine et sur les problèmes qui s'y rattachent*. pp.1–39.

1926c. 'Description de ces temps. Misère de M. Jacques Maritain'. *L'Esprit* 1 (May), pp.258–71.

1927a. 'Notes pour le procès de la chrétiennité'. *L'Esprit* 2, 121–38ff. (Philosophy. Written between the summer of 1925 and the spring of 1926 as a critique of Jean Wahl.)

1927b. 'Reconnaissance de l'unique'. *L'Esprit* 2 (May), pp.5–37.

1929. 'Verdun, par le maréchal Pétain'. *La Revue marxiste* 6 (July), 719–20.

1931. (unpublished) 'Critique de la philosophie'. Proposed publisher: Editions Reider. (Manuscript destroyed by Parti Communiste Français censor.)

1932. Cahier de Revendications 'Du Culte' L'Esprit au matérialisme dialectique. *Nouvelle Revue Française* 231 (December), pp.803–5.

1933a. 'Le fascisme en France: aperçus généraux'. *Avant Poste* 1 or 2 (June), pp.68–71.

1933b. 'P. Allard: Les Dessous de la guerre'. *Avant Poste* 1 (June).

1933c. 'A. Breton: Les Vases communicant'. *Avant Poste* 1 (June).

1933d. 'A propose du livre de L.-F. Céline'. *Avant Poste* 1 (June).

1933e. 'V. Serge: Ville conquise'. *Avant Poste* 1 (June).

1933f. 'M. de Unamuno: Avant et après la révolution'. *Avant Poste* 1 (June).

1933g. (with Norbert Guterman) 'Individu et classe'. *Avant Poste* 1 (June), pp.1ff.

1933h. 'R. Martin du Gard: Vieille France'. *Avant Poste* 1 (June).

1933i. 'Echanges de lettres, L.-F. Céline, H. Lefebvre'. *Avant Poste* 2 (August), p.143.

1933j. 'Autocritique'. *Avant Poste* 2 (August), pp.142ff.

1933k. 'G. Giono: Serpent d'Étoiles'. *Avant Poste* 2 (August).

1933l. 'Les Jeux de l'amour et de la politique'. *Avant Poste* 2 (August).

1933m. 'R. Trintzius: Fin et commencement'. *Avant Poste* 2 (August).

1933n. (with Norbert Guterman) 'La mystification. Notes pour une critique de la vie quotidienne'. *Avant Poste* 2 (August), pp.91ff.

1933o. 'Lettre d'un jeune à la jeunesse'. *Avant Poste* 3 (October/November), pp.183ff.

1933p. (with Norbert Guterman) 'Journal d'un Aryen'. *Avant Poste* 3 (October/November), pp.165ff.

1933q. 'Le Karl Marx de Otto Rülhe'. *Avant Poste* 3 (October/November), 199ff.

1933r. 'B. Mussolini: Le Fascisme'. *Avant Poste* 3 (October/November).

1933s. 'La Revue *Esprit*'. *Avant Poste* 3 (October/November), p.202–3.

1933t. 'G. Suarez: Les Hommes malades de la paix'. *Avant Poste* 3 (October/November).

1933u. L. Lorwin: L'Internationalisme et la classe ouvrière'. *Avant Poste* 3 (October/November).

1933v. (with Norbert Guterman: signed L., G.J.) 'E.H. Lavine: Le Troisième degré méthodes de la police américaine'. *Avant Poste* 2 (August).

1934a. 'Madame 60 bis par Henriette Valet' *Nouvelle Revue Française* 43: 225 (December), pp.921–3.

1934b. (with Norbert Guterman) *Morceaux choisis de Karl Marx* Paris: NRF (numerous reprintings).

1935a. 'Qu'est-ce que la Dialectique?' Part 1. *Nouvelle Revue Française* 45: 264 (September), pp.351–64.

1935b. 'Qu'est-ce que la Dialectique?' Part 2. *Nouvelle Revue Française* 45: 265 (October), pp.527–39.

1935c. 'People's Front in France'. *New Republic* 84: 1088 (9 October), pp.235–7.

1935d. 'On ne m'a pas demandé d'y collaborer'. *Vendredi* (6 October).

1936a. (with Norbert Guterman) *La Conscience mystifiée*. Paris: Gallimard (new edition, Paris: Le Sycomore, 1979).

1936b. 'Anarchie ou Hiérarchie par S. de Madariaga'. *Nouvelle Revue Française* 47: 274 (July), p.241.

1936c. 'Crise du Progrès par Georges Friedmann'. *Nouvelle Revue Française* 47: 275 (August). pp.382–4.

1936d. 'France decides Europe's Fate'. *New Republic* 86: 1116 (22 April), pp.306–8.

1936e. '*Dirigeants de l'Europe* par E. Ludwig et *Pilotes de l'Europe par J. Gunther*'. *Commune* 4: 40 (December), pp.486–8.

1937a. *Le nationalisme contre les nations* (preface by Paul Nizan). Paris: Editions sociales internationales (reprinted, Paris: Méridiens-Klincksieck 1988, Collection *Analyse institutionnelle*, 'Présentation' M. Trebitsch, 'Postface' Henri Lefebvre).

1937b. (with Norbert Guterman) 'Le problème de la conscience'. *Europe – revue mensuelle* 175 (July), pp.384–405 (extract from 1938a; also published as 1937h).

1937c. 'Essai sur les rapports de la critique et du roman'. *Commune* 4: 48 (August), pp.1472–83.

1937d. 'V. Jankélévitch: l'ironie'. *Europe – revue mensuelle* 177 (September), pp.134–5.

1937e. 'Nizan: Les matérialistes de l'antiquité; Friedmann: La Crise du Progrès; Luppol: Diderot'. *Zeitschrift für Sozialforschung* Bd 6, pp.667–8.

1937f. 'Lettres de Lénine à sa famille trad. par Morhange et Matveev'. *Europe – revue mensuelle* 177 (September), p.138.

1937g. 'Affair of the Hooded Men'. *New Republic* 93: 1202 (15 December), pp.162–4.

1937h. 'Le Problème de la conscience'. In M. LeRoy *et al.* (eds) *Descartes* Paris: Rieder (extract from 1938a; also published as 1937b).

1938a. (with Norbert Guterman) *Cahiers de Lénine sur la dialectique de Hegel*. Paris: Gallimard (new edition, Collection *Idées*, 1967. Spanish trans., Mexico: Editorial America, 1939. Introduction written in 1935 to this first translation of Lenin's 1914–15 notebooks into a Western European language).

1938b. (with Norbert Guterman) *Morceaux choisis de Hegel* Paris: Gallimard (three reprints 1938–39; reprinted as Collection *Idées*, two volumes, 1969).

1938c. *Hitler au pouvoir, bilan de cinq années de fascisme en Allemagne*. Paris: Bureau d'éditions (reprinted with an introduction by Michel Trebitsch and postface by Henri Lefebvre, Paris: Méridens Klincksieck, 1988).

1938d. 'Watch France!' *New Republic* 97: 1256 (28 December), p.226.

1939a. *Nietzsche*. Paris: Editions sociales internationales.

1939b. *Le Matérialisme dialectique* Paris: Alcan (edition destroyed in 1940. Numerous reprints: Presses Universitaires de France, beginning in 1947; 5th edition with new foreword, 1961; 7th edition, 1974, Collection *Nouvelle encyclopédie philosophique*; Collection de Poche, 1977; new edition, 1990; German trans., Frankfurt: Suhrkamp Verlag, 1964; English trans. by John Sturrock, London: Jonathan Cape (see 1968l); New York: Grossman, 1973; Spanish trans., Buenos Aires: Argonauta, 1948; Buenos Aires: Siglo XX, 1969; Italian trans., Turin: Einaudi, 1949; Japanese trans., Tokyo: Kisetsu-sha, 1971; Dutch trans., Meppel: Boom Pers, 1972; Portuguese trans., Lisbon: Panorama, 1972).

1939c. 'Nietzsche et le fascisme hitlerien'. *Commune* 7: 66 (February), pp.229–34.

1939d. 'Stendhal et le problème moderne de l'individu'. *Commune* 7: 69 (May), 567–71.

1939e. 'Le Temps des dupes'. *Les Volontaires* (June/July).

1940. *A la Lumière du matérialisme dialectique II: Méthodologie des sciences* Paris: Editions Sociales. (Complete print run destroyed by publisher on orders of Parti Communiste Français censors. Mimeo copy held by author. Copy on file: MacOdrum Library, Rare Books Collection, Carleton University, Ottawa.]

1943–45. Various anonymous articles and notes for the Parti Communiste Français newspaper *Patriote.*

1944. 'Georges Politzer' *La Pensée* New Series 1 (October/November/December), pp.7–10.

1945. 'Existentialisme et marxisme: réponse à une mise au point'. *Action* 40 (8 June), 5–8. (Response to Sartre (1944) 'A propos de l'existentialisme, mise au point' *Action* 12 (17 December).)

1946. *L'Existentialisme.* Paris: Editions du Sagittaire.

1947a. *Critique de la vie quotidienne, I: Introduction.* Paris: Grasset (2nd edition with new foreword, Paris: L'Arche, 1958; Japanese trans., Tokyo: Gendai Shicho-Sha, 1968; German trans., Munich: Carl Hanser, 1974; Italian trans., Milan: Dedalo, 1977; English trans., London: Verso 1991 – see 1991a). (Part I of an occasional series; see 1961j, 1981a, 1991a).

1947b. *Marx et la liberté.* Geneva: Edition des Trois Collines.

1947c. *Descartes.* Paris: Editions d'Hier et Aujourd'hui.

1947d. *Logique formelle, logique dialectique*, Vol. 1 of *A la lumière du matérialisme dialectique* (written in 1940–41; Vol. 2 censored – see 1940, Paris: Editions sociales. 2nd edition with preface, Paris, 1969; 3rd edition, Paris: Messidor–Editions sociales, 1982; Spanish trans., Ediciones 62, 1970; Italian trans., Moizzi, 1975; Japanese trans., Tokyo: Godo-Shuppan-Sha, 1971; Portuguese trans., Civilizaçiao Brasileira, 1973).

1948a. 'La pensée militaire et la vie nationals'. *La Pensée* 17, pp.39ff.

1948b. 'Introduction à l'esthétique, Part I'. *Arts de France* 19–20, pp.42ff.

1948c. 'Le Don Juan du Nord'. *Europe – revue mensuelle* 28 April, 73–104.

1948d. 'La crise du capitalisme français'. *La Pensée* 17 (March/April), 39–50.

1948e. 'Marxisme et sociologie'. *Cahiers internationaux de sociologie* 4, 48–74.

1948f. *Le Marxisme.* Paris: Presses Universitaires de France, Collection *Que sais-je?* (over 20 reprints. Albanian trans., Rilindja, 1977; German trans., Beck, 1975; Arabic trans., Arabes, 1973; Korean trans., Seoul: Tambu-dang, 1987; Danish trans., Copenhagen: Andersen, 1973; Spanish trans., Buenos Aires: Universitaria, 1961; Greek trans., Zacharopoulos, 1960; Indonesian trans., Jakarta, 1953; Japanese trans., Tokyo: Hakusul-Sha 1962; Italian trans., Garzanti, 1960; Dutch trans., Amsterdam: Arbelderspers, 1969; Portuguese trans., São Paulo: Difel, 1958, Lisbon: Bertrand, 1975; Serbo-Croat trans., Belgrade: Bigz, 1975; Swedish trans., Stockholm: Cavefors, 1971; Turkish trans., Istanbul: Gelisim, 1977).

1948g. *Pour connaître la pensée de Karl Marx,* Evreux: Le Cercle du bibliophile Paris: Bordas (some catalogues list this as a revised version of a pamphlet circulated in 1946 as *Marx;* 2nd edition, 1956, with preface, April 1955; 3rd edition, published as *Karl Marx* 1985 with preface, index and bibliography; Catalan trans., Barcelona: Hogar del

Libro, 1982; Portuguese trans., Edicoes 70, 1975; Japanese trans., Tokyo: Minerva-Shobo, 1970).

1948h. 'Introduction à l'esthétique, Part II'. *Arts de France* 21–2, pp.54ff.

1949a. 'L'homme des révolutions politiques et sociales'. In *Pour un nouvel humanisme, Rencontres internationales de Genève*. Neuchâtel: Éditions de la Braconnière pp. 115–35.

1949b. 'Staline et la nation, Part 1'. *La Nouvelle Critique* 11 (December), pp.18–32 (see Part 2: 1950d).

1949c. 'Problèmes de sociologie rurale, la Communauté paysanne et ses problèmes historico-sociologiques'. *Cahiers internationaux de sociologie*, VI, pp.78–100.

1949d. *Diderot*. Paris: Les Editeurs français réunis, Collection *Hier et aujourd'hui* (Republished 1983 as *Diderot, ou les affirmations fondamentales du matérialisme*. Paris: L'Arche, Collection *Le sens de la marché*.)

1949e. 'Autocritique'. *La Nouvelle Critique* 4 (March), 41–57.

1949f. *Pascal*, Vol. 1 of two. Paris: Edition Nagel (see 1954c).

1950a. 'Connaissance et critique sociale'. In Marvin Farber (ed.) *L'Activité philosophique contemporaine en France et aux États-Unis*. Paris: Presses Universitaires de France. pp.298–319.

1950b. 'Sur le régionalisme et la décentralisation'. *Annales de l'institut d'études occitanes* 5.

1950c. 'Knowledge and Social Criticism'. In *Philosophic Thought in France and the USA*. Albany, NY: State University of New York Press. pp. 281–300 (2nd edition, 1968).

1950d. 'Staline et la nation, Part 2'. *La Nouvelle Critique* 14 (March). pp.44–56. (Table of Contents for issue 14 found in issue 12. See Part 1: 1949b).

1951a. 'Les Classes sociales dans la campagne. La Toscane et la Mezzadria classica', *Cahiers internationaux de sociologie* X, pp.70–93.

1951b. 'Lettre sur Hegel'. *La Nouvelle Critique* 22 (January), 99–104.

1953a. 'Perspectives de sociologie rurale'. *Cahiers internationaux de sociologie* XIV, 122–40.

1953b. (panel discussion with J. Daric, P. Gemaehling, Th. Caplow *et al.*, 'Structures familiales comparées', Georges Friedmann (ed.) *Villes et campagnes*. Paris: Armand Colin. pp.327–62 (Semaine sociologique symposium, Paris, 1951).

1953c. *Contribution à l'esthétique*. Paris: Editions sociales, Collection *Problèmes* (translated into 20 languages).

1954a. 'Lénine philosophe', Colloque de Lénine philosophe et savant. *La Pensée* 57 (September/October), pp18–36.

1954b. 'Art et connaissance'. *Les Cahiers rationalistes* 136 (January/February).

1954c. *Pascal*, Vol. 2 of two. Paris: Edition Nagel (see 1949f).

1955a. 'Secteur commercial et secteur non commercial dans révolution du loisir'. In *Journées d'études de Marly-Roi*, Paris: Centre national d'éducation populaire.

1955b. 'La notion de totalité dans les sciences sociales D'. *Cahiers internationaux de sociologie* XVIII (January–June), pp.55–77.

1955c. 'Vie quotidienne et sociologie'. *Recherches sociologiques* 22.

1955d. 'De Lénine philosophe'. *Deutsche Zeltung Philos.* 111: 6.

1955e. 'Une discussion philosophique en URSS, logique formelle et logique dialectique'. *La Pensée* 59 (January/February), pp.5–20.

1955f. 'Le concept de classes: Un dialogue entre G. Gurvitch et H. Lefebvre', *Critique* 11: 97 (June), pp.559–69.

1955g. *Rabelais*. Paris: Les Editeurs français réunis.

1955h. *Musset*. Paris: L'Arche, Collection *Les grands dramaturges* (2nd corrected edition, 1970, Collection *Travaux*).

1956a. 'De l'explication en économie politique et en sociologie'. *Cahiers internationaux de sociologie* XXI (July–December), pp.19–36.

1956b. 'La philosophie en France'. *Mysl Filoz* 4 (Warsaw).

1956c. 'Une philosophie de l'ambiguité'. In *Mésaventure de l'anti-marxisme, les malheurs de M. Merleau-Ponty*, pp.99ff (see 1956e; 1957c).

1956d. 'Théorie de la rente foncière et sociologie rurale'. In *Actes du IIIe Congrès international de sociologie*, two volumes, Amsterdam.

1956e. 'M. Merleau-Ponty et la philosophie de l'ambiguité, Part 1'. *La Pensée* 68 (July/August), pp.44–58 (see 1956c; for Part 2 see 1957c).

1956f. *Pignon*. Paris: Edition Falaise (2nd expanded edition, Le Musée de Poche, Paris: J. Goldschmidt, 1970).

1956g. 'Lois objectives et forces sociales'. *La Nouvelle Critique* 75 (May), pp.59–72.

1956h. 'La Communauté villageoise'. *La Pensée* 66 (March/April), pp.29–36 (interventions in round table discussion: pp.28, 37–8).

1956i. 'Divertissement pascalien et aliénation humaine'. In *Blaise Pascal, l'homme et l'oeuvre. Cahiers de Royaumont* 1, Paris: Editions de minuit, pp.196–203 (discussion: pp.204–24).

1957a. 'Les entretiens philosophiques de Varsovie'. *Comprendre* 19 (December), pp.237–45.

1957b. 'Georges Politzer et la psychanalyse.' *La Raison, Cahiers de psychopathologie* 18, pp.3ff.

1957c. 'M. Merleau-Ponty et la philosophie de l'ambiguité, Part II'. *La Pensée* 73 (May/June), pp.37–52 (see 1956c; for Part 2 see 1956e).

1957d. 'Le Marxisme et la pensée française'. *Les Temps modernes* 13, pp.137–138 (July/August), pp.104–37 (translated and published 1957: 'Marksizm i mysl Francuska'. *Twórczos* 13: 4).

1957e. *Pour connaître la pense de Lénine* Paris: Bordas (Japanese trans., Tokyo: Minerva-Shobo, 1970; Portuguese trans., Lisbon: Moraes, 1972; Swedish trans., Stockholm: AB Raben E Søgren, 1971).

1957f. 'Le matérialisme dialectique'. *Encyclopedie française*, Gaston Berger (ed.).

1957g. (with G. Lefebvre, C. Parain and R. Dauvergne) 'La Communauté rurale'. *Revue de synthèse* 78: 7 (July–September), pp.308–15.

1957h. 'Vers un romantisme révolutionnaire'. *La Nouvelle Revue Française* 58 (October), pp.644–672.

1957i. 'De la morale provisoire à la générosité'. In *Descartes, Cahiers de Royaumont* 2, Paris: no publisher listed.

1958a. 'Besoins et langage'. *Cahiers de l'institut de science économique appliquée* 75, pp.5ff.

1958b. *Problèmes actuels du marxisme*. Paris: Presses Universitaires de France; 4th edition, 1970, Collection *Initiation philosophique* (German trans., Frankfurt: Suhrkamp Verlag, 1965; Arabic trans., Beirut: Al Tall'a, 1963; Spanish trans.,

Cordoba, Argentina: Paidela, 1965; Greek trans., Athens: Grammata, 1980; Japanese trans., Tokyo: Gendai Shicho-sha, 1960).

1958c. 'Réponse au camarade Bessé'. *Les Temps modernes* 14: 149, pp.238–49.

1958d. (with Lucien Goldmann, Claude Roy and Tristan Tzara) 'Le romantisme révolutionnaire'. *Le Romantisme révolutionnaire* Paris: La Nef.

1958e. 'Gallia'. *Voies nouvelles* 5, pp.5ff.

1958f. 'Staline et le marxisme'. *France Observateur* 405 (13 February), p.15.

1958g. 'Rapports de la philosophie et de la politique dans les premières oeuvres de K. Marx'. *Revue de mètaphysique et de morale* 2–3 (April/September), pp.299–324.

1958h. 'L'exclu s'inclut'. *Les Temps modernes* 14: 149, pp.226–37.

1958i. 'Retour à Marx'. *Cahiers internationaux de sociologie* XXV (July–December), pp.20–37.

1958j. 'Marxisme et théorie de l'information, Part 1'. *Voies nouvelles* 1, pp.15ff.

1958k. 'Marxisme et théorie de l'information, Part 2'. *Voies nouvelles* 2, pp.17f.

1959a. 'Le Soleil crucifié'. *Les Temps modernes* 14: 155, pp.1016–29 (extract from 1959i).

1959b. 'Un philosophe se penche sur son passé'. *France Observateur* 456 (29 January), p.15.

1959c. 'La question du programme'. *Voies nouvelles* 7, pp.8ff.

1959d. 'Qu'est-ce que le passé historique? *Les Temps modernes* 14: 161 (July), pp.159–69.

1959e. 'Justice et vérité'. *Arguments* 15: 3, pp.13–19.

1959f. 'Les cadres sociaux de la sociologie marxiste'. *Cahiers internationaux de sociologie* XXVI (January–June), pp.81–102.

†1959g. 'Enquête sur la nouvelle vague'. *L'Express* (May).

1959h. 'Dialogue entre François Chatelet et Henri Lefebvre à propos de *La Somme et le reste*'. *Voies nouvelles* 9, pp.21ff.

1959i. *La Somme et le reste*, two volumes. Paris: La Nef de Paris (new one-volume edition, Paris: Bélibaste, 1973; 1st edition reprinted as one volume; see 1989a).

1959j. 'Mort du Citoyen', *L'Express* (4 June), p.28 (extract from *La Somme et Le reste*; see 1959i).

1960a. 'Les nouveaux ensembles urbains'. *Revue française de sociologie* 2 (April–June), pp.186–201.

1960b. 'De Clausewitz à de Gaulle'. *France Observateur* 513 (18 February), p.24.

1960c. 'Psychologie des classes sociales'. In *Traité de sociologie de Gurvitch* Vol. 2, Presses Universitaires de France, pp.364–86.

1960d. *Allemagne*. Paris and Zurich, Ed. Braun & Cie and Atlantis Verlag.

1961a. 'Critique de la critique non-critique'. *Nouvelle Revue marxiste* 1: 1 (June), pp.57–79. (Response to Sartre's *La critique de la raison dialectique*.)

1961b. 'La planification démocratique'. *La Nouvelle Revue marxiste* 2, pp. not available. (Rare issue.)

1961c. 'Introduction à la psycho-sociologie de la vie quotidienne'. In D. Huisman (ed.) *Encyclopédie de la psychosociologie*. Paris: publisher not available, pp.102ff.

1961d. 'Le marxisme est l'événement spirituel du XXe siècle'. *Arts* 817.

1961e. 'Une utopie expérimentale: pour un nouvel urbanisme'. *Revue française de sociologie* 3 (July–September), pp.191–98.

1961f. 'Accumulation et progrès'. *Cahiers de l'institut de science économique appliquée* 1: 10, pp.39ff.

1961g. 'Changements dans les attitudes morales de la bourgeoisie, contribution à une sociologie de la classe bourgeoise'. *Cahiers internationaux de sociologie* 31 (July–December), pp.15–40. (Sociology – develops Sartre's *Critique of Dialectical Reason* 717–21.)

1961h. 'Marxisme et politique'. *Revue française de science politique* XI: 2 (June), pp.338–63.

1961i. 'Les dilemmes de la dialectique.' *Médiations* 2, pp.79ff.

1961j. *Critique de la vie quotidienne, II: Fondements d'une sociologie de la quotidienneté.* Paris: L'Arche (German trans., Munich: Carl Hanser, 1975; Italian trans., Milan: Dedalo, 1977; Japanese trans., Tokyo: Gendai Shicho-Sha, 1972). (Part II of an occasional series; see 1947a, 1981a, 1991a).

1961k. 'A propos du XXII Congrès du P.C. de l'U.R.S.S., le vide théorique est-il comblé?'. *La Nouvelle revue marxiste* 3 (February–April), pp.50–5.

1962a. 'Le Procès des monstres (sur le procès de Liège)'. *Arts* 890 (November).

1962b. 'Le destin de la liberté est en lieu'. *Arts* 3 (January).

1962c. 'Les mythes de la vie quotidienne'. *Cahiers internationaux de sociologie* XXXIII (July–December), pp.67–74.

1962d. 'Le bistrot-club, noyau de vie sociale'. *Information bimestrielle des architectes de la Seine* (February).

1962e. 'Marxisme et technique'. *Esprit* New Series 307, pp.1023–8.

1962f. 'Marx et la sociologie.' *Actes du 51e Congrés mondial de sociologie.* International Sociological Association, Washington, 2–8 September.

1962g. 'Idéologie et vérité'. *Cahiers d'études socialistes* 20 (15 October), 7–16. (Debate with François Chatelet; also published as 1962k.)

1962h. 'La signification de la commune'. *Arguments* 27–8, pp.11–19.

1962i. *Introduction à la modernité.* Paris: Editions de Minuit, Collection *Arguments* (English trans., Verso, 1995 (see below); German trans., Frankfurt: Suhrkamp Verlag, 1978; Spanish trans., Madrid: Technos; Japanese trans., Hosci University Press; Portuguese trans., São Paulo: Pas e terra).

1962j. ' Le concept de structure chez Marx'. In Roger Bastide (ed.) *Sens et usage du terme de structure* The Hague: Mouton, pp.100–6 (2nd edition, 1972).

1962k. (with François Chatelet) *Idéologie et vérité.* Paris: Études et documentation internationales (also published as 1962g).

1963a. (in collaboration with Norbert Guterman) *Karl Marx, Oeuvres choisies*, Vol. 1. Paris: Gallimard, Collection *Idées.*

1963b. 'Le marxisme est-il dépassé? un entretien avec A. Parinaud'. *Arts* 903 (13 February).

1963c. 'Réflexions sur les divergences entre les PC chinois et soviétique'. *Le Monde* (4–5 August), p.2.

1963d. 'Réflexion sur le structuralisme et l'histoire'. *Cahiers internationaux de sociologie* XXXV, pp.3–24.

1963e. 'Henri Lefebvre (né en 1905)', In G. Deledalle and D. Huisman (eds) *Les philosophes français d'aujourd'hui par eux-mêmes.* Paris: CDU, pp.282–301.

1963f. *La vallée de Campan – Étude de sociologie rurale.* Paris: Presses Universitaires de France, Collection *Bibliothèque de sociologie contemporaine* (2nd edition, 1991; some volumes misprinted as *Vallée de Campian*).

1964a. 'S'agit-il de penser? La semaine de la pensée marxiste'. *Le Monde* (29 January), p.8.

1964b. 'L'État et la société'. *Les cahiers du centre d'études socialistes* 42–43, pp.17ff.

1964c. *Marx.* Paris: Presses Universitaires de France (Spanish trans., Barcelona: Labor, 1975; Portuguese trans., Lisbon: Don Quixote, 1974).

1964d. (with Norbert Guterman) *Karl Marx, Oeuvres choisies*, Vol. 2. Paris: Gallimard, Collection *Idées.*

1964e. 'Les sources de la théorie marxiste–léniniste de l'État'. *Les Cahiers du centre d'études socialistes* 42–43, pp.31ff.

1965a. 'Les Méthodes et situations des sciences sociales'. *Le Monde* (17 February), p.11.

1965b. 'Sur quelques critiques du développement social et du socialisme'. *Praxis: Revue philosophique* 2–3, pp.156–67.

1965c. 'Classe et nation depuis le "manifeste" 1848'. *Cahiers internationaux de sociologie* XXXVIII (January–June), pp.31–48.

1965d. 'Les mutations intervenues dans les structures des deux grandes sociétés industrielles du monde'. *Le Monde diplomatique* 129 (January), p.10.

1965e. *Métaphilosophie*, 'Envoi' by Jean Wahl. Paris: Editions de Minuit, Collection *Arguments* (German trans., Frankfurt: Suhrkamp Verlag, 1975; Japanese trans., Tokyo: Gendai-Shicho-Sha; Portuguese trans., Rio de Janeiro: Civilizaço; Czech trans., Prague: Svoboda).

1965f. *La Proclamation de la Commune.* Paris: Gallimard, Collection *Trente Journées qui ont fait la France* (Japanese trans., Tokyo: Iwanami-shoten, 1967).

1965g. 'Kostas Axelos: Vers la pensée planétaire'. *Esprit* 338, pp.1114–17.

1965h. *Pyrénées.* Lausanne: Editions Rencontre, Collection *L'Atlas des voyages.*

1966a. 'Preface'. In *L'Habitat pavillionnaire.* Paris: Centre de recherche d'urbanisme, pp.3–24 (collective study by H. Raymond, M.-G. Raymond, N. Haumont and M. Coornaert, directed by H. Lefebvre; 2nd edition published by Institut de sociologie urbaine, Paris, 1971; 3rd edition by Centre de recherche et de rencontres d'urbanisme, n.d.).

1966b. 'Claude Lévi-Strauss et le nouvel éléatisme, Part 1'. *L'Homme et la société* 1 (July–September), pp.21–31 (see 1966g for Part 2).

1966c. *Sociologie de Marx* Paris: Presses Universitaires de France, Collection *Sup* (2nd edition, 1968; 3rd edition, 1974, Collection *Le sociologue*; German trans., Frankfurt: Suhrkamp Verlag, 1972; English trans., London: Penguin, and New York: Pantheon (see 1968k); Danish trans., Copenhagen: Hans Reitzel, 1972; Spanish trans., Barcelona: Ediciones 62, 1969; Greek trans., Athens: Gutenberg, 1980; Italian trans., Milan: Il Saggiatore, 1968; Japanese trans., Tokyo: Serika Shobo, 1970; Dutch trans, Meppel: Boom & Zoom, 1973; Portuguese trans., Rio de Janeiro: Forenze, 1969; Swedish trans., Stockholm: Rabén & Sjögren, 1970).

1966d. *Le langage et la société.* Paris: Gallimard, Collection *Idées* (German trans., Dusseldorf: Pedagogischer Verlag Schwann, 1973; Spanish trans., Buenos Aires: Ed. Siglo Viente, 1977; Italian trans, Florence, 1972; Japanese trans., Tokyo: Serika Shobo, 1972; Portuguese trans, Lisbon: Ulisseia, 1968).

1966e. 'Problèmes théoriques de l'autogestion'. *Autogestion* 1 (December), pp.59–70.

1966f. 'Capitalisme d'État ou secteur public démocratisé'. *Le Monde* (5 February), p.8.

1966g. 'Claude Lévi-Strauss et le nouvel éléatisme, Part 2', *L'Homme et la société* 2 (October–December), pp.81–103 (see 1966b for Part 1).

1967a. '1925'. *La Nouvelle Revue française*. Numéro Spécial sur André Breton 172 (April), pp.707–19.

1967b. *Position: contre les technocrates* Paris: Gonthier (new edition as 1971e; Spanish trans., Buenos Aires: Granita-Gedisa, 1974; Japanese trans., Tokyo: Kinokunia, 1970; Portuguese trans., Lisbon: Livraria Moraes, 1968, and São Paulo: Documentos Edit., 1969).

1967c. 'Sur une interprétation du marxisme: L. Althusser'. *L'Homme et la société* 4 (April–June), pp.3–22.

1967d. 'Le droit à la ville'. *L'Homme et la société* 6 (October–December), pp.29–35.

1967e. 'L'urbanisme aujourd'hui, mythes et réalités'. *Les Cahiers du Centre d'études de socialistes* 72–73, pp.5ff (debate between H. Lefebvre, J. Balladur and M. Ecochard).

1967f. 'Propositions pour un nouvel urbanisme'. *Architecture d'aujourd'hui* 132 (June/July), pp.14–16 (English summary, see p.C11).

1967g. 'Besoins profonds, besoins nouveaux de la civilisation urbaine'. *Revue 2000*.

1967h. 'Quartier et ville de quartier'. *Cahiers de l'Institut d'Aménagement et d'Urbanisme de la Région Parisienne* 7.

1968a. 'Forme, fonction, structure dans le capital'. *L'Homme et la société* 7 (January–March), pp.69–81.

1968b. *Le Droit à la ville* Paris: Anthropos (2nd edition, Paris: du Seuil, Collection *Points* 1974 (incorporates 1973d; English trans., see Lefebvre *et al.* 1996; German trans., Basis Verlag, 1972; Spanish trans., Ediciones 62, 1968; Greek trans., Papazissis, 1976; Italian trans., Turin: Marsilio, 1970; Japanese trans., Chikuma-Shobo, 1969; Portuguese trans., Documentos Ed., 1968; Swedish trans., Bokomotiv, 1982).

1968c. 'Bilan d'un siècle 1867–1917–1967 et de deux demi-siècles'. In Victor Faye (ed.) *En partant du Capital*. Paris: Anthropos, pp.115–42.

1968d. 'Lefebvre parle de Marcuse'. *La Quinzaine littéraire* 52, 3–5.

1968e. 'L'homme unidimensionnel d'Herbert Marcuse, société close ou société ouverte? *Le Monde* (16–17 June), p.9.

1968f. 'Humanisme et urbanisme, quelques propositions'. *Architecture, Formes, Fonctions* 14.

1968g. (with Monique Coornaert) 'Ville, urbanisme et urbanisation'. In *Perspectives de la sociologie contemporaine, Hommage à Georges Gurvitch* Paris: Presses Universitaires de France, pp.85–105.

1968h. *L'irruption de Nanterre au sommet* Paris: Anthropos (German trans., Frankfurt: Voltaire, 1969; English trans., Monthly Review Press (see 1969d); Spanish trans., Extemporaneos, 1970; Italian trans., Moizzi, 1975; Japanese trans., Chikuma-Shobo, 1969).

1968i. *La vie quotidienne dans le monde moderne*. Paris: Gallimard, Collection *Idées* (Albanian trans., Pristina: Rilindja Nigp, 1980; German trans., 1972; English trans, New York: Harper & Row, 1971h; Spanish trans., Madrid: Alianza, 1972; Italian trans., Milan: Il Saggiatore, 1979; Portuguese trans., Lisbon: Ulisseia, 1969).

1968j. 'Erfahrung der Spontaneität, Interview über die Pariser Mai Unruhen'. *Neutralität* (June).

1968k. *Sociology of Marx.* trans. by N. Guterman of 1966c, New York: Pantheon.

1968l. *Dialectical Materialism* (trans. by J. Sturrock of 1939b; incorporates the 1961 foreword to the 5th edition, London: Jonathan Cape).

1969a. 'De la science à la strategie urbaine'. *Utopie* 2–3, pp.57ff.

1969b. 'Preface'. In Phillipe Boudon (ed.) *Pessac, le Quartier Le Corbusier.* Paris: Dunod (English trans. by Lund Hemphries, 1972).

1969c. 'Les paradoxes d'Althusser'. *L'Homme et la société* 13 (July–September), pp.3–37.

1969d. *The Explosion: From Nanterre to the Summit.* Paris: Monthly Review Press (trans. of 1968h).

1970a. *La révolution urbaine* Paris: Gallimard, Collection *Idées* (German trans., Paul List Verlag, 1972, revised edition, Syndikat, 1976; Spanish trans., *La revolucion urbana*, Madrid: Alianza, 1972; Italian trans., Rome: Armando Armando, 1973; Japanese trans., Tokyo: Shobun-Sha, 1976; Portuguese trans., São Paulo: Vertice-Ed. revista dos tribunals Ltd, 1988; Serbo-Croat trans., Belgrade: Nolit Publishing House, 1975).

1970b. (Mario Gaviria (ed.)) *Du rurale à l'urbain.* Paris: Anthropos (includes reprint of Lefebvre's talk 1967e. Spanish trans., Ediciones 62, 1970; Italian trans., Guaraldi, 1971; Portuguese trans., Ulmeiro, 1977).

1970c. 'Réflexions sur la politique de l'espace'. *Espace et société* 1 (November), pp.3–12.

1970c. 'Réflexions sur la politique de l'espace', *Espace et société* 1 (November), pp.3–12.

1970d. 'Preface'. in A. Vachet *L'Idéologie libérale.* Paris: Anthropos, pp.11–14.

1970e. *La fin de l'histoire: épilégomènes.* Paris: Editions de Minuit, Collection *Arguments* 46 (Spanish trans., Buenos Aires: La Pleiade; Italian trans., Milan: Sugar; Portuguese trans., Lisbon: Don Quixote).

1971a. *Le manifeste différentialiste.* Paris: Gallimard, Collection *Idées*, 186pp (Spanish trans., Mexico: Sigio veintiuno, 1972; Italian trans., Bari: Dedalo, 1980).

1971b. 'La classe ouvrière est-elle révolutionnaire?', *L'Homme et la société*, 21 (July–September), pp.149–56.

1971c. 'La reproduction des rapports de production, Part 1'. *L'Homme et la société* 22 (October–December), pp.3–23 (see 1972c for Part 2).

1971d. *Au-delà du structuralisme* Paris: Anthropos (reprinted as 1975d; Portuguese trans., Paz e terra, 1972; Serbo-Croat trans., Jugoslovenska, 1972).

1971e. *Vers le cybernanthrope, contre les technocrates* Paris: Denoél-Gonthier, Collection *Médiations* (revised edition of 1967b; Spanish trans., Buenos Aires: Granita-Gedisa, 1974; Serbo-Croat trans., Belgrade: Radmédcka Stempa, 1973).

1971f. 'La ville et l'urbain'. *Espace et société* 2 (March), pp.3–7.

1971g. 'Musique et sémiologie'. *Musique en jeu* 4, 52–62.

1971h. *Everyday Life in the Modern World*, Sacha Rabinovitch (trans.). Harmondsworth: Penguin (trans. of 1968i).

1972a. *Trois textes pour le théâtre.* Paris: Anthropos.

1972b. *La pensée marxiste et la ville.* Paris-Tournai: Casterman, Collection *Mutations–Orientations* (3rd edition, 1978; German trans., Otto Maier, 1975; English trans., Macmillan, 1984; Danish trans., Reitzel, 1974; Spanish trans., Extemporaneos, 1973; Greek trans., Odysseus, 1975; Italian trans., Mazzota, 1973; Portuguese trans., Ulisseia, 1973).

1972c. 'La reproduction des rapports de production, Part 2'. *L'Homme et la société* 23 (January–March), pp.3–22 (see 1971c for Part 1).

1972d. 'Les institutions de la société post-technologique'. *Espace et société* 5 (April), pp.3–20.

1972e. 'Engels et l'utopie'. *Espace et société* 4 (December), pp.3–9 (extract from 1972b).

1973a. 'Le mondial et le planétaire, *Espace et société* 8 (February), pp.15–22.

1973b. 'Les idéologies de la croissance'. *L'Homme et la société* 27 (January–March), pp.3–18.

1973c. *La survie du capitalisme, la reproduction des rapports de production.* Paris: Anthropos (German trans., Paul List Verlag, 1974; English trans., Allison & Busby, 1974; Spanish trans., Laia, 1974; Greek trans., Nea Synora, 1975; Italian trans., Moizzi, 1975; Portuguese trans., Publicac Escorpiao, 1974; Serbo-Croat trans., Suèt lost, 1975).

1973d. *Espace et politique.* Paris: Anthropos, Vol. 2 of *Droit à la ville* (see 1968b). (Includes conference texts from 1970 to 1972 and extracts from interviews in *Espaces et sociétés* (November1970–December 1971); 2nd edition, Paris: Editions du Seuil, Collection *Points* 1974 incorporates Vol. 1 of *Droit à la ville* (1968b); English trans., (see Lefebvre 1996; Spanish trans., Ediciones 62, 1974; Japanese trans., Shobun-Sha, 1975).

1973f. 'Les autres Paris'. *Espaces et Sociétés* 13–14, pp.185–92.

1974a. 'La production de l'espace'. *L'Homme et la société* 31–32 (January–June), pp.15–32.

1974b. *La production de l'espace.* Paris: Anthropos (2nd edition, 1981; 3rd edition, 1986; Italian trans., Moizzi, 1975; Japanese trans., Fukumura Shuppan, 1975; Danish trans., Archipress 1980; English trans., of 1st French edition, 1991 (see 1991d)).

1974c. (with Leszek Kolakowski) 'Evolution or Revolution'. In F. Elders (ed.) *Reflexive Water: The Basic Concerns of Mankind.* London: Souvenir, pp.199–267.

1975a. *Hegel, Marx, Nietzsche, ou le royaume des ombres.* Paris: Tournai, Casterman. Collection *Synthèses contemporaines* (Spanish trans., Siglo XXI de España, 1976; Greek trans., Kedros, 1976; Italian trans., Missi, 1976; Japanese trans., Sunudra, 1976; Portuguese trans., Ulisseia, 1976).

1975b. 'L'État dans le monde moderne'. *L'Homme et la société* 37–38 (July–September), pp.3–23.

1975c. *Le temps des méprises: Entretiens avec Claude Glayman.* Paris: Stock (Spanish trans., Barcelona: Kalros, 1975; Italian trans., Milan: Ulthipla, 1979).

1975d. *L'Idéologie structuraliste.* Paris: Le Seuil, Collection *Points* (abridged edition of 1971d).

1975e. 'Sur L'Aliénation'. *Social Praxis* 3: 1–2, pp.63–75.

1975f. (ed.) *Actualité de Fourier: Colloque d'Arc-et-Senans* Paris: Editions Anthropos.

1975g. 'Introduction'. in 1975f *Actualité de Fourier*, pp.9–20.

1975h. 'Les autres Paris'. *Espace et société* 13–14 (October–January), pp.185–92 (script for a film, *Le Droit à la Ville*, 26 minutes, 1973).

1976a. *L'État dans le monde moderne*, Vol. 1 of four. *De l'État.* Paris: UGE, Collection *10/18.*

1976b. *Théorie marxiste de l'État de Hegel à Mao*, Vol. 2 of four *De l'État* Paris: UGE, Collection *10/18.*

1976c. 'Le marxisme éclaté'. *L'Homme et la société* 41–42 (July–September), pp.3–12 (English trans., see 1980c).

1976d. (with Y. Bourdet and O. Corpet) 'Interview dans le cadre du débat – Léninisme –stalinisme ou autogestion'. *Autogestion et socialisme* 33–34 (January–March), pp.115–26.

1977. *Le mode de production étatique*, Vol. 3 of four. *De l'État*, Paris: UGE, Collection *10/18*.

1978a. (with Catherine Régulier) *La révolution n'est plus ce qu'elle était*. Paris: Editions Libres-Hallier (German trans., Munich, 1979).

1978b. *Les contradictions de l'État moderne, La dialectique de l'État*, Vol. 4 of four. *De l'État*, Paris: UGE, Collection *10/18* (Spanish trans., Granila Ed., 1979; Italian trans., Bari: Dedalo, 1978; Portuguese trans., Socicultur, 1979; Serbo-Croat trans., Bicz, 1982).

1979a. 'A propos d'un nouveau modèle Étatique'. *Dialectiques* 27. pp.47–55.

1979b. (with B. Bernardi) 'Une Vie pour penser et porter la lutte de classes à la théorie: Entretien,' *Nouvelle Critique* 306: Special issue 125 (June), pp.44–54.

1980a. *La présence et l'absence* Paris: Casterman (Spanish trans., Fonde de Cultura, 1981; Greek trans., Athens: Kedros, 1982).

1980b. *Une pensée devenue monde* Paris: Fayard (Italian trans., Rome: Riuniti, 1983; Serbo-Croat trans., Zagreb: Globus, 1982).

1980c. 'Marxism Exploded'. *Review. Journal of the Research Foundation of the State University of New York* 4: 1 (Summer), pp.19–32.

1981a. *Critique de la vie quotidienne, III: De la modernité au modernisme (Pour une métaphilosophie du quotidien)* Paris: L'Arche (German trans., Carl Hanser 1976). (Part III of an occasional series; see 1947a, 1961j, 1991a).

1981b. *De la modernité au modernisme: pour une métaphilosophie du quotidien* Paris: L'Arche, Collection 'Le sens de la marché'.

1982. 'Henri Lefebvre philosophe du quotidien'. Interview with O. Corpet and T. Paquot, *Le Monde* (19 December – Sunday), pp.ix–x.

1983. *Diderot; ou les affirmations fondamentales de matérialisme*. Paris: L'Arche, Collection 'Le sens de la marché' (reprint of 1949d).

1984a. 'Quo vadis?'. *Revolution* 236 (September).

1984b. 'Pensare la pace'. *Il Ponte* (January–February).

1985a. (with Catherine Régulier-Lefebvre) 'Le projet rythmanalytique,' *Communications* 41, pp.191–9.

1985b. 'Fragments d'un discours politique'. *Révolution* 264 (March).

1985c. 'Culture et citoyenneté'. *Révolution* 258 (February).

1985f. *Qu'est-ce que c'est pour penser?* Paris: Publisud.

1986a. 'Pour une nouvelle culture politique'. *M: Mensuels, marxismes, mouvements* 1, pp.3ff.

1986b. 'Le renouveau philosophique avorté des années trente'. Interview with Michel Trebitsch, *Europe* 683 (March), pp.29–41.

1986c. 'À propos de l'autogestion'. *M: Mensuels, marxismes, mouvements* 2 (May).

1986d. (with Catherine Régulier-Lefebvre) 'Essai de rythmanalyse des villes méditer-ranéennes'. *Peuples méditerranéens* 37 (October–December) (translated in Lefebvre 1996).

1986e. *Le retour de la dialectique, Douze mots clefs pour le monde moderne*. Paris: Messidor–Editions sociales.

1986f. (with P. Tort) *Lukács, 1955*. Paris: Aubier.

1986g. 'Sur la crédibilité politique'. *M: Mensuels, marxismes, mouvements* 2 (May).

1986h. 'M comme machine'. *M: Mensuels, marxismes, mouvements* 6 (December), pp.58–9.

1986i. (with François Châtelet, Jean-Marie Vincent, Françoise Bellue *et al.*) *Marx ou pas? Reflexions sur un centenaire.* Paris: Études et documentation internationales, pp.21–5.

1986j. 'Hors du centre, point de salut?' *Espaces Temps* 33, pp.17–19 (translated in Lefebvre 1996).

1987a. 'Quelques questions sur le questionnement'. *M: Mensuels, marxismes, mouvements* 7 (January).

1987b. 'Introduction au débat: le marxisme aujourd'hui'. *M: Mensuels, marxismes, mouvements* 7 (January).

1987c. 'Crise de l'État'. *M: Mensuels, marxismes, mouvements* 9 (March).

1987d. '12 thèses sur la connaissance'. *M: Mensuels, marxismes, mouvements* 12 (June).

1987e. 'Penser les médias'. *M: Mensuels, marxismes, mouvements* 8 (February).

1987f. 'L'URSS et le modèle étatique'. *M: Mensuels, marxismes, mouvements* 10 (April).

1987g. 'Le quotidien'. *M: Mensuels, marxismes, mouvements* 11 (May).

1987h. 'Lettre de démission'. *M: Mensuels, marxismes, mouvements* 14 (November).

1987i. 'An interview with Henri Lefebvre'. *Environment and Planning: Society and Space* 5, 27–38.

1988a. (with Catherine Régulier-Lefebvre) 'Une nouvelle positivité de l'urbain'. *M: Mensuels, marxismes, mouvements* 17 (February).

1988b. 'Maggio 68 recordi e riflossini di una protagonists, intervista Henri Lefebvre'. *Anni 70* 5 (April).

1988c. 'Entretien avec R. Hess sur la montée de l'extrême droite en France, analyse comparative avec les années 1930'. *Journal d'analyse institutionnelle* 7 (June).

1988d. 'Entretien avec Catherine Régulier et Henri Lefebvre à propos des prisonniers politiques' (ms. AFAPP – Association des familles et des amis des prisonniers politiques, Paris (June); copy available from R. Hess, Dept. de Sociologie, Universitaire de Rouen, France).

1988e. 'Toward a Leftist cultural politics: remarks occasioned by the centenary of Marx's death', D. Reifman (trans.), C.Grossberg and L. Nelson (eds) *Marxism and the Interpretation of Culture.* Urbana: University of Illinois Press.; New York: Macmillan, pp.75–88.

1988f. (with Catherine Régulier-Lefebvre) 'Un symptôme du glissement vers la néo-barbarie (à propos des conditions de détention des membres d'Action Directe)'. *Libération* 27–28 (February).

1988g. *Le Nationalisme contre les Nations.* Paris: Méridiens Klincksieck (reprint of 1937a with new postface).

1989a. *Le Somme et le reste*, 'Preface' by Réné Lorau, Paris: Méridiens Klincksieck (reprint of 1st edition, see 1959i)

1989b. 'L'Urbain en question'. *Société Française* 33, pp.44–7 (translated in Lefebvre 1996).

1991a. *The Critique of Everyday Life, Volume 1*, John Moore (trans.). London: Verso (translation from the 1958 French 2nd edition with Preface; see 1947a).

1991b. (with Groupe de Navarrenx – Armand Ajzendberg, Lucien Bonnafé, Katherine Coit, Yann Couvidat, Alain Guillerm, Fernando Iannetti, Guy Lacrois, Luci Martini-Scalzone, Serge Renaudie, Oreste Scalzone) *Du Contrat de citoyenneté* Paris:

Syllepse/Périscope/Archipel Transéd, Collection *Explorations* (preface by Armand Ajzenderg).

1991c. (with Patricia Latour and Francis Combes) *Conversation avec Henri Lefebvre* P. Latour and F. Combes (eds). Paris: Messidor, Collection *Libres propos*.

1991d. *The Production of Space*, N. Donaldson-Smith (trans.). Oxford: Basil Blackwell (translation of 1974a with preface by Michael Trebitsch and postscript by David Harvey).

1991e. 'Les illusions de la modernité'. *Manières de voir* 13, *Le Monde Diplomatique*, pp.14–17.

1991f. 'Une intervention inédite'. *M: Mensuels, marxismes, mouvements* 50, pp.32–3.

1992a. (with Catherine Régulier-Lefebvre) *Eléments de rythmanalyse: Introduction à la connaissance des rythmes*, preface by René Lorau. Paris: Editions Syllepse, Collection *Explorations et découvertes* (Ch. 3 translated in Lefebvre 1996).

1992b. (with Patricia Latour and Francis Combes) 'Conversation avec Henri Lefebvre'. *Le Monde* (20 January), p.7c (extract from 1991c).

1995. *Introduction to Modernity: Twelve Preludes September 1959–May 1961*, J. Moore (trans.). London: Verso (translation of 1962i).

1996. *Writings on Cities*, E. Kofman and E. Lebas (trans. and eds). Oxford: Basil Blackwell (translation of 1968b and 1973d, together with 1980d, 1986d, 1989b and 1992a, Ch. 3).

Planned work: *La Découverte et le secret* (no publisher has announced plans to publish this work, which Lefebvre projected in 1988, three years before his death).

SECONDARY SOURCES

Abercrombie, N. 1986. *Sovereign Individuals of Capitalism*. London: Allen.

Ajzenberg, A. 1991. 'Toujours engagé'. *M. Mensuel, marxisme, mouvement* 50, 30–1.

—— 1994. 'A partir d'Henri Lefebvre. Vers un mode de production écologique'. *Traces de futurs. Henri Lefebvre, le possible et le quotidien*. Paris: Société Française, 1–5 (this text of conference proceedings is not available outside France or listed with books in print).

Althusser, L. and Balibar, E. 1972. *For Marx*. London: Verso.

Amiot, M. 1986. *Contre l'État, les sociologues*. Paris: Maison des Sciences de l'Homme.

Anderson, B. 1981. *Imagined Communities*. London: New Left Books.

Anderson, K. 1992. 'Lenin, Hegel and Western Marxism: From the 1920s to 1953'. *Studies in Soviet Thought*, 44 (2), 79–129.

Anderson, P. 1976. *On the Tracks of Western Marxism*. London: New Left Books.

—— 1983. *Historical Materialism*. London: Verso.

Anon. 1991. 'List of works of the philosopher Henri Lefebvre'. *Le Monde*, 1 July, p. 2, 15b.

Anon. 1991. 'Obituary for the philosopher Henri Lefebvre, retrospective'. *Le Monde*, 1 July, p. 2, 1b, 15a–b

Ansay, P. and Schoonbrodt, R. (eds) 1989. *Penser la ville, choix de textes philosophiques*. Brussels: Aux Archives de l'Architecture Moderne.

Aragon, L. 1953. *Les Paysans de Paris*. Paris: Gallimard.

Arato, A and Brienes, P. 1979. *The Young Lukács and the Origins of Western Marxism*. New York: Seabury.

Ardener, S. (ed.) 1993. *Women and Space: Ground Rules and Social Maps*, rev. ed. Oxford: Berg.

Axelos, Kostas 1963. *Marx, penseur de la technique*. Paris: Minuit.

Bachelard, G. 1931. *L'Intuition de l'instant*. Paris: Stock.

—— 1938. *La psychanalyse du feu*. Paris: Stock.

—— 1950. *La dialectique de la durée*. Paris: PUF.

—— 1957. *La poétique de l'espace*. Paris: PUF.

Barreau, H. 1985 'Les théories philosophiques de la connaissance face à la relativité d'Einstein'. *Communications* 41, 95–109.

Barthes, R. 1959. *Mythologies*. Harmondsworth: Penguin.

Bataille, G. 1957. *L'Eroticisme*. In collection *10/18*. Paris: UGE.

—— 1970. *Oeuvres completes*, two vols. Paris: Gallimard.

—— 1987. *Eroticism*. London: Marion Boyars.

—— 1992. *On Nietzsche*, B. Boone (trans.). London: Athlone Press.

Baudrillard, J. 1981. *For a Critique of the Political Economy of the Sign*. New York: Telos (originally published, Paris: Gallimard, 1972).

—— 1983. *The Precession of Simulacra*. New York: Semiotexte.

Baurain, N., Lourau, R. and Savoye, A. 1985. 'Entretiens avec Henri Lefebvre' (January–March) (cited in R. Hess 1988. *Henri Lefebvre et l'aventure du siècle*. Paris: A. M. Métailié.

Béchillon, D. de (ed.) 1994. *Les défis de la complexity, Vers un nouveau paradigms de la connaissance?* Paris: Harmattan.

bell hooks 1990. *Yearning*. Toronto: Between the Lines.

Bellos, D. 1994. *Georges Perec. Une vie dans les mots*. Paris: Editions du Seuil (original English *Georges Perec. A Life in Words*. New York: HarperCollins 1993).

Benjamin, W. 1989. *Paris, capitale du XIXe siècle, le livre des passages*. Paris: Editions du CERF.

Benveniste, E. 1966. *Problèmes du langage*. Paris: Gallimard.

Berger, J. 1980. *About Looking*. New York: Pantheon.

Bernié-Boissard, C. 1994. 'Henri Lefebvre, sociologue du quotidien, philosophe de la modernité'. *Espaces et Sociétés* 76 (1), 13–29.

Bey, H. 1991. *TAZ: Temporary Autonomous Zones*. New York: Autonomedia.

Bhabha, H. 1989. *Nation and Narration*. London: Routledge.

Blanchot, M. 1971. *L'Amitié*. Paris: Gallimard.

Blum, V. and Nast, H. 1996. 'Where's the difference? The heterosexualization of alterity in Henri Lefebvre and Jacques Lacan'. *Environment and Planning D: Society and Space* 14 (4), 559–80.

Body-Gendrot, S. 1993. *Ville et violence. L'Irruption de nouveaux acteurs*. Paris: PUF.

Bonnafé, L. 1991. 'Sur l'audience d'Henri Lefebvre'. *M. Mensuels, marxismes, mouvements* 50, 20–2.

Bonnett, A. 1992. 'Art, ideology, and everyday space: subversive tendencies from Dada to postmodernism'. *Environment and Planning D: Society and Space* 10, 69–86.

Bonnett, A. 1996. *LandRanger 168. Colchester and Blackwater Area* 1:50,000 by Ordnance Survey 1992, Southampton, Ordnance Survey. *Transgressions* 2, 132–3.

Boschetti, A. 1985. *Sartre et 'Les Temps Modernes'*. Paris: Minuit.

Bourdieu, P. 1971. 'The Berber House or the World Reversed'. In Mary Douglas (ed.) *Rules and Meanings*. Harmondsworth: Penguin, 98–110.

Braidotti, R. 1994. 'Foucault. La convergence avec le féminisme'. *Magazine Littéraire* 325, 68–70.

Breton, A. 1924. *Les manifestes dadaïstes* (second set of manifestos published in 1930).

Bürger, P. 1984. *Theory of the Avant Garde*. Minneapolis: University of Minnesota Press.

Burkhard, F. B. 1986. 'Priests and Jesters: Henri Lefebvre, the "Philosophies" Gang and French Marxism between the Wars'. Ph.D. thesis, Department of History, University of Wisconsin, Madison.

Butler, J. 1993. *Bodies that Matter: on the Discursive Limits of Sex*. London: Routledge.

Cahiers de Philosophie 1993. *Le Philosophe dans la cité* 17.

Campbell, J. 1995. *Paris Interzone: Richard Wright, Lolita, Boris Vian and Others on the Left Bank, 1946–60*. London: Minerva; Mandarin by Reed Paperbacks International.

Carraro, D. 1981. *L'Avventura umana nel mondo moderno: Henri Lefebvre e l'uomo quotidianus.* Milan: Unicopli.

Castells, M. 1977. *The Urban Question: A Marxist Approach*, A. Sheridan (trans.). London: Edward Arnold (originally published as *La question urbaine.* Paris: Maspero, 1972).

Castells, M. 1989. *Informational City.* Oxford: Basil Blackwell.

—— 1994. 'L'École française de sociologie vingt ans après. Retour au futur?' *Les Annales de la Recherche Urbaine* 64, 58–60.

—— 1996. *The Rise of the Network Society*, Vol. 1 of *The Information Age: Economy, Society and Culture.* Oxford: Basil Blackwell.

Castoriadis, C. 1984. *Crossroads in the Labyrinth*, K. Soper and M. H. Ryle (trans.). Brighton: Harvester (originally published as *Les carrefours du labyrinthe.* Paris: Seuil, 1978).

Castro, R. 1994. *Civilisation urbaine ou barbarie?* Paris: Plon.

Caute, D. 1964. *Communism and the French Intellectuals 1914–1960.* New York: Macmillan.

Chemetov, P. 1991. 'Henri Lefebvre nous parle' *M. Mensuel, marxisme, mouvement* 50, 40–1.

Clement, W. 1986. *The Canadian Corporate Elite : An Analysis of Economic Power.* Ottawa : Carleton University Press.

Cohen, G. 1978. *Karl Marx's Theory of History.* Oxford: Oxford University Press.

Courbon, J. 1994. 'Pour une définition du concept d'écologie politique et urbaine. In *Traces des futurs. Henri Lefebvre, le possible et le quotidien.* Paris: Société Française.

Couvelakis, E. 1994. 'L'Espace entre philosophie de l'histoire et pratique politique'. *Espaces et Sociétés* 76 (1), 99–122.

Couvidat, Y. 1994. 'L'Anthrope, le cybernanthrope et les technopoles'. In *Traces des futurs. Henri Lefebvre, le possible et le quotidien.* Paris: Société Française.

Cremieux, B. 1931. 'Examens de Conscience'. In *Inquiétude et reconstruction.* Paris: Corrëa (essay dated 1926).

Csikszentmihalyi, M. 1990. *Flow; The Psychology of Optimal Experience.* New York: Harper.

Current Digest of the Soviet Press 1949–1992. Washington: The Joint Committee on Slavic Studies.

Curry, M. 1996. 'Finding the space in the text and the text in space'. In *The Work in the World: Geographical Practice and the Written Word.* Minneapolis: University of Minnesota Press, 175–200.

Davidson, A. 1992. 'Henri Lefebvre'. *Thesis Eleven* 33, 152–5.

Dear, M. 1994. 'Les Aspects post modernes de Henri Lefebvre', *Espaces et Sociétés* 76 (1), 31–40.

Debord, G. 1977. *Society of the Spectacle.* Chicago: Black and Red.

—— 1957. 'Report on the Construction of Situations and on the International Situationist Tendency's Conditions of Organisation and Action' (pamphlet, no place: no publisher).

—— 1961. *Situationniste Internationale* 6, 22ff.

—— 1994. 'Guide de psychogéographie de discours sur les passions de l'amour'. In *Asger Bjorn Exhibition.* Amsterdam: Stedlijk Museum.

DeCerteau, M. 1994. *L'Invention du quotidien, I. Arts de faire*, 2nd edn. Paris: Gallimard.

Delbo, C. 1969. *Théorie et pratique, dialogue imaginaire mais pas tout à fait apocryphe entre Herbert Marcuse et Henri Lefebvre*. Paris: Anthropos.

Deleuze, G. 1968. *Différence et répétition*, Paris: PUF.

—— 1993. *The Fold: Leibniz and the Baroque*. Minneapolis: University of Minnesota Press (originally published as *Le Pli*. Paris: Minuit, 1988).

Deleuze, G. and Guattari, F. 1976. *L'Anti-Oedipe, Capitalisme et schizophrenie*. Paris: Minuit.

Deutsche, R. (ed.) 1991. *If You Lived Here*. New York: Dia Art Foundation.

Dieuaide, P. and Motamed-Nejad, R. 1994. 'Méthodologie et hétérodoxie en économie: retours sur Henri Lefebvre'. *Espaces et Sociétés* 76 (1), 69–98.

Drieu la Rochelle, P. 1934. *Socialisme fasciste: Marx contre Nietzsche*. Paris: Gallimard.

Easthope, A. 1979. 'Liberal and Theoretical Discourse: An Opposition Assessed'. *Social Praxis* 6 (3–4), 217–5.

Engels, F. 1954. *Dialectics of nature*, 2nd edn, C. Dutt (trans.). Moscow: Progress.

Eribon, D. 1994. *Michel Foucault et ses contemporains*. Paris: Fayard.

Featherstone, M. 1995. *Undoing Culture; Globalization, Postmoderism and Identity*. London: Sage.

Ferenczi, T. 1988. *Le Monde* (June 26–27). 'Nationalisme'.

Flanner, J. 1946. 'Underwear'. *New Yorker* (22 May) (also published in J. Flanner *Paris Journal, 1944–65*, W. Shawn (ed.). New York: no publisher.

Foucault, M. 1966. *Les Mots et les choses*. Paris: Gallimard (translated as *The Order of Things*. New York: Vintage, 1970).

Foucault, M. 1975. *The Birth of the Clinic*. A. M. Sheridan-Smith (trans.). New York: Vintage/Random House (originally published as *Naissance de la clinique*. Paris: Presses Universitaires de France, 1963).

—— 1984. *The Foucault Reader*, P. Rabinow (ed.). Harmondsworth: Penguin.

—— 1986a. *Power/Knowledge*, C. Gordon (ed.). Brighton: Harvester.

—— 1986b. *The History of Sexuality, Vol. 2: The Use of Pleasure*, R. Hurley (trans.). London: Viking (originally published as *L'usage des plaisirs*. Paris: Gallimard, 1984).

Friedmann, G.-P. 1925. 'Une direction dans la Nouvelle Génération'. *Europe* 26 (May), 125ff.

Gambacorta, C. 1989. 'Experiences of Daily Life'. *Current Sociology: The Sociology of Everyday Life* 17 (1) (Spring), 121–40.

Garaudy, R. 1960. 'Questions à Jean-Paul Sartre, précédées d'une lettre ouverte'. *Revue Clarté*, np.

Gardiner, M. 1995. 'Utopia and Everyday Life in French Social Thought'. *Utopian Studies* 6 (2), 90–123.

Garnier, J. P. and Goldschmidt, D. 1978. *La comédie urbaine*. Paris: Maspero.

Garnier, J. 1994. 'La vision urbaine de Henri Lefebvre: des previsions aux révisions'. *Espaces et Sociétés* 76 (1), 123–45.

Gaudin, J. 1994. 'La ségrégation et la recherche urbaine. Chassés-croisés entre chercheurs et décideurs'. *Les Annales de la Recherche Urbaine* 64, 28–33.

Genestier, P. 1994. 'La banlieue au risque de la métropolitisation'. *Le Débat* 80, 192–218.

George, P. 1985. 'Cinquante ans qui ont transformé les rapports avec l'espace'. *Communications* 41, 59–67.

Giard, L. and Mayol, P. 1994. *L'Invention du quotidien. II. Habiter, cuisiner*. Paris: Union générale d'éditions.

Giblin, B. 1977. 'La nation-paysages. "The National Geographic Magazine"'. *Hérodote* 7, 149–57.

Giedeon, S. 1941. *Space, Time and Architecture*, Cambridge, Mass.: Harvard University Press.

—— 1962. *The Eternal Present*, two vols. New York: Pantheon.

Giscard d'Estaing, V. 1976. *La Démocratie française*. Paris: Fayard.

Goffman, E. 1969. *The Presentation of Self in Everyday Life*. London: Allen & Unwin (originally published, 1959).

Gosselin, Y. 1991. 'État et sociétés industrielles avancées: la perspective d'Henri Lefebvre'. M.A. thesis, University of Ottawa.

Gottdiener, M. 1985. *Social Production of Urban Space*. Austin: University of Texas.

—— 1993. 'A Marx for our Time: Henri Lefebvre and *The Production of Space*'. Book review in *Sociological Theory* 11 (1) (March), 129–34.

—— 1996. 'Alienation, Everyday Life and Postmodernism as Critical Theory'. In F. Geyer (ed.) *Alienation, Ethnicity and Postmodernism*. London: Greenwood, 139–48.

Grawitz, M. 1994. *Lexique des sciences sociales*, 6th edn. Paris: Dalloz.

Gregory, D. 1994. *Geographical Imaginations*. Basil Blackwell, Oxford.

Grenier, J. 1936. 'L'Âge des orthodoxies'. *Nouvelle Revue Française* (April).

Grönlund, B. 1993. *Lefebvre's Ontological Transformation(s) of Space*. Stockholm: Nordplan.

Grosz, L. 1994. *Volatile Bodies*. Bloomington, Ind.: Indiana University Press.

Grosz, E. 1995. *Space, Time and Perversion: Essays on the Politics of Bodies*. London: Routledge, 207–27.

Gusdorf, G. 1991. 'Henri Lefebvre, témoin de son siècle'. Colloque L'homme modern, hommage à Henri Lefebvre (Hagetmau 1985).

Habermas, J. 1989. *The Structural Transformation of the Public Sphere; An Inquiry into a Category of Bourgeois Society*. Cambridge, Mass.: MIT Press.

Hall, E. T. 1966. *The Hidden Dimension*. Garden City, NY: Doubleday.

Hamel, P. and Poitras, C. 1994. 'Henri Lefebvre, penseur de la postmodernity'. *Espaces et Societés* 76 (1), 41–58.

Haraway, D. 1991. *Simians, Cyborgs and Women*. London, Free Association Books.

Harvey, D. 1973. *Social Justice and the City*. Edward Arnold.

—— 1982. *The Limits to Capital*. Oxford: Basil Blackwell.

—— 1989. *The Condition of Postmodernity*. Oxford: Basil Blackwell.

—— 1991. 'Afterword'. H. Lefebvre *The Production of Space*, D. Nicholson-Smith (trans.). Oxford: Basil Blackwell, 425–32.

—— 1993. 'From Space to Place and Back Again: Reflections on the Condition of Postmodernity'. In J. Bird, B. Curtis, T. Putnam, G. Robertson and L. Tickner (eds) *Mapping Futures: Local Cultures, Global Change*. London: Routledge, 3–29.

Hayden, D. 1981. 'Two Utopian Feminists and their Campaigns for Kitchenless Houses'. In *Building for Women*. no place: D.C. Heath & Co.

Hegel, G. W. F. 1892. *History of Philosophy*, E. Haldans (trans.), Vol. 1 of three. *Lectures on the History of Philosophy*. London: Routledge.

—— 1949. *The Phenomenology of Mind*, revised 2nd edn, J. B. Baillie (trans.). London: Allen & Unwin.

—— 1969. *Hegel's Science of Logic*, A. V. Miller (trans.). London: Allen & Unwin.

Heidegger, M. 1962 [1928]. *Being and Time*, J. Macquarrie and E. Robinson (trans.). New York: SCM Press.

Heine, 1976. 'Préface à Lutèce'. *Sämtliche Schriften*, Vol. 9. Munich: Hanser.

Heller, A. 1984. *Everyday Life*, G. L. Campbell (trans.). London: Routledge.

Hess, R. 1988. *Henri Lefebvre et l'aventure du siècle*. Paris: Editions A. M. Métailié, 1988.

—— 1994. 'La théorie des moments, ce qu'elle pourrait apporter a un dépassement de l'interactionnisme'. In *Traces de futurs. Henri Lefebvre, le possible et le quotidien*. Paris: Société Française.

Hindess, B. and Hirst, J. 1977. *Mode of Production and Social Formation: An Auto-critique of Pre-capitalist Modes of Production*. London: Macmillan.

Hirsh, A. 1981. *The French New Left: An Intellectual History from Sartre to Gorz*. Boston: South End Press.

Hocquenghem G. 1974. *L'Après-mai des Faunes*, Paris: Editions Lebovici.

Home, S. 1988. *The Assault on Culture: Utopian Currents from Lettrisme to Class War*. London: Aporia Press and Unpopular Books.

Horkheimer, M. and Adorno, T. 1944. *The Dialectic of Enlightenment*, J. Cumming (trans.). New York: Herder and Herder.

Huisman, D. 1984. *Le Dictionnaire des philosophies*. Paris: PUF.

—— 1993. *Dictionnaire des mille oeuvres clés de la philosophie*. Paris: Nathan.

International Situationist Anthology 1986, K. Knabb (trans. and ed.). Berkeley, Calif.: Bureau of Public Secrets (originally published as *Situationniste Internationale*. Paris: Ed. G. Lebovichi).

Ilcan, S. *et al.* 1999. *Postmodern Ethics*. Montreal: McGill-Queen's University Press.

Irigaray, L. 1993. *An Ethics of Sexual Difference*. London: Athlone.

Jacoby, R. 1981. *Dialectic of Defeat: Contours of Western Marxism*. London: Cambridge University Press.

Jameson, F. 1984. 'Postmodernism, or the Cultural Logic of Late Capitalism', *New Left Review* 146 (July–August), 53–93.

Jameson, F. 1991. *Postmodernism, or the Cultural Logic of Late Capitalism*. London: Verso.

Jay, M. 1973. *The Dialectical Imagination*, Boston: Little, Brown & Co.

—— 1984. *Marxism and Totality: The Adventures of a Concept from Lukács to Habermas*. Berkeley: University of California Press.

Jehl, B. 1994. 'La ville-image'. In *Traces de futurs. Henri Lefebvre, le possible et le quotidien*. Paris: Société Française.

Jenks, C. 1995. *Visual Culture*. London: Routledge.

Jessop, B. 1991. *The Politics of Flexibility; Restructuring State and Industry in Britain, Germany and Scandinavia*. Aldershot, UK: Edward Elgar.

Joseph, I. 1994. 'Le Droit a la ville, la ville a l'oeuvre. Deux paradigmes de la recherche urbaine'. *Les Annales de la Recherche Urbaine* 64, 4–10.

Kanapa, J. 1948. 'Un debat sur la logique en U.R.S.S., la logique d'Henri Lefebvre'. *La Pensée*, 17 (March–April), 111–21.

Katznelson, I. 1992. *Marxism and the City*. Oxford: Clarendon Press.

Kelly, M. 1982. *Modern French Marxism*. Baltimore: Johns Hopkins University Press.

King, A. 1990. *Global Cities*, two vols. London: Routledge.

Kleinspehn, T. 1975. *Der Verdrängte Alltag: Henri Lefebvre's marxistische Kritik des Alltagslebens*. Giessen: Focus Verlag.

Kofman, E. 1993. 'La politique de la ville'. *Modern and Contemporary France* 1 (4), 379–83.

Kofman, E. and Lebas, E. 1996. 'Lost in Transposition – Time, Space and the City'. Introduction to *H. Lefebvre Writings on Cities*, E. Kofman and E. Lebas (trans.). Oxford: Basil Blackwell, 1–60.

Kofman, M. 1995. *Edgar Morin: From Big Brother to Fraternity*. London: Pluto.

Korsch, K. 1970. *Marxism and Philosophy*, F. Halliday (trans.). London: New Left Books.

Kristeva, J. 1981. 'Woman's Time'. *Signs* 7 (1) (Autumn).

Kurzweil, E. 1980. *The Age of Structuralism: Lévi-Strauss to Foucault*. New York: Columbia University Press.

Laberenne, P. 1979. 'Du Cercle de la Russie Neuve (1928–1936) et l'Association pour l'Étude de la Culture Sovietique (1936–1939)'. *Pensée* 205 (May–June), 15–19.

Lacroix, G. 1994. 'Autour de cybernantrope. Informatique et identité'. In *Traces de futurs, Henri Lefebvre, le possible et le quotidien*. Paris: Société Française.

Latour, P. and Combes, F. 1991. *Conversation avec Henri Lefebvre*. Paris: Messidor.

Le Grignou, B. 1985. 'H. Lefebvre ou les miroirs de l'intellectuel enagé'. Thesis, Université Rennes-I, Rennes, France (copy available at the Bibliothèque Nationale, Paris).

Lebas, E. 1983. 'The State in British and French Urban Research, or the Crisis of the Urban Question'. In V. Pons and R. Francis (eds) *Urban Social Research: Problems and Prospects*. London: Routledge and Kegan Paul.

Letopis' Gazetnykh Statei, 1936–1993. Moscow: Izdatel'stvo Kniga.

Levitas, R. 1993. 'The Future of Thinking about the Future'. In J. Bird *et al.* (eds) *Mapping Futures*. London: Routledge, 257–66.

Lévy, J. 1994. 'Urbanité: à inventer. Villes: à décrire'. *Annales de la Recherche Urbaine* 64, 10–15.

Lipovetsky, G. 1983. *L'Ere du vide. Essais sur l'individualisme contemporain*. Paris: Gallimard.

Loubet del Bayle, J.-L. 1969. *Les Non-conformistes des années trente*. Paris: Ed. du Seuil.

Löwy, M. 1991. 'Le marxisme romantique'. *M. Mensuel, marxisme, mouvement* 50, 6–8.

Lufti, B., Sochaczweski, S. and Janel, T. 1994. 'Henri Lefebvre et la critique de la représentation'. *Traces de futurs. Henri Lefebvre, le possible et le quotidien*. Paris: Société Française.

Lukács, G. 1914. 'Soziologie des modernen Dramas'. *Archiv für Sozialwissenschaft und Sozialpolitik*, 305–45 and 663–706.

—— 1972. *History and Class Consciousness*, R. Livingston (trans.). Cambridge, Mass.: MIT Press.

—— 1974. 'Metaphysics of tragedy'. In *Soul and Form*, A. Bostock (trans.). Cambridge, Mass.: MIT Press, 152–74. (Originally published 1910 in *A lelek es a format*.)

Lutz, C. and Collins, J. 1993. *Reading 'National Geographic'*. Chicago: University of Chicago Press.

Lyotard, J.-F. 1974. *Economie Libidinale*. Paris: Minuit.

—— 1990. *Heidegger and 'the Jews'*. Minneapolis: University of Minnesota Press.

Lyotard, J.-F. and Thebaud, J.-L. 1985. *Just Gaming*. Manchester: Manchester University Press.

MacCannell, D. 1992. *Empty Meeting Grounds: The Tourist Papers*. London: Routledge.

Macey, D. 1993. 'Review. Everything is Dangerous'. *Radical Philosophy* 65, 45–6.

Macpherson, C. B. 1962. *The Political Theory of Possessive Individualism: Hobbes to Locke*. Oxford: Clarendon Press.

Maffesoli, M. 1995. *The Shadow of Dionysos*. Albany, NY: State University of New York Press (originally published as *L'Ombre de Dionysos*. Paris: Méridiens Klincksieck).

—— 1996. *The Time of the Tribes*, D. Smith (trans.). London: Sage.

Mannheim, E. 1956. *Essays on the Sociology of Culture*. London: Routledge.

Marcus, G. 1989. *Lipstick Traces*. Cambridge, Mass.: Harvard University Press.

Marcuse, H. 1964. *One Dimensional Man*. Boston: Beacon.

Martins, M. 1982. 'The Theory of Social Space in the Work of Henri Lefebvre'. In R. Forrest, J. Henderson and P. Williams (eds) *Urban Political Economy and Social Theory: Critical Essays in Urban Studies*. Aldershot, UK: Gower. 160–85.

Marx, K. 1975. '1844 Economic and Philosophical Manuscripts'. *Early Writings*. London: Penguin, 322–30.

Marx, K. and Engels, F. 1934. *Correspondence, 1846–1895*. London: Martin Lawrence.

—— 1965. *The German Ideology*, S. Ryanzanskaya (trans.). London: Lawrence & Wishart.

Massey, D. 1992. 'Politics and Space/Time'. *New Left Review* 196, 65–84.

—— 1993. 'Power-geometry and a Progressive Sense of Place'. In J. Bird *et al.* (eds), *Mapping Futures*. London: Routledge, 58–68.

Melly, G. and Woods, M. 1991. *Paris and the Surrealists*. London: Thames & Hudson.

Merleau-Ponty, M. 1945. *Phénoménologie de la perception*. Paris: Gallimard.

Merrifield, A. 1993. 'Space and Place: A Lefebvrian Reconciliation'. *Transactions of the Institute of British Geographers* 18 (4), 516–31.

Meschonnic, H. 1988. *Modernité modernité*. Paris: Gallimard.

Meyer, K. 1973, *Henri Lefebvre: ein romantischer Revolutionnär*. Vienna: Europa Verlag, 175pp.

Michael, G. 1925a. 'Philosophies 5/6'. *Clarté* 74, 38–9.

Michael, G. 1925b. 'Sur *Philosophies*'. *Clarté* 71 (May), 86.

Michaux, B. 1994. 'Le manifeste différentialiste et après? Quelques considérations sur le métissage et l'autoproduction de l'espèce humaine'. In *Traces de futurs. Henri Lefebvre, le possible et le quotidien*. Paris: Société Française.

Miller, I. 1981. 'Space and Values: Urbanism and Gardens'. *Building for Women*. No Place: D.C. Heath and Co., 119–50.

Moore, J. 1991. Translator's endnotes. Henri Lefebvre *Critique of Everyday Life*. London: Verso 1991, 258–95 (see Lefebvre 1991a; originally published 1947a).

Morhange, P. n.d. 'L'absolu ne s'exprime que par la loi selon laquelle le vouloir s'aventure.' P.

—— 1924. 'Billet de John Brown où l'on donne le la'. *Philosophies* 3 (September), 18.

—— 1936. *Le Poème sorti du vide*. Paris: Gallimard – Poètes de la NRF.

Morin, E. 1994. *La complexité humaine*. Flammarion.

Morris, M. 1988. 'Things to Do with Shopping Malls'. In S. Sheridan (ed.) *Grafts: Feminist Cultural Criticism*. London: Verso, 193–226.

Mounier, E. 1949. *Le Personnalisme*. Paris, Presses Universitaires de France.

—— 1966. *Communisme, anarchie et personnalisme*. Paris, Editions du Seuil.

Nadeau, M. 1965. *History of Surrealism*, R. Howard (trans.). New York: Macmillan.

Nast, H. 1994. 'Henri Lefebvre'. Paper presented to the Association of American Geographers Conference, San Francisco.

Naville, P. 1926. 'Les tendances confusionnistes du groupe "L'Esprit"; de l'incompatibilité du jargon judéo-philosophique avec le matérialisme historique'. *Clarté* (August/September), 85ff.

Nettl, J. P. 1969. 'Ideas, Intellectuals and Structures of Dissent'. In Philip Rieff (ed.) *On Intellectuals: Theoretical Studies, Case Studies*. Garden City, NY: Doubleday.

Nicholson, L. J. 1990. *Feminism/Postmodernism*. New York: Routledge.

Olalquiaga, C. 1992. *Megalopolis*. Minneapolis: University of Minnesota Press.

Osborne, P. 1994. 'The Politics of Time'. *Radical Philosophy* 6 (8), 3–9.

Ostrowetsky, S. 1994. 'L'urbain comme acte de langage, espace et sociologie'. *Annales de la Recherche Urbaine* 64, 39–45.

Pacquot, T. 1993. 'Civilité, urbanité et citadinité'. *Les Cahiers de Philosophie* 17, 121–48.

Pellegrino, P. and Neves, J. 1994. 'L'architecture et la projection des rapports sociaux sur le sol: Effet, representation ou production de l'espace'. *Espaces et Sociétés* 7 (1), 59–68.

Perec, G. 1965. *Les choses. Chronique des années soixante*. Paris: Les Lettres Nouvelles (D. Bellos (trans.) *Things, a Chronicle of the Sixties*).

—— 1974. *Espèces d'espaces*. Paris: Editions Galilée.

—— 1978. *La vie mode d'emploi*. Paris: Hachette (D. Bellos (trans.) *A User's Manual*).

Petitjean, G. 1994. 'Le Paris secret de Jacques Chirac'. *Le Nouvel Observateur* 22 (September), 90–3.

Philosophes collective (Pierre Morhange, Norbert Guterman, Henri Lefebvre, Georges Politzer, Gabriel Beauroy, Emile Benveniste, Henri Jourdan, Maurice Muller, Jean-Paul Zimmerman and André Barsalou) 1925. 'Révolution d'abord et toujours'. Collective manifesto, *Clarté* 76 (15 July), 23 (reprinted in José Pierre (ed.) 1979 *Tracts surréalistes et déclarations collectives*. Paris: Terrain Vague.

Pitkelthy, L. 1979. 'Hegel in Modern France (1900–1950)'. Ph.D. thesis, University of London.

Plant, S. 1990. 'The Situationist International: A Case of Spectacular Neglect'. *Radical Philosophy* 55, 3–10.

—— 1992. *Most Radical Gesture: The Situationist International in a Postmodern Age*. London: Routledge.

Podgórecki, A. 1986. 'Polish Society; A Sociological Analysis'. Sociology and Anthropology Working Papers 1986–08. Carleton University, Ottawa, 39pp.

Podgórecki, A., Alexander, J. and Shields, R. 1996. *Social Engineering*. Ottawa: Carleton University Press.

Politzer, G. 1924. 'Billet de John Brown où l'on donne le la'. *Philosophies* 3 (September), 18.

—— 1927. 'Introduction'. *L'Esprit* 1 (May), 70–114.

Poster, M. 1975. *Existential Marxism in Postwar France: From Sartre to Althusser*. Princeton, NJ,: Princeton University Press, B2424. D4P68.

Racine, N. 1967. 'Une revue d'intellectuelle communiste dans les années vingt: *Clarté*'. *Revue Française de Science Politique*, 17 (3) (June).

Rée, J. 1994. 'Return of the Translator'. *Radical Philosophy* 67, 41–3.

Renaudie, S. 1988. 'Henri Lefebvre. Une nouvelle positivité de l'urbain'. *M. Mensuel, marxisme, mouvement* 17, 62–6.

Ricoeur, P. 1988. *Time and Narrative*, three vols, K. Balmey and D. Pellauer (trans.). Chicago: University of Chicago Press.

Rose, G. 1993. *Feminism and Geography*. Cambridge: Polity Press.

Ross, A. 1989. 'The Death of Day'. In L. Henihan and B. Watten (eds) *Poetics Journal* 8, 70ff.

Ross, K. 1988. *The Emergence of Social Space: Rimbaud and the Paris Commune*. New York: Macmillan.

—— 1996 [1995]. *Fast Cars, Clean Bodies: Decolonization and the Reordering of French Culture*. Cambridge, Mass.: MIT Press.

Roure, L. 1928. 'Esprit'. *Études* 194 (January–March), 370–1.

Ruby, C. 1989. *Les archipels de la différence. Foucault, Derrida, Deleuze, Lyotard*. Paris: Editions du Félin.

—— 1990. *Le champ de bataille. Post-moderne/neo-moderne*. Paris: Harmattan.

Sartre, J.-P. 1944. 'À propos de l'existentialisme, mise au point'. *Action* 17 (12 December).

—— 1958. *Being and Nothingness*, H. E. Barnes (trans.). New York: Methuen/Philosophical Library (originally published as *L'Être et le Néant*. Paris: Gallimard, 1943).

—— 1961. *Critique of Dialectical Reason*. London: New Left Books (originally published as *Critique de la raison dialectique. Vol. 1: Theorie des ensembles pratiques*. Paris: Gallimard, 1960).

Sassen, S. 1991. *The Global City; New York, London, Tokyo*. Princeton, NJ: Princeton University Press.

—— 1994. 'La ville globale. Eléments pour une lecture de Paris'. *Le Débat* 80, 146–64.

Saunders, P. 1981. *Social Theory and the Urban Question*. London: Hutchinson.

Sayer, A. 1994. 'Henri Lefebvre: *The Production of Space*'. Book review, *Journal of Urban and Regional Research* 17 (3) (September), 458–9.

Schelling, F. Von. 1926. *Recherches philosophiques sur l'essence de la liberté humaine et sur les problèmes qui s'y rattachent*, G. Politzer (trans.). Paris: Rieder.

—— 1936. *Schelling: Of Human Freedom*, J. Gutmann (trans.). Chicago: Open Court.

Schmidt, A. 1972. 'Henri Lefebvre and the Contemporary Interpretations of Marx'. In D. Howard and K. E. Klare (eds) *The Unknown Dimension: European Marxism since Lenin*. New York: Basic Books.

Schnaidt, C. 1994. 'Fragments pour penser le moderne. Complément tardif a l'introduction a la modernité de Henri Lefebvre'. In *Traces de futurs. Henri Lefebvre, le possible et le quotidien*. Paris: Société Française.

Schopenhauer, M. 1958. *The World as Will and Representation*. New York: Dover.

—— 1970. *Essays and Aphorisms*. Selection and trans. of *Parerga und Parlipomena*. Harmondsworth: Penguin.

Sève, L. 1960. *La Différence, de Lénine à 'La Somme et le reste d'Henri Lefebvre*. Paris: Editions Sociales, collection *Les Essais de la nouvelle critique* 7.

Shields, R. 1986. 'Henri Lefebvre, the Postmodern Hypothesis and the Question of Space'. M.A. thesis, Department of Sociology and Anthropology, Carleton University, Ottawa.

—— 1989. 'Social Spatialisation and the Built Environment: The Case of the West Edmonton Mall'. *Environment and Planning D: Society and Space* 7 (2) (Summer), 147–64.

—— 1990. *Places on the Margin: Alternate Geographies of Modernity*. London: Routledge.

—— 1992. 'A Truant Proximity: Presence and Absence in the Space of Modernity'. *Environment and Planning D: Society and Space* 10 (1) 181–98.

—— 1994. 'Body, Spirit and Production: The Geographical Legacies of Henri Lefebvre'. unpublished paper, Association of American Geographers Conference, San Francisco.

—— 1995. 'Fancy Footwork: Walter Benjamin's Notes on Flânerie'. In K. Tester (ed.) *The Flâneur*. London: Routledge, 61–80.

—— 1997. 'Flow as a New Paradigm'. *Space and Culture* 1 (1), 1–7.

Short, R. S. 1966. 'The Politics of Surrealism 1920–1936'. *Journal of Contemporary History* 1 (2) (April), 3–26.

—— 1979. 'Paris Dada and Surrealism'. *Journal of European Studies* 9 (1–2) (March–June), 75–98.

Sintomer, Y. 1994. 'Le soleil crucifié'. *M. Mensuel, marxisme, mouvement* 50, 12–15.

Sirinelli, J.-F. 1990. *Intellectuels et passions françaises*. Paris: Gallimard, collection *Folio*.

Smith, N. 1984. *Uneven Development; Nature, Capital and the Production of Space*. Oxford: Basil Blackwell.

—— 1993a. 'Homeless/Global: Scaling Places'. In J. Bird *et al.* (eds) *Mapping Futures*. London: Routledge.

—— 1993b. 'Grounding Metaphor'. In M. Keith and S. Pile (eds) *Place and the Politics of Identity*. London: Routledge.

Société Française 1994. *Traces de futurs. Henri Lefebvre, le possible et le quotidien*. Papers for conference held 3–5 June.

Soja, E. 1980. 'The Socio-Spatial Dialectic'. *Annals of the Association of American Geographers* 70 (2), 207–25.

—— 1985. 'The Spatiality of Social Life: Towards a Transformative Retheorisation'. In D. Gregory and J. Urry (eds) *Social Relations and Spatial Structures*. London: Macmillan, 90–127.

—— 1989a. 'Modern Geography, Western Marxism, and the Restructuring of Critical Social Theory'. In R. Peet and N. Thrift (eds) *New Models in Geography. The Political-economy Perspective*. London: Unwin Hyman, 318–47.

—— 1989b *Postmodern Geographies, The Reassertion of Space in Critical Social Theory*. London: Verso.

—— 1996. *Third Space*. Oxford: Basil Blackwell.

Spigel, L. 1997. 'From Theatre to Space Ship: Metaphors of Suburban Domesticity in Postwar America'. In R. Silverstone (ed.) *Visions of Suburbia*. London: Routledge, 217–39.

Stokvis, W. 1987. *Cobra. An International Movement in Art after the Second World War*. Barcelona: Ediciones Poligrafa.

Trebitsch, M. 1986. 'Le Renouveau Philosophique avorté des années trente: Entretien avec Henri Lefebvre'. *Europe* 683 (March), 29–41.

Trebitsch, M. 1987a. 'Le groupe Philosophie, de Max Jacob aux surréalistes'. *Les Cahiers de l'Institut de l'Histoire du temps présent* 6 (November), 29–38.

—— 1987b. 'Les Mésaventures du group Philosophies (1924–1933)'. *La Revue des revues* 3 (spring), 6–9.

—— 1988. 'Présentation'. Henri Lefebvre *Le Nationalisme contre les Nations*. Paris: Meridiens Klincksieck, 7–17.

—— 1990a. 'Le groupe Philosophies, et les Surréalistes (1924–1924)'. *Mélusine* 9, 63–86.

—— 1990b. 'Henri Lefebvre et la revue *Avant Poste*: une analyse marxiste marginale du fascisme'. *Lendemains* 57, 77–87.

—— 1990c. 'Philosophie et marxisme dans les années trente: le marxisme critique d'Henri Lefebvre'. *Actes du colloque l'engagement des intellectuels dans la France des années trente* (Montréal, May 1989) 13–44. Montréal: Université du Québec à Montréal.

—— 1991. 'Preface'. Henri Lefebvre *Critique of Everyday Life*, John Moore (trans.). London: Verso, ix–xxviii.

—— 1992. 'Correspondances d'Intellectuels: Le cas des lettres d'Henri Lefebvre à Norbert Guterman (1935–1947)'. In N. Racine and M. Tretisch (eds) *Les Cahiers de l'Institut de l'Histoire du temps présent* 20 (March) 70–84. Sociabilités Intellectuelles: Lieux milieux réseaux. Paris: Centre National de la Recherche Scientifique.

Urry, J. 1990. *The Tourist Gaze*. London: Routledge.

—— 1996. *Consuming Places*. London: Sage.

Vaneigem, R. 1994. *Revolution of Everyday Life*. D. Nicholson-Smith (trans.). San Francisco: Rebel Press (originally published as *Traitéde savoir-vivre a l'usage des jeunes generations*. Paris: Gallimard, 1967).

Valentine, G. 1989. 'The Geography of Women's Fear'. *Area* 21 (4), 385–390.

Vernes, J. 1994. *Paris au XXe siècle*. Paris: Hachette.

Wahl, J. 1926. 'Hegel: La Phénoménologie'. *L'Esprit* 1.

—— 1928. *La Malheur de la conscience dans de la philosophie Hegel*. Paris: Reider.

Weber, M. 1979. *Economy and Society: an Outline of Interpretive Sociology*, two vols, G. Roth and C. Wittich (eds), Ephraim Fischoff *et al.* (trans.). Berkeley : University of California Press (originally published as *Wirtschaft und Gesellschaft*, with appendices from *Gesammelte Aufsatze zur Wissenschaftslehre*, 4th edn. Tubingen: J. C. B. Mohr (Paul Siebeck), 1956).

Wicke, P. 1991. *Rock Music*, R. Fogg (trans.). Cambridge: Cambridge University Press.

Williams, R. 1973. *The Country and the City*. London: Chatto & Windus.

—— 1989a. 'Drama in a Dramatized Society'. In A. O'Connor (ed.) *On Television: Selected Writings*. London: Routledge, 3–13 (originally presented as an inaugural lecture, Cambridge University, October 1974).

Wilson, E. 1991. *The Sphinx and the City*. London: Virago.

Winock, M. 1975. *Historie politique de la Revue Esprit 1930–1950*. Paris: Editions du Seuil.

Wollen, P. 1990. 'Bitter Victory. The Situationist International'. *A Situationist Scrapbook. An Endless Passion . . . an Endless Banquet*. London: ICA and Verso.

Zevi, B. 1974. *Architecture as Space: How to Look at Architecture*, M. Gendel (trans.). New York: Horizon Press.

Zimmerman, M. 'Polarities and Contradictions: Theoretical Bases of the Marxist–Structuralist Encounter'. *New German Critique* 3 (1) (winter), 69–90.

INDEX

eros 12
Esprit 15, 33, 51
L'Esprit 15, 16, 33, 34
essentialism 40, 48, 77, 111, 113, 123, 145, 167, 178, 182
estrangement 40–2, 45, 67
ethics 30, 69, 183
ethnicity 64, 138, 177
ethnography 88, 97, 166
everyday life 11–12, 57–61, 65–78, 91–100, 102–5, 107, 118, 129, 134, 139, 145–6, 149, 153–4, 157, 160, 162, 172, 180, 186–7; and alienation 20, 28, 93; and consciousness 36–42; and Debord 92; and Heller 69; and Marxism 38; and moments 52, 61; and philosophy 32–3, 135–7; and structuralism 122, 125–6; and women 97; banality of 15, 61; material conditions of 15; mystifications of 37, 46–8
existential philosophy 82, 127
existentialism 3, 28, 82–3, 105, 126–32, 135

false authenticity 38, 44, 47, 78
family 96, 121, 148
Fascism 19, 25, 44, 46–8, 50–1, 67, 116, 130
Featherstone, M. 94
female agency 175
feminism 4, 124, 130; *see also* women
Ferenczi, T. 88
festivals 31, 71, 103–4, 118
fetish 25, 41, 44, 46, 78
feudal social relations 176
film 4, 55
First World War 1, 8–9; aftermath of 11–15, 29, 65
Flanner, J. 84, 129
Flaubert, G. 147, 148
Flore, J. de 31, 81, 161
flow 60, 64, 71, 147, 152, 178
form 13, 21, 23, 34, 36, 39, 42, 44–6, 48–53, 63–4, 96, 104, 112–15, 162, 168–70, 185; and abstract space 180; and Renaissance 175; as moment 60–1; of space 79; of thought 115; urban 178
formlessness 73
Foucault, M. 74, 108, 122, 124–5, 127, 135–6, 156

Frankfurt school 24–5, 35, 137; *see also* Adorno, T. *and* Horkheimer, M.
Freud 12
Friedmann, J. 11, 13, 21, 23, 67

Garaudy, R. 86
Gardiner, M. 29, 61, 100, 139
gender 64, 134, 158, 174, 177
geography 61, 140–1, 145–6, 150, 156–8, 163, 176, 187; anglophone 6; intellectual 2; of capitalism 188; of consciousness 41; social 140
geometry 155, 175
German Green movement 143
ghettos 77, 141, 148, 169, 178, 182
Giblin, B. 166
Giedeon, S. 79
global 77, 85, 134, 142–5, 155, 169–70, 172–3, 180, 188
globalisation 187–8
God 13, 30, 34
Goffman, E. 154
Gottdiener, M. 58, 145–6, 157, 160, 169, 177
Gramsci 16, 23, 46–7, 95
Green Party 5, 29
Grosz, E. 124, 158, 181
groupe de recherche 92
Gusdorf, G. 89
Guterman papers, Butler Library, Columbia University 19, 20, 21, 60

Haraway, D. 4
Hardy, T. 148
Harvey, D. 29, 58, 61, 87, 143, 150, 153, 177
Hayden, D. 158
Hegel, G. 3, 6, 12, 20, 21, 24, 25, 43, 45, 56, 74, 84, 86, 87, 110, 130, 136, 152, 159, 175; and *Aufhebung* 33–8, 71–2, 119; and dialectical logic 112; and dialectical materialism 29, 31; and theology 34; dialectic 111–17
Heidegger, M. 14–15, 60, 66–8, 131, 134, 152
Heine 38
Heller, A. 69
Heraclitus 136
Hess, R. 7, 9, 12–15, 17, 19, 20, 21, 23, 26, 31–4, 59, 62–3, 70, 73, 85, 89–90, 98, 104–5, 118, 132

Resistance, the: and Communist Party 4;
and Occupation 22; and Sartre 82, 88;
and Tzara 26–7; in Toulouse 27;
romanticism of 26
revolution 11–12, 24, 26, 30–2, 38, 48,
59, 61, 67, 70, 72, 86, 88, 90–4,
96–7, 118, 134–5, 139, 141, 144,
146, 184; and art 1–2, 56–7, 94; and
difference 108; and Fascism 51; and
May 1968 16; and Situationists 91;
Marxist 15; mystical 21; of everyday
life 107; of spirit 15; political 14–17
Romanticism 26, 33, 57, 73, 77
Rose, G. 50, 71, 158
Ross, K. 6, 39–41, 66, 95, 103, 119, 122,
129, 139–41
rural peasantry 85
rural sociology 5, 9, 23, 85, 87, 97, 147

sacred space 170, 173
Sartre, J.-P. 7, 11, 17, 23, 70, 72, 74,
87–8, 90, 108, 125–34, 137; and
Lefebvre 133; non-rational 130; Parti
Communiste Français (PCF) 81–3
Sassen, S. 77
Saunders, P. 182
Saussure, F. 57
Schelling 3, 34, 71, 94
Schopenhauer 9
scientific revolution 86
Second World War 11, 19, 26–7;
aftermath of 39–40, 65, 96, 147; see
also Resistance, the
self: alienation 67; definition 32, 133;
expression 32; production of 127, 137
self-consciousness 43
semiotic codes 151
semiotics 2, 135, 165
senses 34, 63, 86
sexual freedom 12
sexuality 116, 185
Short, R. 18
sign 22, 24, 35, 63, 88, 99, 107, 121, 165
Simmel, G. 67
Sirinelli, J.-F. 18, 88
Situationists 39, 61, 73, 76, 78, 89–92,
103–7, 118, 184, 187; activism of 4;
and Debord 8, 91, 103–5, 137; and
May 1968 28, 53, 103; and Surrealism
100, 143–4, 184; expulsion from 103
Situationniste Internationale (SI) 91,
103–4, 107

slogans 107, 185
slum 164
Smith, N. 49, 161
social: groups 121; power 121; reality 65,
94; relations of production 100, 151,
160, 162, 168, 178; revolutions 94
social construction 141, 154
society of the spectacle 104; see also
Debord, G.
sociology 19, 23, 27, 47, 75, 90, 91, 106,
135, 145, 156, 158, 169, 188;
American 85; cultural 5; feminist 96–7;
industrial 20; of classes 42–3; rural 5,
9, 85, 87–8, 97, 147–8; urban 29, 142
Socrates 82
Soja, E. ix, 58n, 77, 119, 143, 146,
150–3, 156n
space 38, 52, 58, 60–1, 63, 76, 95, 102,
113, 116, 125, 132, 136, 140–7,
172–85, 188; abstract 48, 79–8; and
capitalism 149–70; and dialectics 144;
and history 170; and production 167;
and time 6, 119–20, 123, 143, 156–8,
168, 172–3, 188; as contradictory 181;
Cartesian 30; natural 133; of
domesticity 140; of leisure 98–100;
social 3, 5–7, 25–6, 30, 78, 90,
119–20, 153–5, 157–61, 170; social
attitudes 5; urban 2
Spanish-Moroccan war 24, 51
spatial: dialectic of the body 185; practice
154, 160, 162–3, 165, 168, 177, 180;
routines 95
spatiality 90, 95, 99, 144, 146, 149, 151,
153, 162, 165, 187
spectacle 65, 77–8, 94, 104–5, 133, 166;
and alienation 77; see also society of the
spectacle and Debord, G.
Spigel, L. 39
spirit 9, 12, 14–15, 22, 31–4, 36, 45,
56–7, 59, 90, 94, 99, 115, 124, 131,
136, 155, 161, 181, 187–8; and Hegel
117
spirituality 13
spontaneity 7, 33, 35, 62, 65, 89, 95, 136,
139
Stalinism 17, 21, 31, 85–6, 92, 131, 134,
139
state 7, 14, 16, 22, 35–6, 45, 48, 72–3,
75, 78–9, 85–6, 92, 95, 102–4, 108,
115, 117, 124, 128, 138, 139, 141,